D1431115

THE
BONDS
OF
WICKEDNESS

THE FRANK S. AND
ELIZABETH D. BREWER
PRIZE ESSAY
OF THE
AMERICAN SOCIETY
OF
CHURCH HISTORY

THE
BONDS
OF
WICKEDNESS

AMERICAN
EVANGELICALS
AGAINST
SLAVERY,
1770–
1808

JAMES D. ESSIG

TEMPLE UNIVERSITY PRESS
PHILADELPHIA

Temple University Press,
Philadelphia 19122
© 1982 by Temple University
All rights reserved
Published 1982

Printed in
the United States of America

Library of Congress Cataloging in Publication Data

Essig, James D.
The bonds of wickedness.

Includes bibliographical references and index.
1. Evangelicalism—United States.   2. Slavery—
United States.   I. Title.
BR1642.U5E85   1982   241'.675   82-10670
ISBN 0-87722-282-7

FOR JANET

IS not this the fast that I choose:
to loose the bonds of wickedness,
to undo the thongs of the yoke,
to let the oppressed go free,
and to break every yoke? . . .
Then shall your light break forth
like the dawn,
and your healing shall spring up speedily;
your righteousness shall go before you,
and the glory of the Lord
shall be your rear guard.

Isaiah 58: 6; 8

AMERICA! be wise; revere the rod;
Break off thy sins, and turn to Jacob's God. . . .
Arise betimes, and break off every yoke,
Let go the oppressed before you feel his stroke;
For he who captive leads must captive be,
And he who freedom gives shall be made free.

J.P., EZEKIEL
COOPER PAPERS

CONTENTS

PREFACE

LIKE MOST HISTORICAL INVESTIGATIONS, the following study owes its beginning to a sense of curiosity and dissatisfaction. In the course of work on the relationship between evangelicalism and abolitionism in the antebellum years, I learned of an earlier period of evangelical concern about slavery, a brief but significant length of time during which prominent evangelicals worked to eliminate slavery in America. Their concern about slavery seemed to emerge in the 1770s, a period of deteriorating relations between Britain and her colonies, and it appeared to persist, in a greatly diminished form, into the opening years of the nineteenth century. Many of the individuals involved had undergone their formative religious experience during the Great Awakening or in its aftermath. I became interested in the origins, the depth, and the durability of their antislavery commitment, but I found no satisfying interpretation of their activity in existing secondary works.

For the most part, this early evangelical attack on slavery had been treated as one example of what Bailyn called a general "contagion of liberty" in the Revolutionary era,[1] or it had been divided into discrete denominational compartments that isolated representative individuals from each other in an artificial way.[2] Denominational historians often showed a sectarian preoccupation with listing antislavery quotations in order to prove that their forebears had been on the "right" side of the issue from the beginning.[3] The work of David Brion Davis and Winthrop D. Jordan provided a welcome and challenging exception, but their treatment of the antislavery evangelicals represented one part of much more inclusive studies.[4] The first evangelical attack on slavery had not been considered as a movement animated by religious concerns that cut across denominational boundaries.

This study explores the origins and nature of evangelical antislavery commitment. It seeks to explain why slaveholding emerged as a pressing issue for evangelicals in the Revolutionary and early national periods, when it had not troubled such worthies as George Whitefield, Samuel Davies, or, so it seems, the great Jonathan Edwards. By assessing the fragility of their antislavery commitment, it also attempts to explain why evangelicals began to lose interest in the slavery issue in the early nineteenth century. I have tried, on the one hand, to avoid what Perry Miller once described as an "obtuse secularism"[5] in the examination of religious movements, a tendency to see such movements solely as expressions of social and political trends. On the other hand, I have sought to break out of static denominational categories and go beyond a survey of ecclesiastical opinion on the slavery issue. I have tried to relate the genesis of evangelical antislavery commitment to attitudes, values, and tensions within evangelicalism itself, while taking developments within denominations into account when they appeared relevant. This approach does not ignore the impact of republican ideas on the thinking of evangelicals, but it does reflect a belief that their antislavery convictions derived from something more than a desire to be consistent in the application of natural rights theory.

The following chapters represent the result of these efforts. Chapter I introduces the prominent figures of the study and examines the way in which the imperial crisis led some evangelicals to see slavery as an emblem of America's bondage to sin. Chapter II deals with the role that evangelical spirituality played in encouraging pious whites to identify with the black victims of oppression. Chapter III shows how the strains that accompanied the transition to respectability could provoke fierce denunciations of slaveholding in the postwar era. Chapter IV evaluates the impact of republicanism on the thinking of David Barrow, James O'Kelly, David Rice, and Samuel Hopkins—Baptist, Methodist, Presbyterian, and Congregationalist, respectively. Chapter V examines the work of evangelical Congregationalists in Connecticut to determine whether the privileged status of Congregational ministers produced antislavery sentiment at all different from that of less favored believers. Chapter VI chronicles the decline of evangelical interest in pursuing antislavery goals. Chapter VII traces the careers of antislavery advocates who carried on a lonely battle in the early 1800s. The Epilogue attempts to link their work with a later period of abolitionist activity.

With the exception of some background material in Chapter I, the study is confined to the years between 1770 and 1808, dates which set useful and uncontrived limits for the scope of the investigation. Before 1770, I can find little evidence of evangelical opposition to slavery, and 1808 marks the year when the congressional ban on American participation in the slave trade went into effect. Evangelical response to this event, however, amounted to more of a retrospect on antislavery activity than a call to further action, for by 1808—as the study will show—evangelical opposition to domestic slavery had largely subsided. Within this span of years, evangelicalism facilitated antislavery commitment by fostering a distinctive style of spirituality which, in certain contexts, could result in a deep aversion to slaveholding.

I would like to acknowledge my debt to the individuals who gave generously of their time in reading and commenting on this study. Edmund S. Morgan, Sydney E. Ahlstrom, C. Duncan Rice, and David Brion Davis offered suggestions which helped to clarify my thinking and sharpen my perceptions. Friends such as Ann F. Withington, Thomas Hietala, and Jeffrey Merrick provided encouragement, advice, and good company while I wrote this study. As colleagues in the fullest sense, C. P. Darcy, Theodore Evergates, and Ralph B. Levering have warmly supported this project in its latter phases.

Sections of the book use material previously published as "A Very Wintry Season: Virginia Baptists and Slavery, 1785–1797," *Virginia Magazine of History and Biography* 88 (April 1980), and "Connecticut Ministers and Slavery, 1790–1795," *Journal of American Studies* 15 (April 1981). The editors of these journals have kindly allowed me to use this material here.

Other individuals and institutions have provided assistance in the preparation of this study. The following libraries and historical societies have granted permission to quote from their manuscript collections: Beinecke and Sterling Libraries; the Historical Society of Pennsylvania; the Presbyterian Historical Society; the Filson Club, Louisville, Kentucky; and Garrett-Evangelical Seminary, Evanston, Illinois. The staffs of the following libraries have also been gracious in their assistance: Yale Divinity School; Union Theological Seminary of Richmond, Virginia; the Virginia Baptist

Historical Society at the University of Richmond; Vanderbilt Divinity School; the New York Public Library; Princeton University; the Rhode Island Historical Society; and the Library of Congress. Carol Quinn at the Hoover Library of Western Maryland College has been extremely kind in obtaining volumes through interlibrary loan. Margaret Griffin lightened the work of revising the manuscript by performing some of the labor of typing.

The book is dedicated to Janet, who already knows the extent of my gratitude.

THE
BONDS
OF
WICKEDNESS

I

BREAK
EVERY
YOKE

ATE ONE AFTERNOON IN DECEMBER OF 1739, George Whitefield lectured representatives of the Maryland gentry on a subject that was about to have lasting impact on American culture. The young Anglican minister had recently arrived from England to conduct a whirlwind evangelistic tour of the colonies. In England, Whitefield had preached to crowds of farmers, tradesmen, coal miners, and assorted ruffians who gathered in open fields, but on this December afternoon he sat in a parlor acting as an apostle to the genteel. He told the gentry about the new birth, a spiritual event which brought the convert into an intensely personal relationship with God and which inaugurated a life of simplicity and self-denial. Adapting his remarks for the benefit of those surrounding him, the evangelist warned of "the Folly and Sinfulness of those Amusements, whereby the polite Part of the World are so *fatally diverted* from the Pursuit after *this One Thing needful.*"[1] The gentry's fondness for gaming, dancing, and other fashionable pastimes struck Whitefield as a formidable obstacle to the Kingdom of God.

Some of the gentry accused him of being excessively strict; surely, they protested, there was nothing wrong with a friendly game of cards or an innocent round of dancing. Whitefield responded to their defense of those "falsely call'd *innocent* Entertainments" by insisting that "Cards, Dancing, and such like, draw the Soul from God, and *lull* it *asleep* as much as Drunkenness and Debauchery."[2] At that point, most of the gentry must have decided that they were dealing with an incurable fanatic. As the gathering broke up, probably few in the audience realized that evangelicals like Whitefield, growing in numbers and audacity, would continue to denounce the fashionable lifestyle in years ahead. Even fewer of the gentry could have guessed that one day some evangelicals would find that an attachment to slaveholding was just as sinful as dancing or card playing.

In the months following his encounter with the gentry, Whitefield and other evangelists proclaimed the message of the new birth to larger, more appreciative, audiences. Thousands of Americans underwent a conversion experience in a revival of religion known as the Great Awakening. Friends of the revival, called New Lights, praised God for the long-awaited renaissance of piety, while opponents, or Old Lights, censured the revival as a riot of emotionalism and an affront to common decency. Itinerant preachers traversed the land, invading the territory of hostile clergymen to bring the word of salvation to all who would listen. Sinners wept, converts rejoiced, and skeptics laughed, but almost no one remained unaffected by the revival. By 1743, the major outburst had subsided, although the aftereffects of the Awakening continued to send shock waves through American culture for the rest of the century, and the repercussions are still being felt.

What had it all meant? That was the question asked by New Lights and Old Lights as the revival began to fade into memory, and historians continue to ask it. The evangelicals beheld a heightened concern for religion and an encouraging display of Christian unity, but critics pointed to the divided churches, maligned clergymen, and scores of itinerants still wandering about the countryside like latter-day prophets. Historians, for their part, have described the Awakening as a mass movement and a revolt of the masses, an expression of antiintellectualism and a major intellectual event, a purely religious phenomenon and a prologue to the American Revolution.[3] If the friends, foes, and historians of the revival have taught us anything, it is that the doctrine of the new birth could generate a number of social, intellectual, and political by-products, not all of them compatible, and not all of them foreseen or even welcomed by the leading participants.

The evangelical response to slavery is a case in point. When Whitefield introduced the gentry to the new birth, he breathed no hint that holding slaves might distract them from the pursuit of the "one thing needful." Indeed, in later years, Whitefield fervently endorsed the practice of slaveholding. And yet, by the early 1770s, prominent evangelicals throughout the colonies had come to see the continued existence of slavery as an unacceptable prospect. They viewed the advent of the American republic as a birth conceived and nurtured in the iniquity of the slave system. Before the young nation could find favor in the eyes of the Lord, they believed, it had to be redeemed from the sin of holding Africans in bondage. They perceived their own spiritual deliverance, as well as that of the new nation, to be related to the emancipation of the slave. In their worship services, in private conversations, in newspaper columns, and in printed tracts, these evangelicals denounced slaveholding as a sin and labored to convince other Americans of the wickedness of the practice.

The antislavery evangelicals broke with the precedent that their forebears established on the question of whether slaveholding was inherently evil, or whether it merely had sinful accessories that could be removed without abolishing the practice itself. Earlier in the century, evangelicals like George Whitefield and Samuel Davies admitted that slavery had its objectionable features, but they sought to eradicate those features by converting both the master and the slave. Although this solution continued to satisfy many of their successors in the Revolutionary era, other evangelicals denied that slavery could ever be hallowed by converting all the individuals involved. Unable to divorce a concern for the souls of black people from the fact of their enslavement, they attacked slavery and maintained that only emancipation would be acceptable to God.

What had brought about this momentous shift in evangelical values? What was there about evangelicalism that could produce a hatred of slavery in some evangelicals, but not others? This study explores the evangelical experience for answers.

I

IN THE EYES OF NEW LIGHTS, the Great Awakening jolted Americans out of their spiritual drowsiness and revived an emphasis on the experiential dimension of faith. The Awakening also shaped the contours of a religious consensus known as evangelicalism. For years before Whitefield's arrival in the colonies, leading religious figures had complained that church members were going through the motions of religiosity in a joyless and somnolent manner, and that many Protestants deluded themselves by thinking that a routine performance of duty would earn them a place in Heaven. Critics branded this sort of piety as nothing more than dead formalism or "works righteousness." Some ministers accused their colleagues of perpetuating spiritual dullness by preaching what Whitefield would call an "unknown, unfelt Christ," a Christ of the creed and catechism, but not an intimate presence in the life of a believer. Throughout the colonies, discontented Protestants concluded that too many would-be professors of Christianity remained strangers to "experimental religion"; that is, they had never personally experienced a deep and abiding relationship with God. Before the Awakening, this discontent with the religious situation produced small-scale revivals such as the "harvests" that took place in the Connecticut River Valley under Solomon Stoddard and his grandson Jonathan Edwards, as well as the stirrings of faith generated by Gilbert Tennent and Theodore Frelinghuysen in the Middle Colonies.[4]

During the Awakening itself, evangelists labored to demolish the false security of sinners by pointing up the woeful inadequacy of "works righteousness." At the same time, they held out the prospect of forgiveness and joyous release from the bondage of sin. If sinners would repent and believe, they would be born again into the Kingdom of God. The new birth was a dramatic, often cataclysmic, moment of conversion when the repentant sinner experienced God's mercy and transforming love. Through this spiritual crisis, the convert achieved a radically new perception of God and reality: Edwards described it as a "divine and supernatural light," while Frelinghuysen spoke of it as a "new light," using the term that came to be applied to the evangelical movement as a whole.[5] To borrow the words of the apostle Paul, "all things became new" for the born-again individual.

Evangelicals differed on the question of how the new birth took place. Working within the doctrinal framework of Calvinism, most American evangelicals continued to believe that God had predestined some people for salvation before the world was made, and that at the moment of conversion God acted to validate a choice made long ago. In this view, individuals did nothing to obtain their salvation, but neither could they do anything to lose it; salvation was a free, irresistible, and eternal gift. Other evangelicals rejected the idea of predestination. In England, John Wesley, the founder of Arminian Methodism and friend of George White-field, preferred to maximize the element of human choice in the process of conversion. Wesley argued that, contrary to the doctrine of predestination, there was nothing irresistible or permanent about grace: a person had the power to accept or reject God's offer, and a person might lose salvation through careless living.[6] This difference in theological opinion developed into a permanent rift between Calvinist and Wesleyan evangelicals.

Evangelicals realized that beneath their differences lay an informal agreement on the nature of religious experience and the hallmarks of a godly life. Wesley reprinted abridged versions of five works by the Calvinist Edwards, including *The Distinguishing Marks of a Work of the Spirit of God* and *A Treatise concerning Religious Affections*.[7] Francis Asbury, Wesley's foremost disciple in America, thoroughly enjoyed Edwards' treatise on the affections, except for "the small vein of Calvinism" running through it. Asbury also professed to revere the memory of Gilbert Tennent, a Presbyterian Calvinist.[8] Samuel Davies, another Calvinist, corresponded with Wesley on the progress of evangelistic work in Virginia.[9] And George Whitefield's career as the Grand Itinerant stands as a testimony to the ecumenical dimension of evangelicalism. Whitefield preached in the church of Edwards, conferred his blessing on Wesley's first two missionaries to America, and envisioned heaven as a place where sectarian labels had no meaning.[10] Evangelicals had their differences, but whether they were Calvinists or Wesleyans, erudite theologians or barely literate exhorters, they were united by a shared experience and a common desire to see men and women born anew in Christ.

Once converts emerged from the trauma of the new birth, they entered an entirely new phase of life. As the literal meaning of the word implies, conversion involved a turning away, a decisive break with a previous life of sin and a resolution to begin a new, holy life in Christ. Converts frequently inaugurated this new life by renouncing certain pastimes and the company of unconverted associates. More importantly, however, the convert embarked on a strenuous program to subdue the unruly forces still at work within the self: pride, lust, love of money, anger, and any tendency that might occasion a lapse into sin. The struggle against inward corruption was painful, but through the process evangelicals matured in godliness and experienced more of God's power and love.[11] Theologians refer to this process of spiritual growth as sanctification. For evangelicals, sanctification provided assurance that their conversion had been genuine, that God had indeed touched them, and that they were attaining mastery over the evil within.

God had not left individual believers to themselves in their quest for self-mastery, but had provided assistance in the form of the Bible and the holy community. Although evangelicals delighted in profoundly moving spiritual experiences, they never elevated their experiences to an authority equal to that of the revealed Word. That, they would say, was the mistake of the Quakers, who believed that God still spoke directly to people as in the days of the apostles.[12] Evangelicals remained staunchly biblical in orientation, maintaining that direct revelation ended with the last page of the Bible, and that the external authority of Scripture was needed to interpret and discipline the impulses that came from within. Without such authority, they feared, people would too easily veer off into heresy or forms of ungovernable spirituality. Evangelicals studied the Bible avidly in an effort to understand what God demanded of them and how well they were fulfilling His requirements.

Besides submitting themselves to the authority of Scripture, evangelicals submitted themselves to the discipline of the religious community. Wherever the influence of the revivals was felt, believers joined fellowships of like-minded Americans. Sometimes these fellowships were institutional churches, but they might be informal gatherings which featured prayer, singing, and exhortation. An institutionalized fellowship acted as a monitor of personal conduct: if a member engaged in some illicit form of behavior, he would receive an admonition, censure, and if all else failed, an order of expulsion from the group. But if the expelled member demonstrated repentance, he would be welcomed back to the fellowship with loving arms.[13] Evangelicals valued group discipline as a mechanism to aid each other in the quest for sanctification.

Evangelicals overcame the world by using Scripture and religious fellowship to attain mastery over the self, but they might also overcome the world by transforming it with the power of the gospel. As a movement, evangelicalism was characterized by a militant sense of mission to convert the world to Christ. The zeal for converts propelled evangelicals into a hostile world and sustained them through periods of discouragement and persecution. They were certain that the world would be transformed as converts multiplied and more people adopted an evangelical lifestyle. Sin, cruelty, and injustice would roll back before the evangelical surge as individuals learned to live in Christian love. Evangelical preachers frequently paused in their labors to excoriate wealthy sinners and warn that God would judge them for their selfishness, oppression of the poor, and callousness toward human suffering.[14] As a consequence of missionary efforts, the world would become a safer, more hospitable place for the evangelical self. Evangelicals could not be certain when, but they believed that one glorious day the entire world would enjoy the universal reign of righteousness known as the millennium.[15]

The evangelical movement was pervaded by tensions which would give rise to conflicting tendencies in its history. In the evangelical outlook, church and world stood in uncompromising opposition, but believers would have to wrestle with the age-old problem of remaining separate from the world while living in it. Evangelicals wished to keep the world at a distance at the same time that they wanted to win it for Christ. The first desire pulled evangelicals in the direction of exclusivity, cross-grained indifference to popular opinion, and scrupulosity about standards for group purity. The second desire pulled them in the direction of inclusivity, concern about appealing to a mass audience, and reluctance to alienate prospective converts by placing unnecessary roadblocks to membership. Evangelicalism also fostered a divided outlook on social evil. Individuals might find themselves torn between an impulse to turn aside from evangelistic work to fight social evil, and an urge to race past such evil in the knowledge that all would be well if they kept to the work of preaching the gospel. The issue of slavery aggravated these tensions and eventually created painful dilemmas for the evangelical movement.

II

JUST BEFORE THE HEIGHT OF THE GREAT AWAKENING, Whitefield
interrupted his frenetic labors to draft an open letter to the inhabitants of Maryland, Virginia, and South Carolina. As a self-pro-
fessed friend and spiritual adviser to the slaves, the evangelist was
"touched with a Fellow-feeling of the Miseries of the poor Negroes" in the course of his excursion through the southern colonies.[16] Whitefield composed a strongly-worded letter in which he
rebuked slaveholders for abusing the bodies of their slaves and
neglecting to care for their souls. The Grand Itinerant fused two
modes of persuasion in his epistle. In seeking to reassure masters
that Christianity would make blacks better slaves, Whitefield employed a strategy that had been in use for quite some time before
he set foot on American shores. His abrasive criticism of the slaveholding class, however, and his prophecy of divine judgment on
the offending provinces pointed in a direction which led away
from accommodation to a rejection of slavery.

Long before Whitefield gave any thought to the problem, Anglican ministers and missionaries sent by the Society for the Propagation of the Gospel in Foreign Parts had learned how uncoop-
erative southern planters could be when it came to teaching slaves
the religion of Jesus. During a visitation conducted on the eastern
shore of Maryland in 1731, commissary Henderson received a
dismal account of Anglican evangelistic work among the slaves.
One minister reported that his parishioners were "generally so
brutish" that they would not permit their slaves to be instructed,
believing that "it made them the greater Rogues & vill[ai]ns, &
they would not suffer it." Another minister found his people "in-
clinable" to such instruction, "but they will not be at the pains and
trouble of it." After repeated calls for proper care of the souls of
slaves, yet another clergyman stated that "the best answer he can
get, even from the best people, is that they are very sorry, and
Lament that they cannot comply with it."[17] Apathy, evasion, and
suspicion characterized the planter response to Anglican initiatives to convert the slaves.

The Anglican missionaries discovered that planter resistance to
slave evangelism grew partly out of a reluctance to apply the New
Testament ideal of spiritual equality to blacks, and partly out of a

fear about the effects that Christianity would have on the slave system. Deeply chagrined by the suggestion that she should look after the spiritual welfare of her servants, one eminent South Carolinian woman responded, "Is it possible that any of my slaves could go to heaven, and must I see them there?" A young gentleman found the idea of fellowship with slaves so distasteful that he refused to take communion with them.[18] As a result of an older association between slavery and heathenism, some planters thought that a slave would be entitled to freedom after he was baptized into Christianity. Other masters blamed Christianity for what they saw as an increased haughtiness on the part of their slaves. And then there was the enduring fear that religious gatherings would furnish slaves with an opportunity to hatch conspiracies against their masters.[19]

Despite the best efforts of Anglican ministers and missionaries to dispel anxieties about the effect of Christianity on slaves, the planters still took a dim view of slave evangelism at the time of Whitefield's arrival. Like other Anglicans before him, Whitefield attempted to allay fears that the gospel would foster slave discontent. "I challenge the whole World to produce a single Instance of a Negroe's being made a thorough Christian, and thereby made a worse servant," he declared confidently. "It cannot be."[20] But along with bold assurances, Whitefield presented slaveholders with an ultimatum: repent or face divine judgment.

Though he never attacked the institution of slavery itself, Whitefield assailed the godless master for his arrogant disregard of his slave's spiritual and temporal welfare. "Go to now, ye rich Men, weep and howl for your Miseries that shall come upon you!" he thundered, echoing sentiments expressed in the New Testament Book of James. God did not reject the prayer of the "poor and destitute," he minded them, "nor disregard the Cry of the meanest Negroes!" "The Blood of them spilt for these many Years in your respective Provinces, will ascend up to Heaven against you." The evangelist even expressed surprise that a just God had not permitted more frequent uprisings, though he quickly added his prayer that such a calamity would not take place. Whitefield concluded that all arguments in favor of converting the slaves would be futile until the masters themselves were convinced of the need for salvation. "A general Deadness as to divine Things, and not to say a general Prophaneness, is discernible both in Pastors and People," he wrote, perhaps remembering his fruitless discussion with the gentry, If the masters would but turn to God, Whitefield told them, treat their slaves better, and provide them with religious instruction, then the inhabitants of the southern provinces might yet escape divine judgment and enjoy God's blessing.[21]

Samuel Davies, another prominent figure in the Great Awakening, also encountered resistance to slave evangelism in the course of his ministry in Hanover County, Virginia. After his arrival there in 1747, Davies found his ministry among the slaves to be so satisfying that their mere presence transported him to heights of heavenly joy. He fondly recounted one experience when, after being awakened at two or three in the morning by slaves singing in his kitchen, "a torrent of sacred harmony poured into my chamber, and carried my mind away to heaven." He rhapsodized about the attendance of slaves at his services, describing the interior of his meetinghouse as a place "adorned (so it has appeared to me) with so many black countenances, eagerly attentive to every word they heard, and some of them washed with tears."[22] Regarding fellowship with slaves as something of a sacramental occasion, Davies sought money from British evangelicals to purchase Bibles and catechisms for pious blacks. At one point, Davies estimated that he had three hundred slaves under his care.[23]

In his less effusive moments, the Presbyterian revivalist realized that local slaveholders did not share his enthusiasm about converting slaves, nor did members of the gentry have much interest in experimental religion themselves. One of Davies' few gentry sympathizers remarked about the predominance of common people and slaves at evangelical meetings. "The gentlemen that even incline to come are afraid of being laughed at," Colonel Gordon observed disconsolately.[24] As if this were not bad enough, slaveholders great and small showed a reluctance to have their slaves instructed in Christianity. The spectacle of blacks remaining unconverted in a Christian land weighed so heavily upon Davies that he attributed "the burden of guilt under which my country groans" to Virginia's neglect of slave evangelism.[25]

Like Whitefield, Davies reassured the planters that pious slaves made better slaves, and that religion would not disrupt work routines on the plantation. In *The Duty of Christians to Propagate Their Religion Among Heathens,* Davies informed the slaveholders of Hanover County that "Your own Interest inclines you to wish, they would become good Servants; faithful, honest, diligent and laborious."[26] Responding to the fear that religion would undermine the master's authority over the slave, Davies told his listeners that Christianity did not destroy the distinctions between master and slave, but rather "establishes and regulates them." Only beyond the grave would temporal distinctions be removed, he said.[27] Far from fostering discontent among slaves, Davies contended, Christianity would actually reconcile the black to his situation, for religion could "render the lowest and most laborious Station in Life so insignificant, that a Man need *not care* for it, but continue in it with generous Indifference!" By providing slaves with the blessings of the gospel, masters could ensure the eternal happiness of their servants and thereby compensate them for their labor on earth, Davies concluded.[28] But also like Whitefield, Davies issued warnings of God's impending judgment upon the planters for their abuse of the slaves. In the midst of the gloom surrounding General Braddock's defeat in 1755, Davies listed the iniquities that brought about this visitation of God's displeasure: swearing, drinking, gaming, neglect of religion, and "a general Neglect of the Souls of the poor Negroes, and in some instances, what Barbarities toward them. . . ." More calamities would follow, Davies implied, unless Virginians repented.[29]

Such remarks hardly qualify Davies or Whitefield as firebrands on slavery, but their contemporaries interpreted their statements as, at best, injudicious, and at worst, inflammatory. An Anglican clergyman in New York maintained that a careful reading of Whitefield's letter to the southern provinces would prove that the revivalist's unguarded remarks "gave great countenance" to a recent slave insurrection in the city.[30] Colonel Edwin Conway described *The Duty of Christians* as a pamphlet in which "Mr. Davies hath much Reproached Virginia. And informs the Negroes they are Stronger than the Whites, being Equal in Number then, & having an Annual addition of thousands."[31] The fact that Davies' real sentiments could be so misconstrued indicates that, as far as the planters were concerned, any criticism of the master's conduct constituted a menace to plantation stability.

Neither Whitefield, Davies, nor any other leading figure of the Great Awakening ever denounced the practice of holding slaves. In 1748, Whitefield begged the trustees of Georgia to allow the importation of slaves so that their labor might be used to support his orphanage in the colony.[32] In 1750, Davies cheerfully acknowledged that about one hundred slaves under his care "are the property of my people."[33] Jonathan Edwards, the eminent theologian of the Awakening, apparently owned a slave, as did Gilbert Tennent, the Presbyterian revivalist who crusaded against unconverted ministers.[34] Everywhere, converted slaveholders were joining evangelical fellowships without having to free their slaves. Evangelicals like Whitefield and Davies bequeathed a mixed legacy to their successors with regard to slavery. Both could express concern about the treatment of slaves and yet assert that from the perspective of eternity, the slave's temporal status did not really matter. Both could promise the slaveholder God's blessing if he took an interest in the slave's spiritual welfare, and they could prophecy God's judgment if the slaveholder did not mend his ways. Some of their successors resolved the ambiguity by assuming the prophet's mantle, taking up the retributive theme, and fashioning it into an attack upon slavery itself.

III

GEORGE WHITEFIELD DIED IN 1770, stricken in the course of yet another evangelistic tour through the colonies. Other giants of the Awakening had passed on before him: Jonathan Edwards in 1758, Samuel Davies in 1761, Gilbert Tennent in 1764, and Samuel Finley in 1766. The passing of these figures did not leave the forces of evangelicalism leaderless, however, for by 1770 a new company of evangelicals had risen to prominence, dedicated to consolidating the intellectual and numerical gains of the Awakening and to extending the frontiers of experimental religion. Many of these individuals had undergone their conversion in the days when the New Light shone at its brightest, while others had experienced the new birth in the soft afterglow of the Awakening. There were not only new leaders on the scene by 1770, but with the arrival of John Wesley's emissaries in 1769, there was also a new sect in America. In order to understand the role that some of these individuals played in the attack on slavery, it is necessary to highlight some developments that took place between the Awakening and the Revolution, which had a bearing on evangelical antislavery activity.

When Jonathan Edwards died, he left behind a body of divinity and a coterie of disciples who defended his variety of Calvinism against all its critics. Edwards' disciples have not fared well at the hands of historians. The group portrait that historians have drawn depicts a contentious brood of metaphysicians who became so fascinated with intricacies of consistent Calvinism that they lost touch with large sectors of churchgoing New England.[35] This portrait faithfully reproduces the less endearing features of the New Divinity spokesmen, as they came to be called, but it fails to convey either the depth of their devotional life or their genuine concern for the success of the new republic. Nor does it give any indication of why some of them took time off from their polemical labors to engage in antislavery work. Of all the spokesmen for the New Divinity, Samuel Hopkins and the younger Jonathan Edwards were the foremost antislavery activists.

Samuel Hopkins had a contemplative, some would say vacant, look about him. He fell under the spell of Edwards after hearing him deliver the commencement sermon at Yale in 1741. One January evening in 1742, while Hopkins was studying with Edwards in Northampton, Mrs. Sarah Edwards told those present that she would be willing "to die in darkness and horror, if it was most for the glory of God."[36] Her resignation of spirit made a deep impression on the youth, for in later years a willingness to be "damned for the glory of God" became for Hopkins a sign of true holiness. After an unsuccessful ministry at Great Barrington, he accepted a call to the First Congregational Church of Newport, Rhode Island. When he arrived in 1769, this tall, ungainly figure began to make visits to the docks of a major slavetrading port, and there he beheld the ships unloading Africans onto the piers. It was perhaps this experience that first made Hopkins directly aware of the horrors of the slave trade and started him on his antislavery career.

As one expression of his concern about the slave trade, Hopkins initiated a proposal to train two blacks for missionary work in Africa. Hopkins managed to interest Ezra Stiles in the project, but only after Stiles, a moderate Calvinist, had satisfied himself that Hopkins did not intend to make Africa a laboratory for the New Divinity. In a circular published in 1773 to raise money for the project, the two ministers called upon "those who are convinced of the iniquity of the *slave trade*" to consider whether the proposed mission was not "the best compensation we are able to make the poor Africans, for the injuries they are constantly receiving by this unrighteous practice and all its attendants."[37] The plea for contributions met with an encouraging response from believers in New England, New York, and Scotland. By attempting to channel antislavery sentiment into an overseas missionary venture, Hopkins anticipated the kind of appeal that New England ministers would make later in the century.

The younger Jonathan Edwards—another theologian of the New Divinity—inherited little of his father's imagination or temperament. A stiff-looking man who lacked pulpit grace and ease in social situations, the younger Edwards assumed pastoral duties at a church in New Haven, Connecticut in 1769, the same year that Hopkins arrived in Newport. In New Haven, Edwards cloistered himself in his study to prepare reprints of his father's work and carry on a pamphlet war with the enemies of Calvinism. "In the pulpit," one who had heard him recalled, "he was too profound to be interesting, or always intelligible to ordinary minds."[38] In antislavery work, Edwards found a cause which engaged his considerable polemical talents. "The more I consider it," Edwards wrote of slavery in 1774, "the more the subject enlarges in my view."[39] The subject so absorbed his attention in the 1770s that he collaborated with Ebenezer Baldwin, another Connecticut Calvinist, on a series of antislavery articles that appeared in the local newspaper.[40]

By gathering the greatest number of new members as a result of the Awakening, the Baptists of New England succeeded where New Divinity Congregationalists had failed. The desire for a pure church, which had guided the American Puritans in the seventeenth century, led a significant number of born-again New Englanders to view the Congregationalist practice of infant baptism as a source of corruption, an unscriptural ceremony that allowed unregenerate people into the church. Individuals of this persuasion left their Congregational churches to form new ones, where only those adults who could demonstrate their conversion were baptized and admitted as members. Their insistence on adult rather than infant baptism—later regarded as a harmless religious preference—reminded their contemporaries of the radical German Anabaptists, those sixteenth-century zealots who staged a bloody uprising at Münster in 1534. The Separate, or New Light, Baptists of New England found themselves laboring under a cloud of suspicion as a result of the Münster episode. The taint of fanaticism and the militant refusal to pay taxes in support of Congregational churches made the Baptists vulnerable to harassment, imprisonment, and distrainment of their goods.[41] Yet in spite of adversity, in many ways because of adversity, the Baptists of New England prospered: between 1740 and 1770, the number of Baptists churches in Massachusetts increased from eight to thirty-two, while in Connecticut the number grew from three to twenty-three.[42]

Despite their strength and aggressiveness, however, the Baptists of New England did not figure prominently in the antislavery activity of the region.[43] But by exporting revival fervor to the southern colonies, where evangelical sentiment against slavery flourished briefly, the New Light Baptists of New England made an indirect contribution to the evangelical attack on slavery.

The New Light Baptists gained a foothold in the southern colonies through the labors of Shubal Stearns and Daniel Marshall, two energetic Yankees who arrived with their families in Virginia in 1754. They traveled extensively throughout the Old Dominion and North Carolina and earned the name "strollers" for their itinerant mode of preaching. The Separate Baptists overcame the initial distrust of another group of Baptists in the area known as the Regular, or Particular Baptists, and encouraged them to expand their own evangelistic efforts.[44] Like their brethren in New England, the southern Baptist groups were accused of plotting sedition and all manner of unspeakable crimes against society. "What evil has not been reported of us?" David Thomas demanded to know in a forceful defense of Virginia Baptists. "Yea, what atrocious villa[i]ny can be mentioned, that has not been laid to our charge?" North Carolina's Governor Tryon stated the official position when he branded Baptists as "enemies to society and a scandal to common sense."[45] The Baptist rejection of the Anglican Church, their simple lifestyle, and their pleas for religious liberty set them apart as a disaffected group, especially in Virginia and North Carolina. Schooled in the experience of dissent, the Baptists applied some of their more memorable lessons to interpret the meaning of slavery.

American Presbyterians emerged from the controversies of the Awakening years to produce three antislavery spokesmen, two of whom had been students of Davies. Born in Hanover County, Virginia, David Rice followed Davies to the College of New Jersey in 1759, after Davies had accepted an offer to serve as president of the institution. When Rice returned to Hanover County a few years later, he was licensed by the presbytery, and he enjoyed more success among blacks than whites in his preaching. Rice had an eccentric streak that hindered him from achieving Davies' eminence as a pastor, but he occupied important posts in the councils of Virginia and Kentucky Presbyterianism.[46] Rice continued to voice his opposition to slavery well into the nineteenth century, long after many other evangelicals had fallen silent on the matter. Another student of Davies, the physician Benjamin Rush, retained an allegiance to evangelical Calvinism until at least 1780, at about which time he adopted a belief in the universal salvation of mankind. Even this position, according to a recent interpreter, represented an extension of his "youthful revivalistic faith," which was nurtured by Gilbert Tennent and Samuel Finley.[47] When Rush penned an address on slavery in the early 1770s, his piety had been deepened by the Scottish Enlightenment and given a social dimension by Davies' doctrine of "public spirit." Jacob Green, the third antislavery Presbyterian of note, had been profoundly affected by the preaching of Tennent and Whitefield while he was a student at Harvard in the early 1740s. Green launched his attacks on slavery from Hanover, New Jersey, using his pulpit and the press to set forth his convictions.[48]

The Congregationalists, Baptists, and Presbyterians had to compete with an entirely new religious group in the years following 1770. In 1769, John Wesley—the founder of Arminian Methodism—dispatched his first two itinerants to the colonies, and they were soon followed by six more preachers. Wesley's movement got its name back in the late 1720s, when John Wesley, his brother Charles, George Whitefield, and other members of Oxford's Holy Club met with ridicule for their "methodical" Bible study and devotional exercises. The movement spread far beyond the confines of Oxford in the 1730s and 1740s as a result of an extensive preaching ministry undertaken by the British evangelicals. A group of Irish emigrants in New York organized the first Methodist society in the colonies in 1766, but with the arrival of Wesley's missionaries, the Methodist initiative in America began in earnest. Until they constituted themselves as a separate church in 1784, the Methodists in America remained the revival wing of the Episcopal Church. They were organized into societies rather than churches, and subdivided into classes for intensive Bible study and discipline. At worship services called "love feasts," Methodists gathered to sing, pray, exchange testimonies, and partake of bread and water as a token of their mutual love.[49]

Of particular importance for the history of American Methodism and the evangelical antislavery movement was the arrival of Francis Asbury in 1771. Asbury, a man of a serious turn of mind, bid farewell to "dear old Daddy," as he referred to John Wesley, and set sail for America, never to see England again. On board ship he asked himself what this journey was all about, what he was going to do in America. "I am going to live to God, and to bring others so to do," he answered firmly.[50] In a journal entry which later editors saw fit to suppress, Asbury revealed that living unto God in America involved work on behalf of the slave. "I have lately been impressed with a deep concern, for bringing about the freedom of slaves in America," he wrote during the Revolution, "and feel resolved to do what I can to promote it." After acknowledging the need for divine assistance in this mission, Asbury continued, "I am strongly persuaded that if the Methodists will not yield on this point, and emancipate their slaves, God will depart from them."[51] Some American-born Methodists shared Asbury's conviction that there was a link between Methodist success and a stance against slavery and, in the course of their preaching duties, they attempted to persuade other Methodists to liberate their slaves.

By the eve of the Revolution, American evangelicals had taken up positions that brought them into contact with slavery or the slave trade. They could report no major revival in progress, but they had laid the institutional and intellectual foundations that would ensure the continuity of experimental religion through periods of trial. Many Americans read the signs of the times in the early 1770s: the colonies were entering a critical period.

IV

IN 1774, DEACON BENJAMIN COLMAN began circulating ideas that would lead to his expulsion from the church of Byfield, Massachusetts. Unlike other disturbers of the Congregational peace in New England, Colman laid no claim to immediate revelation, uttered no blasphemies, and committed no sexual offense. The deepening imperial crisis had plunged the deacon into a mood of introspection as solemn as that of a Puritan searching out his hidden sins. Colman's reflections brought him to the conclusion—so distasteful to his fellow churchmembers—that the colonies lay under God's judgment for the sin of keeping blacks in slavery. Until the colonists removed the "cruel yoke" of bondage from the necks of their slaves, Colman maintained, they should not expect the Lord to deliver them from the hand of British oppression.[52]

Colman was not alone in his interpretation of America's difficulties. In the 1770s, other evangelicals—many of them more influential than the deacon—began to see slavery as an emblem of colonial iniquity. As relations between Great Britain and the colonies deteriorated, clergymen from Massachusetts to Georgia mounted pulpits to call America to repentance. Along with their more secular-minded contemporaries, the ministers took stock of colonial virtue and found America's moral resources to be in an alarming state of depletion. Regarding the Coercive Acts and other British measures as afflictions sent by God to chastise a wanton people, the ministers led their flocks in rituals of fasting, humiliation, and prayer, for if the colonists confessed their sins and collectively resolved to do better, then and only then might the Lord give heed to their prayers for help against the British.[53] It was during this period of introspection, self-criticism, and fear that evangelical opposition to slavery first surfaced into public view.

By evincing a concern about the moral fiber of their contemporaries, evangelicals participated in a larger debate about whether or not republicanism was a suitable form of government for America. Republicanism, its advocates knew, required a great deal from a people; it demanded a willingness to turn aside from greed, envy, and luxury as well as a readiness to work for the common good. Americans scrutinized themselves carefully in the years before the Revolution, trying to decide what sort of people they were, whether they really had the virtue necessary to sustain a government based on the consent of the governed. A wide variety of religious and political leaders decided that not only were Americans bad, but they were getting steadily worse.[54]

Evangelicals agreed with this gloomy assessment of American moral character and blended their voices with southern philosophers and republican theorists to lament American depravity. In 1774, a Methodist preacher named Thomas Rankin surveyed what he regarded as America's abounding wickedness and concluded: "The judgments of God are spread abroad in these lands; and a most portentous cloud hangs over these provinces." Rankin attempted to lead the colonists to a "proper improvement of the present alarming tokens."[55] Deacon Benjamin Colman grew particularly exercised about a proposed dancing school in his area. He appealed to the friends of "experimental Religion" to consider whether it was appropriate to "indulge mirth & Carnal Recreation" when the Almighty called people to "Mourning & Humiliation." The times demanded a mood of seriousness about American corruption, according to Colman, not one of frivolity or merriment.[56]

To assist the colonists in a consideration of their manifold iniquities, evangelical leaders joined other clergymen in drawing up lists of sins that required attention. Like the prophets of ancient Israel, from whom the ministers borrowed some of their favorite sermon texts, they held up the sins that kindled the Lord's anger against them: neglect of religion, covetousness, profanity, drunkenness, and extravagance. The Puritan heritage gave New England clergymen a high degree of proficiency in this sort of exer-

cise, but ministers from the middle and southern colonies participated as well. Once hostilities had broken out, victory over British
arms became the goal of American exertions against their own
wickedness. The clergymen labored so diligently in their office
that by 1776, as Perry Miller phrased it, "the day of humiliation
was demonstrably one with the summons to battle."[57]

As some evangelicals recited the lists of sins, they included an
item that had never before appeared on the agenda for reformation, at least not outside Quaker fellowships. In a fast day sermon delivered during the war, for example, Jacob Green added
slavery to the catalogue of traditional sins: "Infidelity, profane
cursing and swearing, neglect and contempt of religion; selfishness, avarice and extortion; supporting and encouraging slavery;
criminal lang[ou]r and negligence in defence of our civil and
sacred rights."[58] Ebenezer Baldwin placed the enslavement of the
"poor African" at the top of his "dreadful catalogue," above even
worldliness, covetousness, and selfishness.[59] Deacon Coman urged
his fellow citizens to refrain from any "bitter reflection" upon the
British government and to search instead among themselves for
the causes of their misery. "Among the innumerable evils, that
abound among us," Colman volunteered, "I look upon the oppression, bondage and slavery exercised upon our poor brethren
the Africans to be a God-provoking and a wrath-procuring sin."[60]
Thomas Rankin took the occasion of the Congressional Fast Day
in 1775 to discourse on one aspect of Anglo-American apostasy,
proclaiming that "the sins of Great Britain and her colonies had
long cried aloud for vengeance; and in a peculiar manner, the
dreadful sin of buying and selling the souls and bodies of the
poor Africans . . ."[61] Benjamin Rush warned ministers about the
futility of their efforts to obtain God's favor without first addressing the sin of slavery. "In vain will you command your flocks to
offer up the incence of Faith and Charity, while they continue to
mingle the Sweat and Blood of the Negro slaves with their sacri-
fices," Rush told them.[62]

The strength of evangelical conviction about slavery owed as
much to the compelling demands of the fast day ritual as to the
logic of Revolutionary thought. To be sure, the language of colonial protest prompted such evangelicals as Jacob Green, Samuel

Hopkins, and Nathaniel Niles to highlight the inconsistency of professing a great love of liberty while denying freedom to blacks in their midst.[63] In pointing out the discrepancy between American profession and practice, however, these evangelicals did not differ at all from Revolutionary leaders like Patrick Henry and Thomas Jefferson, or even from a Loyalist like Thomas Hutchinson. But for antislavery evangelicals, the practice of keeping blacks in bondage represented something more than a failure to be consistent. Their concept of oppression resonated with meanings derived from the prophetic books of the Old Testament, which supplied them with texts and illustrations to impress the colonists with the need for genuine repentance. This dimension of their thinking gave their antislavery appeals a note of urgency that was absent from the sermons of liberal clergymen who touched upon the subject.[64]

The ritual of the fast day involved a resolution to behave better toward one's fellow men and women as well as toward God. In remarks delivered before the Philadelphia Association of Baptists, Abel Morgan outlined the social duties that would accompany the fast ritual as an indication of a people's sincerity. A truly repentant people should strive to "avoid all acts of oppression, and to show kindness to the needy," Morgan stated. Paraphrasing a verse in Isaiah 58, Morgan stressed that "the fast which the Lord has chosen . . . is to loose the bands of wickedness, to undo the heavy burdens, and to let the oppressed go free, to break every yoke, to deal bread to the hungry, to relieve the poor, to cover the naked." Morgan regretted the fact that American fast days were seldom accompanied by these acts of kindness.[65]

Antislavery evangelicals would have offered a hearty concurrence with Morgan's observations, but they went further and applied Old Testament injunctions against oppression and extortion to the case of the enslaved black. "Wo unto him that buildeth his house by Unrighteousness," Deacon Colman wrote, quoting the prophet Jeremiah, "and his Chambers by Wrong; that useth his Neighbor's Service without Wages, and Giveth him not for his Work." Colman then related his text to slaveholding.[66] Both Jacob Green and Benjamin Rush resorted to the Old Testament book of Amos to prove the sinfulness of slaveholding. In his fast day sermon, Green used the first two chapters of the book to remind Americans of the heavy punishments that God brought upon Tyre, Gaza, Edom, and Moab for their "cruelty to fellow creatures."[67] Rush referred to the fourth and eighth chapters, which dealt with the oppression of the poor and needy.[68] In a similar fashion, Samuel Hopkins alluded to biblical passages forbidding the exploitation of the defenseless. "Are not the African slaves among us the poor, the strangers, the fatherless, who are oppressed and vexed, and sold for silver?" he asked.[69] For these evangelicals, the existence of slavery mocked colonial pretensions of sorrow for sin; it revealed that Americans had not been sincere in their contrition because they had not been thorough in their reformation.

So abominable had slavery become to a few evangelicals that they verged on depicting it as the most concentrated form of evil on earth. "Slavery is an Hydra sin, and includes in it every violation of the precepts of the Law and the Gospel," Benjamin Rush declared.[70] When Elhanan Winchester summoned Virginians to consider some reigning abominations in 1774, he was still a Baptist in good standing, though in later years he would embrace the doctrine of universal salvation. In the sermon of 1774, Winchester contended that the slave trade involved "almost every vice that blackens and degrades human nature."[71] Hopkins may have sensed the perils of reducing the origins of American iniquity to a single practice, and he may have discerned a tendency within himself to do so; he hastily reminded his readers of their other failings. "When I speak of our being under divine judgments for this sin of enslaving the Africans," he wrote in 1776, "I do not mean to exclude other public crying sins found among us, such as impiety and profaneness, . . . intemperance and prodigality, and other instances of unrighteousness. . . . " It was just that slavery was a sin "most particularly pointed out" to Americans, and one so contrary to the laws of righteousness and a professed love of liberty that "we have no reason to expect, nor can sincerely ask deliverance, so long as we continue in a disposition to hold fast this iniquity."[72]

Whether slavery was a sin among sins or a particularly intense expression of evil, some evangelicals of the Revolutionary years had come to perceive it as a grave disability in the pursuit of righteousness. This belief was not solely a product of the Revolution, nor were its implications fully apparent to evangelicals who expressed it in sermons, newspapers, and pamphlets in the 1770s. What aspects of their religious experience contributed to this belief? Why was the prophetic role so congenial to evangelicals? Why did they assign slaves a place among traditional unfortunates such as orphans and widows? How did republicanism influence evangelical ideas about slavery? What would the antislavery evangelicals do to implement their beliefs within the churches? To understand the origins and durability of evangelical antislavery commitment, one must turn to the evangelical experience for attitudes that could issue in an aversion to slaveholding.

II
OUTCASTS
OF
MEN

URING HIS VISIT TO THE AMERICAN COLONIES in the late 1740s, Swedish botanist Peter Kalm noted the widespread reluctance of whites to have their slaves instructed in Christian doctrine. Kalm, careful observer of American behavior, attributed part of that reluctance to "the conceit of its being shameful, to have a spiritual brother or sister among so despicable a people. . . ."[1] At mid-century, Kalm could not foresee the spread of a style of spirituality that placed a high value on association with those thrust beyond the pale of social respectability. Evangelicals who typified the new religious vogue were far from regarding fellowship with slaves as a shameful, distasteful affair; they counted themselves blessed when they could associate with those held in low esteem by the great and mighty of this world.

This chapter examines the role that evangelical spirituality played in the formation of antislavery commitment. In the years that led up to the Revolution, American evangelicals cultivated a lifestyle which expressed their renunciation of the world and their devotion to the ideal of apostolic simplicity. This style of spirituality enabled white believers to associate slavery with more familiar evils, thereby creating the possibility, but not the certainty, of antislavery commitment. For all its limitations, this distinctive religious style helped to sustain an antislavery concern among evangelicals in the last quarter of the eighteenth century.

I

ONE OF JOHN WESLEY'S FIRST MISSIONARIES to America embodied the attributes of the model circuit rider. "Pain and Poverty, reproach and tribulation, sufferings and death, all is nothing so I may but win Christ and promote his kingdom in the world," Joseph Pilmore wrote in 1770.[2] The Christ of Pilmore's gospel was the lowly Jesus, the suffering servant who ministered to the needy and who associated with disreputable types. For evangelicals like Pilmore, the promotion of Christ's kingdom required a willingness to forsake worldly comforts and endure the rigors of the godly life. As exponents of what H. Richard Niebuhr termed the "Christ against culture" viewpoint,[3] these evangelicals, Methodists and Baptists for the most part, defined themselves in opposition to the dominant structures of power and social prestige. They made much out of the fact that their followers often came from the ranks of the poor and illiterate, for in their estimation this gave an apostolic character to their movement. They imagined themselves standing on the edge of the social order, calling people out from the corruptions of an ungodly world to a life of simplicity and humility. No one crossed any geographical boundaries, for the evangelicals' separation occurred on the level of value and attitude. Through their conduct, their dress, and even through the company they kept, the Methodists and Baptists displayed their disengagement from worldly concerns.

To convince people of the urgent need for repentance and separation from evil, Methodist preachers frequently employed biblical texts announcing God's judgment. "Turn ye, turn ye from all your evil ways," declared Pilmore after the prophet Ezekiel, "for why will ye die O house of Israel."[4] James Meacham, a preacher in Virginia, also took his cue from the Old Testament prophets; Meacham never simply delivered a sermon, but "cried" his message up and down the land in the manner of Isaiah.[5] Freeborn Garrettson revealed his fondness for Revelation 6:17 by referring to it as "my old text": "The great day of his wrath is come, and who shall be able to stand."[6] Following the lead of John the Baptist, Pilmore warned his contemporaries to "flee from the wrath to come."[7] Through the use of such texts, the Methodist preachers sought to detach their listeners from a preoccupation with earthly affairs and impress them with the transience of the social world that they inhabited. The preachers tempered their message of judgment with assurances of God's mercy to the sinner, but their central purpose remained to gather a people out from the world and form them into holy communities. Indeed, in the early years of American Methodism, the only requirement necessary for a person to be admitted into a Methodist society was a professed desire to "flee from the wrath to come."[8] But how could such a desire be expressed as the Methodist converts went about their daily business? How would they manifest a godly indifference to the blandishments of wealth and social prestige?

For those who would flee from the wrath to come, Methodist leaders prescribed a lifestyle in which self-effacement and humility figured prominently. As the founder of American Methodism, Francis Asbury exemplified many of the hallmarks of Methodist spirituality. He maintained such a deep concern about his own humility that he underwent a spiritual crisis when some friends were so "imprudent" as to compliment him to his face. As he related the incident, Satan immediately filled him with "self-pleasing, self-exalting ideas" until God stepped in to deliver him from pride. "May he ever keep me humble," Asbury prayed, "and little, and mean, in my own eyes!"[9] To guard against pride, and to keep a proper self-image, members of Methodist societies were "to be as the filth and offscouring of the world," an identity taken from St. Paul's description of the apostle's lot (I Cor. 4:13).[10]

Besides maintaining a concern about their humility, pious Methodists chose pastimes and clothes that would deepen their sense of separation from the world, even as they went about their daily tasks. They avoided costly apparel and any ornamentation betraying an inclination toward "Softness and needless self-indulgence." Frivolous pursuits like gambling, card playing or horse racing had no place in the godly life, and Methodist leaders condemned the acquisitive impulse as an unholy desire to lay up treasures on earth.[11] In a versified journal entry, Asbury condensed the elements of self-denial and social alienation that went into the Methodist identity: "Nothing on earth I call my own:/ A stranger, to the world unknown. . . ."[12]

In its renunciation of worldly vanities, the lifestyle of the Baptists bore a strong resemblance to that advocated by their Methodist counterparts. Much in the manner of the Methodists, the Baptists thought of themselves as a "poor despised company"[13] of believers, existing on the borders of social respectability, refusing to conform to the tastes and conventions of polite society. As one

Virginia gentleman told it, this meant that the Baptists were "quite destroying pleasure in the Country; for they encourage ardent Pray'r; strong & constant faith, & an entire Banishment of *Gaming, Dancing,* and Sabbath-Day Diversions."[14] Moreover, no pleasantries, rhetorical graces, or verbal conceits adorned the Baptist proclamation of the gospel. David Thomas found "our present gravity" more suitable for preaching than the jesting and bantering demanded by the "polite airs" of the world.[15] A lack of gentility could even be a spiritual asset. Robert Semple, an early historian of the Virginia Baptists, celebrated an era when Baptist ministers, "unrefined in their manners, and awkward in their address," turned these shortcomings to advantage and reaped a harvest of souls.[16]

The Baptists further demonstrated the depth of their spirituality through the way they dressed. Semple believed that God blessed the labors of the early Baptist itinerants because they were, among other things, "very plain in their dress," while "pampered" Anglican ministers lay "rolling on the bed of luxury."[17] The Separates of Virginia refused to unite with the Regulars in 1772, suspecting them of indulging their members in "superfluity of apparel."[18] John Leland, a Baptist preacher from New England who was certainly no fop when it came to clothes, found himself in violation of the Virginia Baptist dress code by adhering to the custom of his native region, "each one putting on such apparel as suited his own fancy."[19] This casual attitude toward one's personal appearance simply would not do among people who advertised their separation from the world by means of a stylized simplicity. The Separates who entered South Carolina maintained such a "preciseness" about their clothes and speech that another Baptist in the region compared them to the Quakers.[20] Plain dress, plain talk, and plain manners ranked high in the Baptist scheme of values and kept members a safe distance from "the glittering world."[21]

As a measure of their success in developing a distinctive style of spirituality, the evangelicals could be clearly identified on the American landscape. When some Presbyterian students at Hampden-Sydney College began meeting in private for devotional exercises, their fellow students berated them for carrying on in a "methodistic manner."[22] Colonel Landon Carter, a Virginian planter of strong opinions and little appreciation for religious enthusiasm, detected "the demure air of a new light or an Anabaptist" in the behavior of one of his tenants.[23] John Leland recalled an incident from his school days in Grafton, Massachusetts, when his Latin master ordered him "not to preach like a new light, but to speak like a scholar." Leland's schoolmates teased him by calling him a New Light, but when he asked them what a New Light was, "they would be as confused in their answers as if they did not know B from a bull's foot."[24] Although a precise definition might have eluded them, eighteenth-century Americans recognized one of those pious types when they saw one.

Both the Methodists and the Baptists marveled at the unlikely instruments that God had chosen to carry out His will, for just as in the days of the apostles, they believed, God had chosen the despised and lowly to confound the wisdom of the mighty. Asbury enthusiastically noted the role of "such simple men, of such small abilities, and no learning" in the growth of Methodism.[25] "The truth is," David Thomas asserted, "poverty, the want of erudition, and the malice of an ungodly world, are just so many more likely characters of God's election, than of the contrary."[26] For William Fristoe, the shortage of rich converts "gave clearer proof of the genuine quality of religion among us," for in the early Christian era it was the "common people" who received the Word with gladness. Not that poverty placed the Almighty under obligation to bestow grace, as Fristoe quickly pointed out, but it permitted Christians to escape "a gaudy, superfluous appearance, a stream whose rapid current has swept the polite world away."[27] The Baptists and Methodists never tired of pointing out their humble circumstances, for a lack of gentility strengthened their claim to an apostolic descent.

Although evangelicals drew most of their recruits from the lower and middling ranks of society, they could count a well-to-do convert here and there. Biographical sketches of early leaders sometimes describe an individual as a "man of considerable fortune," "a man of reputation," or a man of "respectable parentage."[28] Pennsylvania Presbyterians could claim socially eminent members like General Roberdeau, Virginia Baptists had the likes of Robert

Carter of Nomini Hall in their midst for a time, and Baptist Isaac Backus came from a fine Connecticut family. A sprinkling of respectable converts, however, did nothing to undermine evangelical confidence in the movement's apostolicity. After all, two Baptists observed, I Corinthians 1:26 declared that "not *many* wise men after the flesh, not *many* mighty, not *many* noble" were called to salvation; the text did not say "not *any*."[29]

Furthermore, born-again gentlefolk were expected to conform to the vogue of stylized simplicity when they entered the evangelical community. In a self-conscious display of power and social standing, Colonel Samuel Harriss showed up at a Virginia Baptist meeting in full military regalia. But as Harriss' sense of conviction deepened in the course of the service, he discarded his sword, badges, and other ornaments, thus signifying his passage from the old life to the new. And Garrettson expressed approval when two "very dressy women" underwent conversion and attended a subsequent meeting "dressed very plain."[30] In their class analysis of the movement, evangelicals therefore had it both ways. When a stray gentry convert wandered into the fold, they would rejoice in the fact that not even the most fashionable sinner was beyond redemption. But when the wellborn held aloof, evangelicals remembered that few rich men would enter the Kingdom of God.

Once they joined an evangelical community, rich, poor, and middle-class believers often assumed roles quite different from those to which they had been accustomed. Evangelical commentators were correct in their assertion that people of negligible wealth, intellect, and social standing rose to positions of prominence in the movement. Through religious activities, these individuals discovered gifts which opened new avenues for leadership and self-expression.[31] Genteel converts shed their finery and accepted instruction from their social inferiors. An awareness of social distinctions did not disappear entirely in the fellowship of the Spirit, for evangelicals could still identify the rich and the poor among their simply-clad brethren. But in the early years of evangelicalism, believers esteemed only those who possessed a wealth of religious experience and the favor of the Lord, and such people could come from any level of society.

For evangelicals who gloried in their simplicity, who flaunted their lack of refinement as a badge of spirituality, the company of other social outcasts provided a source of edification and instruction. Among those individuals traditionally classified as needy, such as the sick, the imprisoned, and the poor, evangelicals tested their humility as they enhanced their self-image. This kind of ministry was, as Joseph Pilmore said of visiting sick persons, a "*painful* but very *profitable*" task,[32] a labor fraught with challenges, but which promised to yield spiritual benefits for the persevering believer.

By exercising a concern for the victims of misfortune, Wesley's early missionaries to America carried on a work that dated back to the 1730s. At that time, members of Oxford's Holy Club conducted visitations to local jails and poorhouses.[33] After Pilmore's arrival in Philadelphia, he ministered to the "poor distressed creatures" in the prison and the "distressed fellow creatures" in the poorhouse.[34] Pilmore was repeatedly struck by the spiritual discernment of these unfortunates; he contrasted their piety favorably with that of their social betters. During an errand of mercy to the inmates of a poorhouse, Pilmore "found more satisfaction in their conversation than that of the most refined & polite Citizens who are strangers to God."[35] Instead of going to church on one Sabbath in 1772, Pilmore preached to the "poor neglected prisoners in the Gaol, who were greatly affected under the word, and their flowing tears encouraged me to hope that some of them may enter into the kingdom of God, though many self-righteous Pharisees be shut out."[36] Thus was the Kingdom of Heaven in Pilmore's eyes: the unfortunate somehow enjoyed God's favor, while the worldly person of substance lacked in spiritual insight.

Black slaves comprised one group of afflicted humanity not included in the Holy Club's routine of visitation but, in the late 1730s, John Wesley inadvertently prepared the way for their eventual inclusion in the ranks of the unfortunate. During his first and only visit to the American shores, Wesley conducted an unspectacular evangelistic tour through parts of Georgia. An interview with a black woman in the province led him to exclaim, "When shall the Sun of Righteousness arise on these outcasts of men, with healing in his wings!"[37] By recording his exclamation, Wesley supplied devoted readers of his journal with a conceptual device in the form of a phrase, a convenient designation which they could use to interpret the slave's status. For Wesley's successors in America, work among black "outcasts of men," whether slave or free, became an extension of their ministry to traditional objects of charity.

Methodist preachers enrolled slaves into the ranks of the unfortunate by several means. Jesse Lee simply added one more item to his duty roster. "This morning I met the black class, visited a sick person, and then went and visited the prisoners before preaching," he noted casually on one occasion.[38] While recording the progress of work among slaves in South Carolina, Asbury grouped slaves with individuals who had long been a target of Methodist endeavor: "these are the poor; these are the people we are more immediately called to preach to."[39] And, as they had done with the inmates of jails and poorhouses, Methodist preachers drew comparisons between the faith of the needy and the prosperous. Upon hearing some New York blacks deliver accounts of their religious experience, Thomas Rankin remarked, "If the rich in this society were as much devoted to God as the poor are, we should see wonders done in this city."[40] In Pilmore's mind, the pious slave occupied a position analogous to the penitent prisoner who would enter the Kingdom, while the master, cast in the role of the self-righteous Pharisee, might find himself excluded. "How many of these poor Slaves will rise up in judgment against their Masters," he asked in 1772, "and porhaps [sic] enter into life, while they [the masters] are shut out."[41] Similarly, William McKendree predicted that many slaves would see heaven's glories while their "proud oppressors" would be denied admission.[42]

White evangelicals of differing denominational backgrounds beheld in the pious black, slave or free, someone who seemed to conform to their ideal of spirituality in almost every respect. Here, they discerned, was another member of despised, downtrodden humanity, alienated from centers of power and social prestige, but yet enjoying the Lord's favor. "O condescending Jehovah," William McKendree prayed after speaking to some blacks, "that attends the feeblest indeavours of the least and meanest of thy creatures."[43] William Hill, a Presbyterian, found a source of spiritual uplift in the testimony of a "poor persecuted negro." Baptist

Richard Dozier listened attentively to a black preacher in Virginia and commented, "Oh, see God choosing the weak things of this world to confound the things that are mighty."[44] In the case of the slave, the white evangelical had someone who would not be likely to succumb to worldly affectation or "needless self-indulgence." The fact that the slave's situation left him little room for such temptations did not diminish the white evangelical's admiration for him. And if suffering and privation were heaven-sent opportunities for spiritual advancement, then, according to the white evangelical viewpoint, the religious slaves were entitled to a generous share of blessings. Freeborn Garrettson announced his firm conviction that "the sufferings of those poor out-casts of men, through the blessing of God, drove them near to the Lord, and many of them were amazingly happy."[45] Mean in the eyes of the world, great in the sight of God, the pious slave appealed to the white evangelical imagination as a model of simplicity and faith under trial.

Association with religious slaves became a fashionable pastime for white evangelicals who abjured worldly ornamentation and who desired to perfect their own humility. Freeborn Garrettson cherished the "precious moments" that he could spend with his "poor out-casts of men."[46] Similarly, James Meacham discovered that "my Soul was much blessed indeed among my poor outcast[s] of Men. . . ."[47] Part of the white evangelical's sense of delight derived from an expectation that contact with the downtrodden would enrich his own piety. While the white brethren held a love feast in the parlor of a South Carolina house, Asbury remained in the kitchen with the slaves to practice the way of humility. "I must be poor: this is the will of God concerning me," he told himself.[48] William McKendree relished the thought of abasing himself before slaves. "I think if ever I was truly humble in my life twas this evening," he recalled after one summer service. "I felt [a] little like I was under all their feet[.] . . . thought I could let the dear humble black people that sat praising the Lord . . . walk upon me with pleasure if it would bring Glory to my King."[49] McKendree's contact with slaves nourished such fantasies and confirmed his identity as one of the despised of the earth.

Evangelicals like Meacham, Garrettson, Asbury, and McKendree

embraced the slave as a kindred spirit, invested him with beatific
attributes, and admitted him to the society of outcasts. Had their
interest in the enslaved black ended there, these four Methodists
might have been content to let him stay in bondage, safe from the
snares of the world. Yet they and other white evangelicals went
beyond a desire to associate with the downtrodden slave, and
committed themselves to seek his emancipation. Their antislavery
commitment was encouraged by another aspect of evangelical spirituality, one which promised emotional rewards for measures
undertaken to relieve the distress of someone as afflicted as the
slave.

II

"IT IS EVIDENT, THAT YOU ARE the most melancholy people in the
world," ran a common jibe at the Baptists. "Always sighing! groan-
ing! weeping! mourning! Surely you have no joy on earth."[50] From
the perspective of a detached observer, it must have seemed as
though the Baptists practiced a very dolorous kind of religion, but
from the Baptist point of view, the ability to shed abundant tears
signified a believer's openness to the Spirit of God. As David
Thomas stated forthrightly, "lively Christians are apt to weep
much. . . ."[51]

Ever since the days when George Whitefield and Gilbert Tennent had gone about denouncing cold and lifeless piety, the religious affections had occupied a central place in the American
evangelical experience. Baptists and Methodists had a special fondness for sentimental display, often climaxing their meetings in a
shower of tears. Displays of sentiment accompanied acts of charity
as well as acts of worship, for benevolent evangelicals responded
to human need in an emotional, but stylized, manner. As they
sought to relieve the suffering of slaves, some white evangelicals
arrived at the conclusion that nothing short of emancipation would
secure lasting relief for the enslaved black. The religious sensibility of these evangelicals supplied the emotional incentives for
them to act on behalf of the slave.

As the recorded experience of Baptist and Methodist leaders
makes clear, evangelicals of the Revolutionary period exhibited
their piety through effusions of sentimentality. Francis Asbury,

for example, treasured those moments in his preaching career when "a melting tenderness went through the congregation," reducing everyone present to a state of tears.[52] For such "melting times" to occur, Asbury had to establish a rapport with his audience, and then, through an impassioned mode of address, raise the emotional susceptibilities of his listeners. A cloudburst of tears would release the tensions generated by his emphasis on the sinner's guilt and God's gracious offer of forgiveness. Often, however, Asbury found that his auditors lacked the "spiritual sensibility" to achieve the desired emotional state, a deficiency that he attributed to a preoccupation with worldly concerns.[53] After lackluster performances on his part, Asbury would berate himself for a want of "sensibility." But when he found people sufficiently "tender," and when he himself felt "liberty" in preaching, both preacher and congregation basked in the warm glow of Christian fellowship. Among some New Jersey believers, for example, Asbury discovered that his heart was "warm and expanded in preaching to them."[54]

Baptist and Methodist preachers measured the depth of the worship experience by the amount of tears shed at their meetings. In the wake of one satisfying session, a Baptist minister surveyed the house and noted proudly: "it is a fact, that the floor of it was as wet with the tears of the people, as if water had been sprinkled all over it, or with a shower of rain."[55] At a baptismal service in 1771, Daniel Fristoe and his fellow Baptists expressed their ineffable joy in a manner that outsiders failed to appreciate. "The multitude stood round weeping, . . . when we sang *Come we that love the lord* & they were so affected that they lifted up their hands and faces toward heaven and discovered such chearful countenances in the midst of flowing tears as I had never seen before," Fristoe wrote in his journal.[56] The solvent of tears could even occasionally reduce the better sorts to a state of conviction. Methodist Jesse Lee, overcome by emotion to the point where he could not utter a word, noticed that there was "scarcely a dry eye in the house: some of the most dressy people shook, being deeply affected with the word which reached their hearts."[57]

Needless to say, these performances inspired derision and mirth in many quarters. In an address to the "Anabaptists" imprisoned in Virginia in 1771, an anonymous writer branded Baptist piety as excessively "sour, gloomy, severe."[58] John Taylor's attempt to introduce an evangelical sensibility into the ranks of the patriot army met with a mixed reception. "Some of the poor soldiers became much affected under preaching, and were despised by their officers, declaring that my preaching disqualified them for fighting, their fellow-soldiers also despised their tears and sorrows."[59] In a lampoon of what was then passing for religiosity, a local wit submitted "A Receipe to Make an AnaBaptist Preacher in Two Days Time" to the editors of the *Virginia Gazette*. Mix a potion of pride, discord, and stubbornness, the writer advised, give it to a dissenter, and "he will make a wry Face, wink with his Eyes, and squeeze out some Tears of Dissimulation."[60] The Methodists and Baptists, for their part, were unmoved by such ridicule, for whether they wept for their sins or their salvation, these evangelicals clearly enjoyed a good cry.

The presence of blacks at these tearful sessions had the effect of heightening the emotional intensity of the proceedings. Once again, the Methodists provide the most vivid accounts. After Asbury conducted a meeting in New York, very early in his American ministry, he expressed sentiments remarkably similar to those of Presbyterian Samuel Davies: "To see the poor Negroes so affected in pleasing, to see their sable countenances in our solemn assemblies, and to hear them sing with cheerful melody their dear Redeemer's praise, affected me much, and made me ready to say, 'Of a truth I perceive God is no respecter of persons'."[61] On another occasion, Asbury was "greatly affected with the sight of the poor Negroes, seeing their sable faces at the table of the Lord."[62] Joseph Pilmore also testified that "the number of the blacks that attend the preaching affects me much."[63] These were not simply the responses of the spiritual leaders. In the course of an exceptionally edifying love feast in 1774, Thomas Rankin rose and directed the people to look to that part of the chapel where the blacks were seated. "I then said," he reported, "'See the number of the black Africans who have stretched out their hands and hearts to God!' While I was addressing the people thus, it seemed as if the very house shook with the mighty power and glory of Sinai's God." Many present were so overcome that they nearly fainted.[64]

What was there about blacks, as white evangelicals perceived them, that could provoke such outpourings of sentiment? Why did their presence so arouse the religious affections of pious whites?

To answer these questions, and to better understand the role of sentiment in American evangelicalism, it is necessary to survey the religious, philosophical, and literary trends that culminated in the eighteenth-century cult of sensibility. In Restoration England, a group of Anglican clergymen known as Latitudinarians set forth a view of human nature that emphasized man's capacity to act altruistically. This viewpoint, which the Latitudinarians developed in reaction to Puritan and Hobbesian appraisals of man, stressed the emotional disposition of the altruist. Benevolence, as they defined it, included not only the performance of specific acts of charity, but also the feelings of pity and compassion that accompanied such acts. The truly benevolent man, the "man of feeling," as he would later be called, would cultivate the ability to dissolve into tears at the plight of the unfortunate, for by doing so he would demonstrate a highly refined moral sensibility. In addition to this religious development, a school of ethical sentimentalism— descending from Thomas Burnet and the Earl of Shaftesbury through Francis Hutcheson—defined the moral sense of a faculty which distinguished good from evil by a subjective response. Finally, British poets, playwrights, and novelists of the eighteenth century popularized the vogue of "moral weeping" by depicting human misery in such a way as to call forth an effusion of "tender feelings."[65] As a result of these trends, benevolent individuals indulged themselves in "a sort of pleasing Anguish, that sweetly melts the Mind" when confronted by real or fictitious objects of charity.[66]

In their adapted version of the eighteenth-century cult of sensibility, British and American evangelicals linked outpourings of emotion with godliness: a display of "tender feelings" served principally as an expression of sensitivity to God's Spirit rather than a demonstration of moral refinement. And yet the ethical note was not absent from the evangelical rendering of a cultural theme. As

a "man of feeling" in a sinful world, the new creature in Christ
would expend quantities of tears over the plight of the wretched.
Pity and compassion would accompany his benevolent exertions
on their behalf. Act and feeling blended into a pleasing whole for
the evangelical as he opened his heart and his purse to the victims
of misfortune.

Among early American Methodists, the practice of benevolence
had an almost devotional significance. A benevolent disposition,
according to a hymn sung at Methodist services, followed upon
conversion as a response to God's transforming love:

> pure benevolence and love
> O'erflow the faithful heart:
> Chang'd in a moment, we
>   The sweet attraction find,
> With open arms of charity,
>   Embracing all mankind.[67]

If the embrace of all mankind appeared too vague or too exacting
a demand, the popular literature of Methodism defined suitable
objects of charity with more precision. "Benevolence with generous glow / Hastens to soothe the widow's woe, / And wipe the
orphan's eyes," wrote one Methodist poet.[68] As the poet's reference
to a "generous glow" suggested, the exemplary Methodist would
hurry to the scene of need in a flush of sentiment. Through a
tearful display of sympathy, the Methodist identified with the unfortunate in his distress:

> We weep with those that weep below,
> And burden'd for th' afflicted sigh:
> The various scenes of human woe
> Excite our softest sympathy.[69]

Expansive and lachrymose, Methodist benevolence gave the believer the opportunity to recreate the emotions of the love feast
and the preaching service.

Although he was not given over to great displays of sentiment,
Congregationalist Samuel Hopkins also assigned the affections a
prominent role in the Christian's pursuit of benevolence. True
holiness, as Hopkins defined it, consisted in the exercise of "dis-

interested benevolence," a term which denoted the selfess desire
to seek the good of all beings. During one of his meditations,
Hopkins reflected on the relationship between benevolence and
Christian humility. "How do Christians find out their own humility," he asked himself. "How does it exercise itself with respect to
their fellow-creatures?" His answer reveals that association with
the downtrodden perfected humility for Calvinists as it did for
Methodist believers. We show our humility, Hopkins wrote, in our
disposition

> to set others . . . above ourselves; and not to value our-
> selves, and lift ourselves up above others in our own
> thoughts, because of any external distinctions, and ad-
> vantages we may have above them—In an inclination
> to treat the meanest and lowest with condescention and
> kindness, heartily wishing them well and seeking their
> good.[70]

The man who, in his youth, had heard Mrs. Edwards welcome
suffering for the glory of God found a social outlet for his intense
concern about humility. This meditation, overlooked by students
of Hopkinsian benevolence,[71] sheds much light on his antislavery
commitment, and perhaps that of other New Divinity men as well.

Hopkins' benevolent Christian entered into a sympathetic relationship with other individuals and thereby multiplied the sources
of emotional gratification. Universal benevolence "enlarges and
ennobles the mind, and puts the benevolent person in possession
of the good and happiness of others, so that he enjoys it all in a
great degree, and rejoices with those who rejoice," Hopkins explained.[72] Hopkinsian benevolence contained an element which
strongly resembled the "sweet attraction" of its Methodist counterpart, for as one of its fruits, universal benevolence would "unite
all the particular members of the society to each other, and form
them into a band of brothers. . . ."[73] As for the unregenerate,
Hopkins followed the elder Edwards in admitting that God had
endowed them with "natural pity, or compassion," a faculty which
served useful social purposes even though it fell far short of true
benevolence.[74]

American evangelicals envisioned the good society as a network of benevolent believers, united by ties of sentiment, their hearts quivering with affectionate regard for the well-being of others. But of all the scenes of human woe that could excite sympathy in the evangelical breast, black slavery surely represented one of the most grim. White evangelicals, who had already classed slaves among the downtrodden of the earth, wept over their plight, even those who turned up at their meetings, and sought ways to alleviate their distress. James O'Kelly, a Methodist antislavery spokesman of fiery temperament, testified: "The sorrows of my heart are enlarged by hearing, and mine eye affecteth my soul, in beholding the sorrowful scenes that have lately fallen within my province."[75] The heart of another Methodist, Thomas Haskins, was greatly "affected" by the spectacle of a recaptured runaway forced to walk barefoot in January. Haskins "spoke with compassion for the poor Creature," and the master relented.[76] It was a minor victory, but Haskins undoubtedly went away gratified by the thought that he had been able to help at least one unfortunate that day.

By its sheer immediacy and magnitude, the slave system taxed the ability of some evangelicals to respond to suffering in the prescribed manner. During an excursion through Maryland, Asbury beheld "such cruelty to a Negro that I could not feel free to stay; I called for my horse, delivered my own soul, and departed."[77] Preachers could deliver themselves from isolated instances of cruelty, but the day-to-day brutalities of the system could not be so easily avoided. James Meacham discovered that exposure to the cruelties of slavery cramped his style of spirituality. "I [had] little or no liberty in speaking," he wrote at the close of one day's work, "only a burning fury in my Soul against blood and oppression. . . ."[78] Indeed, the slave system and its attendant horrors weighed upon Meacham's spirits until his depression seemed to be a kind of bondage itself: "O! how terribly I was impressed with the enormous weight of the gaulding [galling] yoke of oppression," Meacham wrote.[79]

O'Kelly, Haskins, Asbury, and Meacham all hated the practice of holding blacks in bondage, and their reflections illustrate the way in which white evangelicals could become emotionally engaged in the cause of the slave. Antislavery evangelicals, greatly affected by the misery of the slaves, realized that only emancipation would secure certain deliverance from oppression—oppression of slaves as well as oppression of the spirit.

As they undertook to persuade others to their way of thinking, the evangelicals directed their appeals to the sensibility of the slaveholder. Taking an opportunity to plead "very affectionately" for the slave, William McKendree achieved results identical to those he would have endeavored to produce at a preaching service. "The hearts of many seem'd truly melted," he noted with satisfaction.[80] Other evangelicals rehearsed the horrors of slavery to sensitize their audience to the suffering of blacks. In *A Dialogue Concerning the Slavery of the Africans,* Samuel Hopkins included particulars about the slave trade to awaken his readers "to feelings of humanity and pity toward our brethren who are the miserable sufferers."[81] Such a response, it will be remembered, even the unregenerate could make through their natural faculties. "Brethren!" the Methodist O'Kelly announced, "do me justice; lay open this evil in its native colours, and surely you will agree that it deserves the abhorrence of every feeling, every good man."[82] David Rice, the Presbyterian protégé of Samuel Davies who enjoyed success in his ministry among the blacks of Virginia, asked: "Where is the heart, that does not melt at this scene of woe?"[83] According to John Wesley's *Thoughts on African Slavery,* written in England and read by Methodists in America, the softening of a slaveholder's heart was a spiritual event comparable to the stirrings of grace:

> Have you no sympathy, no sense of human woe, no
> pity for the miserable? . . . Did not one tear drop from
> your eye, one sigh escape from your breast? . . . But
> if your heart does relent, though in a small degree,
> know it is a call from the God of love. And "to-day, if
> you will hear his voice, harden not your heart."[84]

By itself, the cultivation of an evangelical sensibility did not inevitably produce sympathy for the slave, much less lead to antislavery commitment. Quite conceivably, an evangelical could have wept over the misery of a distant object of pity while keeping blacks in bondage at home. Or, like Davies, he might delight in the company of slaves and do nothing to change their temporal status. But if the white evangelical ever had to face the threat of persecution, there was a greater likelihood that he would view the slave's situation with more sensitivity.

III

EVANGELICALS WHO SUBSCRIBED to the ideal of apostolic simplicity believed that persecution had a salutary effect on the godly life. Christ's Sermon on the Mount taught them to rejoice when they suffered abuse for their faith: "Blessed are ye, when men shall revile you, and persecute you, and shall say all manner of evil against you falsely, for my sake" (Matt. 5:11). Fortified by such texts and by the example of the early Church, evangelicals of the Revolutionary era not only expected persecution, but sometimes welcomed it as a confirmation of their fidelity to the apostolic model. In addition to its role in strengthening religious conviction, the experience of persecution stiffened the antislavery commitment of white evangelicals by bringing them to a deeper understanding of the meaning of oppression.

As privileged members of a religious establishment, evangelical Congregationalists in Connecticut and Massachusetts could hardly be described as the downtrodden of the earth. They enjoyed the protection of the civil authorities and attended churches supported by tax revenues. Yet representatives of these favored groups seized upon every slight, insult, or lukewarm response as evidence that they, like the apostles, had been rejected by the world. At an ordination ceremony, Levi Hart advised ministers not to seek "the empty applause of this vain world," for God's most trusted servants often incurred the reproach of their contemporaries. "Alas!" Hart cried, "that this awful truth should receive additional confirmation, from the treatment given to the gospel, in common, at this day!"[85]

Such statements must have seemed like pure affectation to Methodists and Baptists, for they had to endure more verbal and physical abuse than any other evangelical group in America. In an appraisal of a journey undertaken through the southern colonies in 1773, Pilmore wrote that "the Slanderous reports that were raised of me, together with the opposition I some times met with, made my way sufficiently rough, . . . yet the Lord has brought me safe through all and made me more than conqueror through faith in the Lamb."[86] After encountering opposition to his preaching, Asbury compared his situation to that of a famous biblical personality: "My soul is amongst the lions, but the God of Daniel is with me."[87] American Methodists also bore a stigma as Tories, partly because of their British connections, but mainly because of Wesley's attack on the American position in *A Calm Address to our American Colonies*. Freeborn Garrettson, suspected of Loyalist sentiments, rode into Dover, Delaware in 1778 while a mob shouted, "hang him, hang him."[88] After enduring a beating, Garrettson managed to confess: "My affliction was good for me. . . ."[89] Garrettson was once described as "all meekness and love, and yet all activity," but he displayed considerable courage as he made his rounds. His tormentors pursued him even in his dreams. He related that while asleep one night, "I thought I saw an innocent creature chased almost to death, by a company of dreadful beings. . . ."[90] His line of work exacted a considerable physical and psychological toll from him.

The Baptist quest for religious freedom opened members to forms of harassment ranging from catcalls to physical abuse. In New England, the Separate Baptists endured punishments for their refusal to pay taxes in support of Congregationalism. Detractors circulated rumors that Isaac Backus, the sturdy leader of the New England Baptists, "had Bastards in this or that place."[91] William Fristoe recalled the early years of the southern Baptist movement as a time when preachers "were exposed to sneers, ridicule, reproach, and contempt—bonds, afflictions, persecutions, and distress, marked their way as sheep appointed for the slaughter. . . ."[92] Throughout the colonies, the Baptists thrived on persecution, testing their spiritual mettle and maintaining group identity in the process.

In those instances where Methodist and Baptist leaders provided details about their tribulations, they singled out one class of citizens for special mention as ringleaders and participants. A mob intent on roughing up Freeborn Garrettson searched for him in vain at his friend's house and had to be content with dragging his friend through the streets. "This mob was made up of what they call the first people in the county," Garrettson reported.[93] While Garrettson conducted a meeting on Maryland's eastern shore in

1780, twenty "persecutors" burst into the hall and shoved a pistol against the preacher's chest. Garrettson once again pointed out that "these were under the appellation of gentlemen."[94] The gentry of Virginia subjected local Baptists to similar forms of abuse. Sometimes they acted in an official capacity—like the sheriff who whipped John Waller for disturbing the peace—while at othertimes, they indulged themselves in malicious amusement, like the "gang of well-dressed men" who nearly drowned David Barrow in a mock baptism.[95] As a result of encounters like these, the Baptists of Virginia blamed "the learned, the wealthy, and those of great parentage" for the false accusations and the persecutions that they had to endure.[96] The enmity of the better sorts enhanced the Baptist self-image and allowed them to develop an identity as an "oppressed people."[97]

When they attempted to bring the gospel to the slaves, evangelicals met with victims of another kind of oppression, and there directing it stood a class of familiar antagonists. On the eve of the Revolution, and for some years after it, American evangelicals had yet to overcome gentry resistance to slave evangelism. The source of the gentry's opposition had remained virtually unchanged since the days of Whitefield and Davies: preaching disrupted plantation routine and spoiled good servants, as the gentry told it. Colonel Landon Carter registered disgust when one of his slaves showed evidence of a "new light" persuasion. "I believe it is from some inculcated doctrine of those rascals [the New Lights] that the slaves in this Colony are grown so much worse," he wrote in his diary in 1770.[98] To compound his frustrations, one of Carter's overseers joined the Baptists and informed his employer that "he cannot serve God and Mammon, has just been made a Christian by dipping, and would not continue in my business but to convert my people." Singularly unimpressed by this proposal, Carter deemed such "religious villains" to be as unsatisfactory as "horrid hellish rogues" when it came to the effective management of slaves.[99] Another critic of the Baptists charged that, by breaking up families and drawing "Slaves from the Obedience of their Masters," the Baptists brought Virginia to the brink of social chaos: "The very Heartstrings of those little Societies which form the greater are torn in sunder, and all their Peace destroyed."[100] Southern gentlemen of the Revolutionary years continued to doubt the compatibility of slavery and evangelical Christianity.

Fears about the consequences of slave evangelism were so pervasive that when blacks gathered together for religious meetings, even under white supervision, they ran the risk of incurring the wrath of suspicious whites. James Meacham preserved an account of an incident where some whites "eagerly ran into the Church with sticks clubs and caines—abeating and abusing the poor Slaves them outcast[s] of Men for praising of God." On this occasion, a local magistrate acted as the chief instigator of the mob.[101] While preaching in Culpeper County, Virginia, James Ireland recoiled in astonishment as members of a slave patrol broke up his Baptist meeting by beating blacks in the assembly and placing others under arrest.[102] There were occasions when the worst expectations of the gentry were realized. In 1775, a black preacher named David barely escaped being hanged by the gentlemen of Charleston, South Carolina, for allegedly dropping some "unguarded Expressions" to the effect that "God would send Deliverance to the Negroes, from the power of their Masters, as He freed the Children of Israel from Egyptian Bondage." David's white benefactor expressed regret that the preacher had deviated from his message of spiritual deliverance.[103]

Episodes like the one involving David had an obvious tendency to alarm already skeptical planters, but in the context of an eighteenth-century slave society, almost any religious activity that an evangelical preacher undertook would send reverberations through the plantation. If he attempted to demonstrate a pastoral concern for slaves in the Tidewater region, the preacher would inadvertently challenge the planter's self-designated role as patriarch of his "people." Should the preacher endeavor to attract slaves to his meeting, organize them into classes, or meet with them for prayer, he would rupture the self-contained world of the Chesapeake plantation.[104] The period of evangelical expansion in the Chesapeake area coincided with several demographic trends that could only aggravate tensions between the preacher and the large slaveholder. A decline in the number of imported slaves and a corresponding increase in the proportion of American-born slaves enabled blacks to develop a more stable, cohesive social life. As a result of a trend toward larger plantations in the Tidewater region, masters had difficulty maintaining the proper surveillance over slave activities.[105] Since more slave activities took place beyond their supervision, Tidewater planters could scarcely have welcomed the arrival of itinerants who took a special interest in blacks. In the coastal regions of the Lower South, where planter paternalism was less developed and the density of slave population was much higher, the roving preacher would compound the already formidable problems of maintaining a disciplined labor force.[106] To avoid conflict with the planter, the preacher would have to avoid slaves, an unacceptable prospect for people intent on saving souls.

The gospel imperative, however, generated a militance about slave evangelism that had implications beyond the purely spiritual realm. In 1774, for instance, the Hanover Presbytery addressed a petition to the Virginia House of Burgesses on the subject of religious liberty. The petition, which David Rice signed as moderator of the presbytery, broached the question of slave baptism with deference, but then stated the presbytery's position on the matter with uncompromising firmness. They had always "desired" to baptize slaves with the permission of masters, the petitioners maintained, "but when a servant appears to be a true penitent and makes a profession of his faith in Christ, upon his desire it is our indispensable duty to admit him into our church. . . ."[107] Even as David Thomas attempted to refute the charge that Baptists divided slaves from their masters, he struck a menacing posture towards those who would obstruct the work of spiritual liberation:

> When the LORD JESUS displays the banners of his love,
> and his gospel trumpet sounds proclaiming liberty to
> the captives; Beelzebub will not fail making an horrible
> uproar, we may be sure. . . . The war is most just,
> and it must be carried on, whatever outcries the usurper, or his confederates may think proper to make.
> The strong holds must be demolished, the prison doors
> broken down, and the iron fetters dissolved, let who
> will gainsay it. The elect slaves must be redeemed,
> though others choose to hug their chains and even
> curse their best friends, who offer to set them free.[108]

Such rhetoric, though it fell far short of a revolutionary manifesto, did nothing to allay gentry suspicions about the social consequences of the New Light, while in the evangelical mind it fostered an attitude of defiance toward the gentry.

Beneath the embattled gospel banner, white evangelicals discovered that they held some common ground with the slaves. James Ireland's experience of persecution led him to interpret the violence unleashed on slaves in his congregation as a skirmish in the ongoing struggle for religious liberty. Behind the scene, Ireland pointed out, there lurked those "enemies and opposers of religion" who constantly beset the faithful.[109] In a similar fashion, John Leland depicted the injustice of slavery in categories familiar to the Baptists. "Liberty of conscience, in matters of religion, is the right of slaves beyond contradiction," he stated in *The Virginia Chronicle*, "and yet, many masters and overseers will whip and torture the poor creatures for going to meeting, even at night, when the labor of the day is over."[110] Methodist Philip Cox, with evident distaste for gentry high-handedness, complained that "a great many of the poor blacks are not allowed to join us by their lordly masters."[111] Philip Bruce, writing to a Methodist bishop in England, told of the offense that black conversions gave to the "rich and great." "I suppose if they dared they would tear us in pieces: but through the grace of God we regard them not, and had rather offend one half of the world to save the other, than let them all go quietly to hell together," Bruce decided.[112] No one would go anywhere quietly, but Bruce indicated that neither he nor the converted slaves would see their "lordly" persecutors in the hereafter.

The ordeal of persecution, shared by white and black evangelicals, enabled white evangelicals to identify with limited aspects of the slave's experience. The white Christian, however pious and well-meaning, could never know the oppression endured by his enslaved brothers and sisters beyond the confines of the prayer meeting. But the white Methodist or Baptist had faced the slave-holding gentleman, who emerges from the evangelical narratives as haughty in demeanor, abusive, intent on intimidating the preacher or undermining his effectiveness, and often brandishing a whip or pistol for that purpose. White evangelicals had some familiarity with this sort of oppression. By attempting to deny slaves the opportunity of seeking their spiritual deliverance, the "lordly master" directed the evangelical's attention to an odious feature of the slaveholder's authority. The more certain evangelicals focused on that feature, the more objectionable they found the whole slave system.

Although not all persecuted evangelicals arrived at such a position, at least several leaders translated their hatred of religious oppression into a hatred of slavery itself. John Leland came to see slaveholding and religious persecution as two expressions of the same oppressive spirit. After religious freedom had been obtained in Virginia in 1785, Leland could declare: "As personal slavery exists chiefly in the southern states, so religious slavery abounds exclusively in three or four of the New England states."[113] Before 1785, however, both forms of oppression existed side by side in Virginia, and the slaveholding, persecuting gentleman brought them both into focus for the Baptists. David Barrow had suffered indignities at the hands of the gentry, and in an antislavery pamphlet he raised the question of whether a slave could ever enjoy religious liberty.[114] After witnessing a slave beaten for coming to a worship service, James Meacham asked himself, "O how can I rest when I see my brother unhumanely intreated [treated]."[115] Presbyterian David Rice, who began his career as a dissenting minister in Virginia, stated that laws which recognize slavery support "the severest persecutions" and "rob multitudes" of their "religious privileges" and "the rights of conscience."[116]

The experience of southern dissidents may shed indirect light on the relative weakness of antislavery feeling among New England Baptists. Like their dissenting brethren in the South, New England Baptists waged a protracted struggle for religious liberty and clashed frequently with the authorities. Baptists in New England, however, did not have to contend with the hostility of a planter elite, nor was their local tormentor likely to double as a large slaveholder. The authorities in Connecticut and Massachusetts opposed Baptist work, not because the Baptists disrupted a slave system, but because they disrupted the parish system of the Congregational establishment. In other words, the situation of New England Baptists did not provide them with several ingredients that went into the antislavery commitment of southern dissenters. As a result, the quest for religious liberty did not acquire the same meaning for New England Baptists as it did for a Barrow, a Rice, or a Leland.

In the South, the experience of persecution not only helped white evangelicals to interpret slavery, but it also steeled their resolution to suffer abuse for their antislavery principles. "Twice the clubs have been raised to beat me," O'Kelly stated with regard to his antislavery work, "once the pointed dagger was presented against me . . . yet I must defend this truth, and hope that my testimony will be received among you, my brethren." On one occasion, the portly Thomas Coke emerged from a Methodist meeting to find himself involved in a confrontation with one of the persecuting gentry. A number of those present had walked out angrily when Coke began to hold forth on the iniquity of slaveholding. A "high-headed Lady" had stormed out with them and told the "rioters" that she would "give fifty pounds, if they would give that little Doctor one hundred lashes." Much to the woman's disappointment, the crowd inflicted nothing worse than verbal abuse upon Coke, but this would not be the last mob that he would have to face because of his antislavery convictions.[117] In the summer of 1792, angry whites in Meacham's part of Virginia threatened to lynch Methodist preachers for their suspected involvement in a rumored slave insurrection. Meacham welcomed the prospect of martyrdom: "O! what an honorable death this would have been for a preacher of the Gospel had God seen it best."[118] Freeborn Garrettson, who was no stranger to the experience of persecution, had once been cuffed by a gentleman who swore at him and affirmed that the preacher would "spoil all his negroes." Undaunted, Garrettson continued to meet with slaves and also tried to "inculcate the doctrine of freedom" among their owners.[119] Perceiving their struggle to be intimately tied up with that of their brethren in bondage, antislavery evangelicals took up the slave's cause as their own and worked to secure his spiritual and temporal deliverance.

Far removed from the threat of physical abuse, Congregationalist Samuel Hopkins gloried in the tribulations that his antislavery principles brought him in Rhode Island. Like any Methodist or

Baptist, Hopkins acknowledged the blessedness of being "unconnected with the great and rich in the world, and gay, unprofitable company."[120] Hopkins therefore persevered in his attacks on slavery, even though members of a wealthy family demonstrated their displeasure with his ideas by leaving the church, and the "leading people" of Newport's Second Congregational Church made no secret of their opposition to his antislavery views. Although he expected to fall under "reproach" for preaching to the blacks of Newport, Hopkins performed that duty gladly, embracing "whatever obloquy or suffering may be the consequence."[121] Contact with blacks enhanced Hopkins' self-image, as it did in the case of the Methodists; antislavery activity afforded the New Divinity minister an outlet for his intense concern about humility, a way of showing his "unconnected" station in the world.

By the early 1770s, evangelicalism had established itself as a robust force in American religious life. These same years marked the appearance of an antislavery testimony among exponents of the new birth. The evangelical style of spirituality, which was distinctive enough to be denounced or ridiculed, conditioned the white believer's response to slavery. As the movement expanded, white members had abrasive encounters with facets of the slave system, whether it was the plantation or, in the case of Hopkins, agents of the slave trade. Regarding themselves as the despised, the lowly, and the outcasts of fashionable society, white evangelicals decided that slaves were their kind of people. The evangelical sensibility encouraged whites to invest their emotional resources in the welfare of the oppressed. During the Revolutionary crisis, evangelical leaders assumed a stance as prophets, and applied Old Testament injunctions against oppression to a people in their midst. Evangelical militance about converting slaves, which masters had rarely seen among earlier missionaries, provoked some of the better sorts to react with violence. The experience of persecution drove white believers into a closer identification with their beloved African and helped them to perceive, in a limited way, the evil that slavery wrought for their black brothers and sisters. Of course, these factors did not operate with equal force on every believer. The element of physical abuse was conspicuously absent for evangelicals in the Congregationalist establishments of Connecticut and Massachusetts, and Chapter V will show that this absence produced antislavery sentiment of a different character among Congregationalists in Connecticut. But where the combined influence of these factors was felt, evangelicals began to doubt the efficacy of Christianizing the slave system. Many resolved their doubts by concluding that emancipation was the only Christian response to the evils of slavery.

Doubts about slaveholding also arose for evangelicals as they considered the effect that the practice had on the master's habits. Here again, the gentlefolk unwittingly aided believers in interpreting the meaning of slavery.

III

THE
GLITTERING
WORLD

HE EVANGELICALS DID NOT HAVE TO BE HARASSED by the gentry to know that there was enmity between them. As seen by Christians who discerned a person's spiritual loyalties from his clothes and pastimes, the gentry wore the livery of the world and danced wantonly to its music. If evangelicals ever needed a reminder of how an overfond regard for the things of this world would destroy godliness, they could contemplate the example of the gentry.

In spite of all its sinful vanities, the social world of the gentry had a beguiling splendor for evangelicals, as William Fristoe revealed when he named it "the glittering world."[1] In the postwar decade, evangelicals surrendered themselves to the allurements of that world in numbers large enough to alarm the faithful about the erosion of evangelical identity. As they attempted to root out the traces of worldliness that had grown up among them, some evangelicals turned their attention to a practice that they recognized as a conspicuous feature of the gentry's fashionable but godless lifestyle. That practice was slaveholding.

I

IN HIS UNPUBLISHED HISTORY OF THE BAPTISTS, Morgan Edwards introduced the material on South Carolina with some sprightly observations on life and labor in the colony. "We come now to the polite and wealthy province of South Carolina," he wrote in 1772, "a province whose planters are *Nabobs*, whose merchants are *Princes* and whose inhabitants (for the most part) have slaves to wait on them."[2] By highlighting slavery and gentility as the noteworthy features of South Carolina, Edwards revealed his awareness that the grand style of the planters rested on a foundation of slave labor. Georgia also impressed the Baptist historian as a place where "politeness and slaves" abounded.[3] If, as the evangelicals were convinced, gentility blighted true godliness, and if gentility flourished in the presence of slavery, then perhaps there was something spiritually unwholesome about the use of slave labor.

The southern gentry provided evangelicals with a case study in the debilitating effects of worldliness. Between Virginia's Blue Ridge and the Chesapeake Bay, for instance, James Ireland found that few of the "politest part of the people" had any concern for the state of their souls.[4] The gentry's lack of religious fervor did not surprise evangelicals like Ireland. After observing the behavior of some "gay and giddy-looking folks" in Maryland, Asbury concluded that their background and circle of acquaintance conspired to distract them from a proper consideration of how they would spend eternity.[5] In Asbury's eyes, gaiety and giddiness reigned supreme in Charleston, South Carolina, a city which the Methodist designated as the "seat of Satan, dissipation and folly." Asbury discovered that, in this citadel of wickedness, the gentry indulged themselves in a whirl of activity that left little time for devotional exercises: "the white and worldly people are intolerably ignorant of God; playing, dancing, swearing, racing; these are their common practices and pursuits."[6] The obligation to put on a "genteel parade" extinguished even those flickering signs of spiritual life that the rich showed on rare occasions, William Fristoe declared. For this reason, he explained, one should not expect deep religious commitment from the gentlefolk, for "it is impossible to court popularity and the friendship of the carnal world, and enjoy communion with God at the same time."[7] The gentry showed evangelicals that there could be no concessions for the sake of respectability, no compromises with Mammon, for a love for the things of this world bred indifference to the things of God.

The successful staging of a "genteel parade," the evangelicals realized, required a retinue of slaves. William Fristoe attributed the profligate habits of the gentry to the influences of a plantation childhood. The children of the planters, Fristoe reasoned, contracted sinful habits because they were "freed from hard labor, by having slaves to labor for them, . . ." an exemption that allowed them time to indulge in sports, balls, and other diversions of the "high life."[8] David Rice formulated the causal relationship between slavery and sin more precisely: "Slavery produces idleness; and idleness is the nurse of vice." Although Rice disavowed any desire to reproach "men of fortune," he inveighed against those young slaveholding gentlemen who employed themselves in "scenes of pleasure and dissipation" and who thus became "pernicious pests" of society.[9] According to William Colbert, slavery rendered the inhabitants of Maryland's lower counties impervious to the gospel by filling them with vanity.[10] The rice plantations of South Carolina presented Asbury with a spectacle of unremitting depravity, a place where a godless atmosphere, a vicious gentry, and the use of slave labor combined to produce a hothouse environment for sin. "If a man-of-war is 'a floating hell'," he wrote of the rice plantations, "these are standing ones: wicked masters, overseers, and Negroes—cursing, drinking—no Sabbaths, no sermons."[11] Richard Whatcoat, one of Asbury's Methodist colleagues, also associated slaveholding with a dissolute manner of living, as in the case of the backslidden preacher who "gave way to Drink game and op-[p]ression" before he died.[12]

Slavery intruded upon the evangelical consciousness with a taint of worldliness attached to it, but did this mean that the believer who rejected the world had to renounce slaveholding as well? The position of Morgan Edwards represents one of the possible answers that could be given to this question. Although he sensed the existence of an unholy union between "politeness" and slavery, Edwards had no objections if a pious planter like the Reverend Francis Pelot of South Carolina owned "slaves and stock in abundance," provided that the example of his godliness influenced "other rich planters" to instruct their slaves in Christianity, and perhaps to become pious planters themselves.[13] Through the grace of God, Edwards allowed, both slavery and wealth could be had without a corrupt lifestyle and without the trappings of gentility.

The conversion experience of Freeborn Garrettson, however, suggests another answer. Before he underwent his spiritual rebirth in 1775, this Maryland youth expected to use his inheritance of land and slaves to accumulate the "riches of the world."[14] But in the early stages of his conversion, Garrettson felt two spirits at war within him; God called him to a life of righteousness, while Satan

"seemed to set the world and the things of it in the most brilliant
colours before me. . . ." Even after conversion, Satan continued to
dangle the "splendor" of the world before him.[15] The struggle went
on until a thought entered Garrettson's mind as he led his family
in devotions. "'It is not right for you to keep your fellow creatures
in bondage'," the thought told him; "'you must let the oppressed
go free'." Garrettson testified that at that moment he made a
commitment before God to emancipate his slaves. As a result, he
reported: "All my dejection and that melancholy gloom, which
preyed upon me, vanished in a moment: a divine sweetness ran
through my whole frame. . . ."[16] Garrettson's emancipation of his
slaves marked the resolution of his struggle to obtain release from
the burden of worldly cares.

As these two individual responses demonstrate, the perception
of a link between slavery and worldliness did not inevitably produce convictions against holding blacks in bondage. For a brief
period after the war, however, American evangelicals showed a
readiness to adopt the position that Garrettson took in 1775. It
took a mood of apprehension about worldliness to bring out the
antislavery possibilities embedded in the evangelical experience.
That mood descended over wide sectors of evangelicalism in the
postwar era.

II

WHEN FRANCIS ASBURY HEARD NEWS OF A preliminary peace treaty
between Great Britain and America, he began to worry that the
end of the war would weaken evangelical will to resist the enemies
of the spirit. Peace, he wrote in the spring of 1783, "may make
against the work of God: our preachers will be far more likely to
settle in the world; and our people, by getting into trade, and
acquiring wealth, may drink into its spirit."[17] The anxieties of Asbury and other evangelical leaders mounted during the next several years, for as they surveyed the religious landscape of the
postwar period, they saw numbers of their followers breaking
ranks and going over to the side of the world.

Evidence of wavering commitment appeared almost as soon as
the fighting stopped. Samuel Hopkins returned to Newport after
the British evacuated, and there he discovered that the minds of

people in his church were "more filled with the cares of this world, than they were when I left them!"[18] In the fall of 1783, Richard Dozier recorded his dismay at seeing Virginia Baptists who imagined that "they have taken themselves out of the world, and at the same time following the world."[19] Asbury took no delight from the fulfillment of his prophecies. "I lament the love of the world, covetousness, and other evils that lie heavy on the Church of God," he wrote early in 1784.[20] These privately expressed misgivings would be amplified in the decade after the war as other individuals and ecclesiastical bodies arrived at similar assessments of the religious situation.

Just what was there about the conduct of their fellow evangelicals that so disturbed these leaders? To begin with, the evangelical laity succumbed as readily as the rest of their countrymen to the rage for imported finery and other goods that flooded American ports after the war. Richard Dozier issued a stern warning to those whose new taste in clothes smacked more of "proud profanity" than the religion of the lowly Jesus: "Your boots and spurs and half gloves too, look too much like what worldlings do."[21] At a meeting of Virginia and North Carolina Baptists in 1790, David Barrow took Luke 12:15 as his text and warned his brethren to beware of covetousness, that inordinate desire for material possessions.[22] David Rice observed the same unholy desires out in Kentucky, where the Presbyterian minister had settled after a quarrel with his congregation in Virginia. In Kentucky, Rice saw believers "gaping after every new fashion in dress" and even giving themselves over to the shameful practice of dancing.[23] The "love of shining dress" was also much too prevalent among younger Methodists, Asbury noted sadly in 1793.[24] Samuel Hopkins interpreted the signs of worldliness both within and without his church as a partial fulfillment of St. John's vision of the end times. According to Hopkins' *Treatise on the Millennium,* published in 1793, the sixth vial of Revelation 16 had already been poured out onto the earth, commencing an era when humans would strive to "outshine others in dress and high living."[25] The vogue of stylized simplicity, these evangelicals believed, had gone out of fashion in a variety of religious circles.

Even the ministers, the exemplars of the faith, were subject to temptation. Baptist Henry Toler prayed earnestly: "O that God would deliver me from Pride, and as much as possible from all this World."[26] Out on the preaching circuit, William McKendree personified the allurements of "Voluptuousness" in the form of a woman and disclosed just how seductive the world could be: "her lim[b]s are soft and delicate[,] her attire loose and inviting, wantonness sparkles in her eyes. She woos by her looks, and by the smoothness of her tongue endeavors to deceive."[27]

McKendree managed to reject these advances, but other preachers found the charms of the world too attractive to resist. In the 1790s, Asbury complained about the number of city preachers who had been "spoiled" for a ministry among the poorer sorts, so corrupt had their manners become in an urban environment.[28] At the request of his fellow Baptist ministers in the Boston area, Elias Smith endured the "anti-christian" ceremony of installation, upgraded the quality of his wardrobe, and went so far as to write down his sermons for delivery instead of waiting for the Spirit to give him utterance in the pulpit. When Smith solemnly warned another Baptist minister that "we were going back to the place from whence we came out," the other minister replied calmly, "We wish to make our denomination respectable as well as the rest."[29] The story was the same among their counterparts to the south. In the aftermath of a revival lasting from 1785 to 1792, Virginia Baptist ministers discarded their "odd tones, disgusting whoops and awkward gestures" in favor of a more "correct" style of address.[30] A Presbyterian minister in Virginia lamented that in Hanover Presbytery, once the field of Davies' work, his clerical colleagues sought after the companionship of "the great and influential men" and openly advocated "the frivolous maxims and amusements of the world such as dancing, etc."[31] With the example of at least some of their leaders before them, rank and file evangelicals would have had fewer qualms about deviating from the ideal of apostolic simplicity.

The postwar era presented Baptist and Methodist evangelicals with other developments that threatened to destroy their identity as a separate people, developments for which nothing in their previous experience had prepared them. As in the case of many

groups before and after this period, the transition from a despised, embattled religious movement to a respectable denomination left Methodists and Baptists with a vague sense of loss. After
the Methodists organized themselves into a church at the Christmas Conference in 1784, there were those who felt that the original spirit had gone out of the movement. Richard Allen, a black
preacher who would help to found the African Methodist Episcopal Church, remembered a pamphlet published in the wake of
the Christmas Conference "which stated, that when the Methodists were no people, then they were a people; and now they
have become a people they were no people; which had often
serious weight upon my mind."[32] When William McKendree made
his preaching rounds a few years later, he detected a certain
staleness and formality creeping into Methodist religious life as
"the dear, *precious, sweet* doctrine of *holyness* has become an old
song."[33]

Baptists in some states had to undergo similar strains of transition. The enactment of religious liberty in Maryland, Virginia,
North Carolina, South Carolina, and Georgia, to name just the
southern states, gave Baptists in those areas an unaccustomed
status before the law. But having fought the good fight and won,
how would they maintain morale, discipline, and group identity?
The experience of the Virginia Baptists provides some clues. John
Leland stated that the enactment of religious liberty in 1785 had
been something of a mixed blessing for Virginia Baptists. "The
ways of Zion mourned," he observed. "They obtained their hearts'
desire, (freedom,) but had leanness in their souls." Far from in-
augurating an era of religious prosperity, the legislature's enactment ushered in a time when "iniquity did abound, and the love
of many waxed cold."[34] Baptist historian Robert Semple followed
Leland in relating the Virginia Baptists' spiritual depression to
their unaccustomed status before the law. "As if persecution was
more favorable to vital piety, than unrestrained liberty," he wrote,
"they seem to have abated in their zeal, upon being unshackled
from their manacles."[35] And this was supposed to be a time when a
local revival was in progress. Due to the protracted nature of the
struggle in Virginia, the subsequent depression of Baptists there

was more severe than elsewhere in the southern states, but the Virginia Baptists illustrate the problems of adjusting to a situation which no longer provided a test for a group's spiritual mettle.

In addition to new legal realities, the Baptists in the southern states had to cope with the problem of assimilating a large number of unlikely converts. Before the end of the war, most of the gentry regarded evangelical religion as a crude and joyless fanaticism, a disposition which made conversions like that of Robert Carter of Nomini Hall all the more exceptional and, to the evangelical mind, all the more instructive about how amazing grace could be.[36] After the war, however, the gentry began to undergo a change of heart. In 1790, a Southern Carolinian Baptist reported that, although the gentry had treated the Baptists in a "scandalous" manner before the Revolution, "A great number of rich planters have now joined them."[37] More would follow in the years ahead, but in the decade after the war, they came in numbers large enough to strain the Baptists' ability to keep their apostolic identity intact. Robert Semple noted that the Virginia Baptists "were joined by persons of much greater weight, in civil society." Although Semple recorded this development with pride, a note of wistfulness crept into his appraisal of the changes wrought by having so many of the better sort within the Baptist fold. He concluded that "a great deal of that simplicity and plainness, that rigid scrupulosity about little matters, which so happily tends to keep us at a distance from greater follies, was laid aside."[38] Semple knew that this was not the sort of influence that Baptists needed.

To reverse these unsettling trends and restore some sense of distance between the church and the world, evangelical leaders called their followers back to their former simplicity. At the Christmas Conference of 1784, the Methodist leadership took a dim view of the "high heads, enormous bonnets, ruffles or rings" and stated flatly that this was no time to indulge in superfluity of dress. To the Methodist preachers they directed a particular admonition: "Do not affect the gentleman.—A preacher of the gospel is the servant of all."[39] Quite significantly, Asbury chose the anniversary of Independence as a suitable occasion to remind his listeners in New York that Christians had escaped the pollutions of the world, but that it was possible for them to be "entangled therein again and overcome."[40] David Rice selected a passage from St. Paul's second letter to the Corinthians as a timely message for Christians in the 1790s: "Come out from among them, and be ye separate, saith the Lord."[41] Rice's thunderous denunciations of greed and genteel vice had become so familiar to the inhabitants of Danville that a drunken rhymester could delight the local tavern crowd by poking fun at the minister's sermons:

> O how he would in pulpit storm,
> and fill all hell with dire alarm!
> Vengeance pronounce against each vice,
> And, more than all, curs'd avarice;
> Preach'd money was the root of ill,
> Consign'd each rich man unto hell. . . .[42]

If Rice did not effect repentance, he at least conveyed the substance of his message in a memorable way. Addressing a more responsive audience, the Charleston Association of Baptists asked their members to consider whether they had forgotten that they were only pilgrims on the earth.[43] The Middle District Association of Virginia Baptists named covetousness as one important reason for the languishing state of religion in 1791.[44] Letters from twenty member churches gave delegates to the 1793 meeting of Virginia's Strawberry Association of Baptists "an account of Zion's leanness in general, which calls aloud for lamentation. . . ." When lamentations alone produced no reformation, the Association provided Baptists with a list of soul-searching questions, one of which recalled a neglected style of spirituality: "Do I live a life of self-denial and mortification[?]"[45] The fact that such a question had to be asked at all reveals how far the Virginia Baptists had departed from the ideal of apostolic simplicity.

During the period of religious depression, which persisted until the end of the century, the godly hankered after the trappings of wealth and respectability, while, at least in the southern states, the wealthy showed a newfound desire for godliness. Evangelicals lost their bearings when these two trends combined to erase the familiar boundary between church and world, Christ and culture. Disoriented and apprehensive, some evangelicals advanced toward an antislavery position in an effort to regain some sense of direction and purpose.

III

THERE COULD BE NO RESTORATION of primitive Christian simplicity without the elimination of slavery. So ran the argument of evangelicals who viewed the presence of slavery among them as another sign of apostasy. These evangelicals urged the elimination of slavery upon individuals, churches, and whole denominations as a major objective in the campaign to push back the forces of the world. And, for a brief span of years, they found a receptive audience.

Slaveholders had been worshipping in evangelical communions since the beginning of the movement, but in the postwar period the associations between slaveholding and a forbidden lifestyle took on a disturbing relevance for some evangelicals. They beheld, not the godless gentry, but believers in their midst using slave labor to secure wealth, comfort, and prestige. James O'Kelly declared that it was for their "ease, honor, and self-interest" that Christians held slaves.[46] A Methodist minister from Georgia confessed as much when he wrote that the lure of the good life made it difficult for him to contemplate the thought of freeing his slaves:

> There is one thing that hath long lain on my mind with
> great weight, and that is concerning Slavery, & I am
> more & more convinced it is wrong, though I feel a
> great Struggle in my mind about it, Ease & Self Interest & the grandeur Life & the thought that my Posterity may labour hard for a living, and perhaps may
> not be thought so much of in the World as If they
> had Slaves to Sett them in a more grand & Easy way
> these things Plead hard against it [emancipation].[47]

John Leland's acquaintance with affairs in Virginia led him to link slaveholding with aspirations for social advancement. "The custom of the country is such," he wrote in *The Virginia Chronicle*, "that, without slaves, a man's children stand but a poor chance to marry in reputation." Leland discerned that this widely held belief posed "one of the great difficulties that prevent liberation of the slaves among the common sort."[48] And the "common sort," as Leland well knew, formed the backbone of the Virginia Baptists. As a result of his observations, Leland detected the "voice of covetousness" in reasoned pleas for caution and moderation in handling the matter of slavery.[49] Among believers in South Carolina, Francis Asbury discovered, an ambition to hold political office and traffic in slaves accompanied a rise in circumstances, thus rendering the upwardly mobile evangelicals "much too great to be Methodists."[50] As a vehicle to further their worldly interests, slavery performed an essential service for evangelicals on the make.

A suspicion that slavery had something to do with worldliness prompted evangelicals in a variety of settings to list slaveholding among the corruptions that had come in upon them. On Christmas Day of 1791, one Sister Whitehead stood up before fifty Methodist ministers, including Asbury himself, and spoke her mind about some recent trends that grieved her. She saw young women and young preachers "catching after the modes of fashion of this world which passes away. . . ." What was more, she saw preachers who would denounce slavery in the pulpit and who would then "marry a young woman who held slaves and keep them fast in bloody slavery." She observed Christians who seemed "as happy as saints in Heaven" while they starved and oppressed their slaves. "O! my Lord," she cried, "is this the religion of my adorable master Jesus?" Physically and emotionally exhausted by the intensity of her performance, Sister Whitehead fainted after she finished speaking.[51]

As two preachers who were present for Sister Whitehead's appeal, James O'Kelly and James Meacham must have breathed a hearty amen when she included slavery among the departures from the primitive Christian ideal. In his *Essay on Negro Slavery*, O'Kelly made antislavery commitment a test of fidelity to the way of Jesus. "Where is the true disciple of Christ," he asked, "poor in spirit, meek in heart, thirsting after holiness, crucified with Christ, dead to the world?"[52] He reminded his readers that the primitive Christians, whose example the Methodists professed to admire and imitate, did not support their ministers with money obtained from slave labor.[53] The idea of deriving wealth from slave labor struck Meacham as such a betrayal of gospel principles that he vowed to take his place alongside Judas in hell if he ever became rich because of slavery. Meacham blamed slavery for the "coldness and Dullness" that afflicted the believers under his care.[54]

William McKendree shared Meacham's perception of a link between slavery and the chill that had settled into the marrow of Methodist piety. One morning in the winter of 1791, McKendree felt burdened by the "want of spirituality and faith" among Methodists on his circuit. Dismayed by the errors that seemed to block the believer's way to heaven, he resolved to preach a sermon that would clear iniquity from the congregation just as Christ had driven the moneychangers from the temple in Jerusalem. "Made me a cord," McKendree wrote, describing the verbal lashing that he gave the people, "and as I went [I] thrashed. Covetousness, pride, and sloth. Overturned the tables of self ease." Last of all, McKendree assailed slavery: "And [I] drove that monster; I mean Blood and Oppression, out of the Lord's temple." The preacher cast slavery out of the sanctuary along with other corruptions that enfeebled evangelical piety. The people listened attentively to this tirade, and McKendree retired that day with a "comfortable hope" that he had moved them to serious reflection.[55]

The elimination of slavery also figured prominently in some Baptist programs for reform. In *The Annual Register* for 1790, John Asplund asked his Baptist readers to consider seven "inconsistencies" within the denomination, each a contradiction to Christ's teaching and "our holy profession." Quite significantly, Asplund listed slaveholding as the first item requiring attention. Next came the complaint that fathers had failed to provide enough religious instruction to make their children "at least useful members of society," an indication that young Baptists, like the children of the gentry, were frittering their time away in vain pursuits. After this Asplund named "Extravagance or superfluity, not only in eating or drinking, but especially in dress, that we may not be conformed to the sinful customs of this world; but be a separate people, denying all ungodliness and worldly lust, &c."[56] By liberating their slaves, by supervising their children's pastimes, and by returning to their former simplicity, American Baptists might maintain their "holy profession" and shore up their deteriorating religious identity.

Like Asplund, delegates to the 1796 meeting of Virginia's Portsmouth Association of Baptists raised the matter of slaveholding in conjunction with other signs of Baptist apostasy. When the delegates, with David Barrow as moderator, asked themselves the cause of these "present wretched and distressing times," they came up with an unequivocal answer: *"We believe covetousness is the source."* Covetousness distracted ministers from their duties and made laymen tight-fisted in their contributions to the poor, they stated. The delegates went on to declare that:

> *Covetousness,* leads Christians, with the people of this country in general, to hold and retain in *abject slavery,* a set of our poor fellow creatures, *contrary to the laws of God and nature:*—for these, and on account of that *detested conformity* to the wicked *ways* and *customs* "of this present evil world;" and for the *abominations* practiced among the citizens in common, we think the *Church* and *Land mourns.*[57]

Unless slavery were eradicated, the delegates implied, Baptists had no good reason to believe that they had destroyed the root of covetousness.

These individuals addressed audiences of varying sizes and denominational backgrounds, but the burden of their message was the same: if believers would be separate from the world, they must renounce the practice of slaveholding. Their testimony reveals the existence of attitudes that help to explain why, in the dozen years following the war, the subject of slavery generated intense discussion in evangelical circles. Within this span of years, antislavery evangelicals set the question of slavery before individuals, churches, and whole denominations in an effort to obtain their commitment to the cause of emancipation.

On the grass-roots level, antislavery evangelicals directed their efforts toward winning individual Christians over to their side. In a letter otherwise devoted to the subject of conformity to the world, David Rice expressed his desire to see slavery abolished by

the triumph of gospel principles in the hearts of individual believers.[58] The journal entries of Methodists like McKendree, Haskins, Colbert, and Thomas Coke show that they regarded antislavery activity as part of their day-to-day routine.[59] Sometimes
they denounced slavery from the pulpit, while at other times they
quietly drew a slaveholder aside to discuss the matter in private.
They frequently convinced people of slavery's evil and helped
them to draw up deeds of manumission. The daily activity of
Baptist preachers is much less detailed, but John Leland made his
antislavery opinions known, and David Barrow set an example by
freeing his own slaves in 1784.[60] Through the force of their personality and the closeness of their relationship with their people,
Methodist and Baptist preachers achieved a small measure of success in the upper South. The number of blacks actually freed in
this manner was statistically insignificant compared to the whole
slave population, but for those blacks who did receive their freedom from an evangelical master, the event was certainly of mon-
umental personal significance.

Winning an entire congregation over to an antislavery position
proved a much more difficult task, one accomplished only in
rare cases. Jacob Green had shown that it could be done early in
1782, when he guided his Presbyterian congregation in Hanover,
New Jersey in a decision to exclude slaveholders from membership. In the records of the church, the members entered their
opinion that slavery was an evil, and "therefore we will not use
this slavery ourselves and will prudently endeavor to prevent it in
others."[61] Evidently, Deacon Colman caught wind of this decision,
for in 1783, after his expulsion from the Byfield Church, the
persistent deacon alluded to "the practice of the purest Chhs. in
the Jersey State" to support his suggestion that Byfield deny communion to slaveholders.[62] Interpreting the slave trade as another
evidence of the worldly spirit that St. John had prophesied, Samuel Hopkins made sure that his church would not be polluted by
the practice. On March 5, 1784, members of his Newport church
voted that the enslavement of Africans constituted "a gross violation" of righteousness and benevolence, and "therefore we will
not tolerate it in this church."[63] Two northern ministers, at least,
had been able to cleanse their temples from iniquity.

Similar goals could not be achieved at higher levels of church organization. By 1795, for example, the Presbyterian General Assembly had shown that it would not sanction a policy like the one enacted by Green. In 1787, the Synod of New York and Philadelphia, then the highest governing body of American Presbyterianism, indicated its approval of "general principles in favour of universal liberty" and encouraged masters to educate their slaves in preparation for freedom.[64] In 1795, the General Assembly considered the question of an unnamed believer from Kentucky's Transylvania Presbytery, Rice's home judicatory, who viewed slavery as "injurious to the interests of the gospel" and who asked whether he should hold communion with slaveholders. The Assembly appointed a committee of three, including Rice, to write a reply. The draft of their letter was submitted to the Assembly and debated paragraph by paragraph for a "very considerable time." By deleting the paragraph encouraging masters to prepare their slaves for freedom, the Assembly retreated from the recommendation that Presbyterians issued in 1787. The Assembly finally adopted a letter which counseled "conscientious" persons like the Transylvania Presbyterian to live in peace and charity,[65] which was to say that slavery had nothing to do with communion.

Methodist antislavery advocates made an abortive attempt to clear slaveholders from their midst at the Christmas Conference of 1784, the same gathering which founded the church and which denounced fancy clothes and affected gentility. They enacted a rule which gave Virginians two years, and all other Methodists one year, to draw up deeds of manumission for their slaves. Those who failed to comply would face expulsion. But resistance to this new rule, especially in Virginia, led to its suspension in the spring of 1785.[66] Thereafter, antislavery Methodists continued their efforts on a local level.

Antislavery Baptists in Virginia had difficulty holding a statewide forum on slavery, much less arriving at agreement about it. The General Committee of Virginia Baptists held a discussion of slavery between the years 1785 and 1793, when the problem of worldliness assumed an unexpected urgency for Baptists in that state. The General Committee, a council created by the district associations to administer Baptist affairs, opened the colloquy in

1785 by declaring "hereditary slavery to be contrary to the word of God. . . ."[67] By and large, however, the body of churches ignored this resolution, with only the Black Creek Church deciding that slavery "is unrighteous."[68] The Ketocton Association attempted to formulate a plan of gradual emancipation in 1787, but this proposal excited such a "tumult" that the Association dropped it.[69]

Matters stood unchanged until the 1790 meeting of the General Committee, where delegates debated the "equity, of Hereditary Slavery" for a "considerable time."[70] The minutes of this meeting unfortunately do not include a record of the arguments employed by the opponents of slavery, but they do establish the fact that David Barrow and John Leland were present. Their voices almost certainly made significant contributions to the proceedings. When a group which included Barrow failed to come up with a satisfactory resolution on slavery, the task fell to Leland. His resolution, quoted fondly and frequently by subsequent Baptist historians, blended republican and biblical rhetoric into an antislavery declaration: slavery was "a violent deprivation of the rights of nature" and "inconsistent" with a republican government; Baptists should use "every legal measure to extirpate this horrid evil from the land"; and they should pray to the Almighty that the legislature would "proclaim the great Jubilee" in a manner "consistent with the principles of good policy."[71]

Though Leland's resolution had enough support to pass at the General Committee's meeting, it met with a cool reception at a local level. The unenthusiastic response of the associations revealed the limits of antislavery efforts within the Baptist denomination. Throughout the long struggle for toleration, the Baptists championed liberty of conscience against the forces of "oppression," those who would suppress a diversity of opinion on religious matters. Having won that contest, individual Baptists had no intention of relinquishing their consciences to a new episcopacy of Baptist elders. The high value placed on liberty, which had once permitted white evangelicals to identify with the victims of physical oppression, also prohibited the General Committee from making emancipation a binding policy for all Baptists.

The Baptist response to Leland's resolution can therefore be explained, in part, as resistance to ecclesiasticism rather than anti-slavery itself. Members of the Roanoke Association, for example, reported that they were not clear about the rightfulness of slav-ery, but they were certain that "neither the general committee nor any other Religious Society whatever has the least right to concern therein as a society, but leave every individual to act at discretion in order to keep a good conscience before God. . . ."[72] Believing that members of the General Committee had overreached their authority, the Strawberry Association entered a terse formulation into its records: "We advise them not to interfere with it."[73] Whether the appeal to individual conscience proceeded from high-minded devotion to principle or self-interest, it successfully enervated the antislavery activity of the Committee. Faced with indifference or disapproval from the member associations, the General Commit-tee dismissed the subject of slavery from its consideration in 1793, defining it as a problem for the Virginia legislature to handle.[74]

The antislavery agitation of the 1780s and 1790s highlighted some of the tensions within evangelicalism which would surface again and again in its history. From its beginning, evangelicalism addressed individuals with a compelling message of spiritual re-birth. The movement's mission was to reform individuals, not society, although society would benefit indirectly from the refor-mation of individual conduct. Evangelicals did, however, view the relief of human suffering as part of their ministry, and they often bore powerful testimonies against the greed and callousness which caused it. But how far should they press their criticism if it threat-ened the work of saving souls? Evangelicals separated themselves from the world and formed religious communities designed to provide alternatives to the values and customs of the social order around them. But did believers have to set their faces against every custom found in the world? Suppose believers should dis-agree on what should be retained and what should be renounced? In their communities, evangelicals subjected themselves to the dis-cipline of fellow believers in an effort to subdue a love of the world. These communities also provided support, comfort, and ineffable joy in the midst of sometimes hostile surroundings. As such the evangelical community was both a staging area for missionary activity and a retreat for battle-weary soldiers of Christ. But what if a demand for purity threatened to dissolve the circle of fellowship?

In the context of the movement, a minority of believers went beyond conversionism and insisted that opposition to slavery become part of the evangelical witness. Without abandoning the task of spreading the gospel, they declared that a person touched by grace should renounce the ownership of another human being, for such ownership represented a form of exploiting the poor and defenseless. As an expression of worldliness, they said, slavery undermined the spirituality of the master and inhibited the emotional element in the life of the Spirit. Converts could not continue to hold slaves any more than they could continue to gamble or wear expensive finery. The antislavery evangelicals argued further that the churches could not carry out the preaching mission while they were beset by an evil so crippling as slaveholding. They therefore urged evangelical communions to exercise their disciplinary function and exclude unrepentant slaveholders from their midst. In the postwar decade, antislavery evangelicals beamed this message at a highly susceptible audience, one already wracked by doubts about spiritual health and group identity. Some evangelicals, including those from the rank and file, took the message to heart, liberated their slaves, and joined the antislavery minority. In the name of the mission and the community, antislavery evangelicals called for an exercise of discipline against slaveholders.

Not all evangelicals, however, saw the matter in these terms. A majority of white believers deflected the antislavery appeal as a distraction from the primary work of saving souls. A public stand against slavery, they might reason, would alienate prospective converts, and the Bible warned against placing stumbling blocks to the Kingdom of God. Many evangelicals admitted that slaveholding was inherently evil, but believed that the practice would be eradicated with the spread of the gospel. These evangelicals would be content with antislavery declarations, but would oppose disciplinary action. Other evangelicals, carrying on the tradition of Whitefield and Davies, admitted only that slaveholding had evil features, but that these could be removed once the master was converted and brought under Christian discipline. In other words, a majority believed that converts could safely bring their slaves with them in the passage from the world to the church, the old life to the new. The majority saw the controversy polarizing the churches and turning the sweet communion of saints into a scene of bitter confrontation. In the name of the mission and the community, then, a majority of whites rejected the antislavery minority's plea for discipline. Judging from the frequency and duration of the debates, many white evangelicals at this period found slaveholding to be a genuinely agonizing issue. Moreover, the records indicate that slavery was an issue which aroused the rank and file as well as the spiritual elite, the Sister Whiteheads as well as the McKendrees, nameless lay people in Kentucky and Virginia as well as Rice and Elder Leland.

By the mid-1790s, the antislavery evangelicals realized that they had not carried the argument, but they continued their efforts to make slaveholding Christians aware of their own bondage to the world. Freeborn Garrettson depicted the difficulties and possible rewards of this approach in *A Dialogue Between Do-Justice and Professing-Christian*. As a believer who obtained release from the cares of the world when he freed his slaves, Garrettson wrote out of his own experience when he portrayed an evangelical's decision to renounce slaveholding as the necessary prelude to spiritual liberty.

As Garrettson's story opens, the characters of Do-Justice and Tender Conscience are on a journey from the City of Destruction to Mount Zion, but they decide to stop over in the village of Self-interest for a night's rest. The two pilgrims represent the values of the evangelical style of spirituality. In the village of Self-interest they lodge with Professing Christian, who, suspiciously enough, has taken up permanent residence in the village with his family. When Do-Justice tries to engage his host in a discussion of African slavery, Professing Christian squirms and attempts to return the conversation to "the doctrines of the Gospel, and plain christian experience."[75] Do-Justice, however, will not be put off, and in the ensuing dialogue he convinces his host of the evil of slaveholding. To succeed, Do-Justice has to warn Professing Christian of the danger of flirting with the world: "If any man loves the world, the love of the father is not in him." The pilgrim also has to contend with the objections of Professing Christian's wife, who resists the idea of emancipation because she is preoccupied with her children's "promotion in life."[76] But when Professing Christian rises above such earthly concerns and decides to free his slaves, he becomes Real Christian in the eyes of Do-Justice and experiences "a little heaven on earth,"[77] much as Garrettson himself had done years before.

The outcome of events in real life could be less edifying than those of allegory. Could the antislavery evangelicals succeed in persuading the Professing Christians among them to renounce the world, free their slaves, and resume the journey to Mount Zion? Or would the majority of Professing Christians continue to rebuff the antislavery appeal as an unprofitable departure from "plain christian experience?" The antislavery evangelicals would not know for certain until the early years of the nineteenth century. In the meantime, there was a new nation to think about.

IV

FREE
CITIZENS
OF
ZION

EVEN AS THEY WORRIED ABOUT CORRUPTION IN THE CHURCHES, antislavery evangelicals turned to a wider audience of Americans and warned that the moral integrity of the republic was in danger. Renunciation of the world, after all, did not necessarily imply a renunciation of civil authority, nor did it breed political apathy. American evangelicals retained too lively a sense of human sinfulness to believe that people could dwell in safety without a government of some sort. Also, republicanism complemented evangelicalism in its recognition of depravity and its stress on the need for simplicity, temperance, and self-denial.[1]

Republicanism, as Americans knew it, rested on a body of social and political ideas known variously as the Whig, Commonwealth, or Country ideology. The origins of this ideology lay in the Civil War and Commonwealth periods of English history, but it had been elaborated by a group of eighteenth-century writers before it was transmitted to the colonies. The Whig publicists taught Americans to think of politics as an unremitting contest between power and liberty, in which the rulers relentlessly sought to rob the people of their privileges and reduce them to slavery. In England, the Whigs maintained, the constitution was supposed to preserve liberty from the forces of tyranny and anarchy by balancing the elements of monarchy, aristocracy, and democracy in one government. The Whigs also underscored the importance of the virtuous freeholder in the preservation of liberty, because an individual with property, they reasoned, could not be bribed or intimidated by any aspiring despot. The Whigs admitted that temporary imbalances in the constitution would inevitably occur, but these could

be corrected through a return to the first principles of the constitution. If, however, the people became too corrupt, or too concerned with their own luxury, to care about the disruption of the
constitution, then they would be vulnerable to the designs of a
tyrannous ruler. Americans borrowed heavily from Commonwealth doctrines in the contest with Great Britain, and after they
replaced the monarchy with a government by the people, American Whigs continued to extol virtue as an indispensable source of
strength and stability in the republic.[2]

These ideas provided antislavery evangelicals of the postwar
years with weapons as they carried their struggle beyond the
churches to the nation at large. To assess the impact of republicanism on the antislavery evangelicals, one could search denominational records for declarations laced with Revolutionary rhetoric,
and one could extract quotations which express a high regard for
liberty from works otherwise devoted to religious topics. A more
fruitful approach, however, may be to select recognized antislavery leaders, concentrate on their life and thought, and discover
how personal experience and denominational background influenced their application of republican ideas. The careers of David
Barrow, James O'Kelly, David Rice, and Samuel Hopkins—Baptist,
Methodist, Presbyterian, and Congregationalist, respectively—
show that antislavery evangelicals of the postwar era considered
slavery to be just as much of a menace to the new nation as to the
church, and for many of the same reasons.

I

JESUS CHRIST LIBERATED DAVID BARROW from the despotic sway of
sin. Barrow might well have described his conversion experience
in this way, for in the political discourse of the Revolution he
discovered a vocabulary that allowed him to interpret Christ's
redemptive work as an attack on all forms of tyranny.

Barrow cut a commanding figure among the Baptists of Virginia. Born in Brunswick County in 1753, this son of a small
farmer read books on a variety of topics to satisfy his inquisitive
bent. After experiencing the new birth in 1770, he preached for
several years and then assumed his first pastorate at the Mill
Swamp Church, Isle of Wight County, in 1774. Besides minister-

ing to several Baptist churches in Isle of Wight and Southampton Counties, Barrow traveled through other parts of southern Virginia and North Carolina. He met with his share of rough treatment at the hands of the gentry, but he received an ample reward for his tribulations in the success that he enjoyed as a preacher. During the Revolution, Barrow laid his pastoral duties aside for a short time to fight in the American army. By the end of the war, he had earned the trust, affection, and admiration of scores of Baptists who had benefited from his ministry.[3] But, in 1784, he made a decision that would bring his promising career in Virginia to an untimely conclusion: he freed his slaves "from a conviction of the iniquity, and a discovery of the inconsistancy [sic] of hereditary slavery, with a republican form of government. . . ."[4]

These two convictions were rooted in Barrow's understanding of sin. In the beginning, according to Barrow, God ordained natural laws "to preserve union and harmony" throughout the whole of creation.[5] Sin, however, represented a deviation from "first principles," a concept which Whig theorists had used to signify an ominous disturbance in the stability of the constitution. Barrow's rendering of the Fall closely paralleled the Whig scenario for encroaching tyranny. Satan, the first despot, in effect destroyed the balance and harmony of the divine constitution and placed humans in subjection to "the reigning *tyrant, sin*." Thereafter, humans multiplied the deviations from first principles by imitating Satan's despotic ways. All forms of tyranny, Barrow believed, including monarchy and slavery, entered history along with the other curses that attended the Fall.[6]

So long as humans remained in subjection to the tyranny of sin, Barrow was convinced that they would retain the capacity to exercise a "*devilish usurpation*" over the rights of others. "Upon the whole," he observed, "I find the depravity of human nature to be such, that it constantly seeks to aggrandize, raise and immortalize itself: and this it does . . . by degrading, blaming and finding fault in others with what we think ourselves to be clear of."[7] In this common human failing, Barrow discerned the origins of despotism. "Upon this very foundation tyranny and usurpation have been supported in all ages," he wrote. White Americans provided Barrow with a living illustration of this lamentable truth: imagining themselves to be endowed with some superior attributes, whites had carried out their tyrannical designs on Africans and North American Indians without the slightest doubt as to their own righteousness.[8]

From Barrow's understanding of sin, it followed that the work of redemption involved a return to first principles, a revolution that demolished the spiritual foundations of tyranny and the institutional structures which rested upon them. All evangelicals knew that regeneration required the rooting out of self-exalting ideas; their whole lifestyle was a testimony to that conviction. But Barrow included slavery and monarchy among the works of the devil that Christ had come to destroy. In the utterance which inaugurated Christ's public ministry, Barrow read a message that spelled the overthrow of all kinds of oppressive rule: "The Spirit of the Lord is upon me . . .; he hath sent me to heal the broken-hearted, to preach deliverance (emancipation) to the captives, and recovering of sight to the blind, to set at liberty (or emancipate) them that are bruised, to preach the acceptable year of the Lord."[9] Barrow awaited the glorious day when the work of emancipation would be carried to completion. Combining Old and New Testament prophecies, he depicted the millennium as a period when the world's original harmony would be restored:

> Kings or despots were sent as a scourge or curse on mankind, and at the close of the reign, of the antichristian man of sin, which was to continue, a "thousand, two hundred, and three score," prophetic "days," they will be taken away as a blessing—The happy period is drawing near, when it will be announced, "Babylon the great is fallen, is fallen," the "trump of Jubilee will be blown," slavery cease, and "every man return to his inheritance," and "sit every man under his vine and fig-tree; and none shall make them afraid."[10]

Realizing that the time for sitting under fig trees had not yet arrived, Barrow translated his anticipation into efforts to hasten the onset of the latter-day glory.

When he freed his slaves in 1784, Barrow not only thought that he had furthered the work of redemption, but also that he had contributed to the health of the republic for which he had fought. "I believe it is acknowledged by all men of understanding, that the strength and riches of a civil community, principally consists in the number of its free, virtuous and industrious inhabitants," Barrow declared, setting forth a doctrine originally stated by James Harrington and Algernon Sydney, two republicans of the seventeenth century. Slavery weakened the republic by denying slaves a share in the common good and by affording their owners "an opportunity of living in idleness and extravagancy," a style of life as abominable to Whigs as it was to evangelicals.[11] Moreover, slavery presented Barrow with evidence that Americans had not entirely rid themselves of kings, because "every *slave-holder,* (in his little dominion) certainly is as *absolute, uncontroulable,* and *arbitrary,* as were more of the *ancient* or *modern monarchs.*"[12] The Barrow farm was transformed from a kingdom to a commonwealth in the moment that the preacher freed his slaves.

About ten years after this decision, Barrow's personal affairs started to take a turn for the worse. The action rendered him "suspicious" in the eyes of Baptists who had once welcomed and trusted him. His financial situation deteriorated until he had difficulty maintaining his family in Virginia without resorting to slave labor.[13] Rather than surrender his antislavery principles, Barrow began to entertain the idea of removing his family to a more congenial part of the nation.

In May of 1795, Barrow made a tour of the western country to investigate the possibility of resettling there. The "novelties" that he beheld, and the "wonders" that "burst" upon his sight exhilarated this itinerant with a passion for learning.[14] As he rode through the western part of Virginia, he observed that the inhabitants had fewer slaves than back in the east, a situation which encouraged habits of industry among them. "The women think it no shame to attend to their household and kitchen affairs with their own hands and the men [work?] steadily at their business," he commented.[15] The same conditions prevailed in western Pennsylvania, a state which had enacted a gradual emancipation law in 1780. When Barrow crossed from Kentucky into the Ohio territory, he rejoiced that, as a result of the Northwest Ordinance, he had been able to set foot on a land where slavery would never intrude.[16] But it was

Kentucky that particularly struck Barrow's fancy. Moving southward into Kentucky, Barrow discovered that his antislavery reputation had gone on before him; evangelicals sympathetic to his views "mortified" him by lavishing attention on the traveler and his horse.[17] Barrow deeply regretted that slavery had been permitted in this state. With regard to the religious life of the state, Barrow noticed a "fashionable conformity" like that of believers back home, while of all the denominations that he surveyed in Kentucky, "the Deists, Nothingarians, and anythingarians are the most numerous."[18] With his fact-finding mission complete, Barrow returned to Virginia in September of 1795, impressed by the richness of the land and the hospitality of the people in Kentucky.

In 1798, Barrow had decided that it was time to leave his native state and, in that year, he settled his affairs, bid his friends farewell, and sought out a new home in Kentucky. Why he did not continue on to Ohio is not entirely clear: perhaps he had developed a strong attachment to the people of Kentucky while he was there; perhaps he felt a call to preach to the numerous "anythingarians" in the state. The most likely explanation is the one which his subsequent ministry bears out. In leaving Virginia, Barrow had no desire to withdraw from the struggle against slavery; he wished to continue it from a more advantageous location. He had not retreated but, instead, had executed a flanking movement. In Kentucky, Barrow proclaimed his gospel of liberation and renewed his campaign to clear the Baptist churches of slavery. The next ten years would tell how successful he would be in this endeavor.

II

JAMES O'KELLY PROBABLY CROSSED PATHS WITH BARROW many times in the course of his preaching duties. O'Kelly's mixture of republicanism and evangelicalism proved to be a volatile compound, one which not only fired his hatred of slavery, but which also ignited a controversy in the young Methodist Church that exploded in schism in 1792. Born of Irish ancestry in 1735, and born again of the Spirit sometime in the mid-1770s, this energetic but temperamental Virginian enlisted in the ranks of both the itinerant ministry and the patriot army during the Revolution.[19] Perhaps it was the joint influence of these experiences that fused religious and political values in O'Kelly's thinking, for by war's end he had come to identify the ideals of primitive Christianity with the ideals of republicanism.

O'Kelly's career as a dissident dated almost from the moment that he became a Methodist preacher. In 1779, only a year after his name appeared on the records of the Virginia conference as an itinerant, O'Kelly joined with a group of Virginia Methodists who declared their ecclesiastical independence from the Church of England. At this time, it will be remembered, American Methodists remained officially a part of the Anglican Church; Methodist preachers were only lay preachers, and members of the local societies had to rely on Anglican clergymen for the administration of baptism and the Lord's Supper. The war, however, created a shortage of Anglican ministers and thus left many southern Methodists without the benefit of the sacraments. A group of Methodist preachers took matters into their own hands. In 1779, they gathered at Fluvanna, Virginia, and ordained themselves for the administration of the sacraments. As O'Kelly later explained, it was not only a shortage of Anglican ministers that prompted the southern preachers to take this step, but also a "murmuring" that "the old church had corrupted herself."[20] Asbury, who had watched these unsettling events unfold from a distance, forestalled imminent secession by promising the dissidents that he would lay their grievances before Wesley himself.[21] The rift was healed, but O'Kelly's early disaffection with Anglicanism foreshadowed his ultimate break with the Methodist hierarchy.

For a time after the Fluvanna affair was settled, it looked as though O'Kelly would take his place alongside Methodist worthies in the work of building the movement. In 1780, Asbury traveled with O'Kelly through North Carolina and described the erstwhile rebel as a "dear man" and a "warm-hearted, good man."[22] At the Christmas Conference of 1784, which carried out Wesley's decision to grant American Methodists their independence as a church, O'Kelly was ordained an elder and, the year after, he became the presiding elder of southern Virginia. In 1785, when the Methodists sponsored a petition campaign aimed at persuading the Virginia legislature to pass a gradual emancipation law, O'Kelly played an active role and, as the recently-ordained Bishop Asbury noted with approval, "let fly" at critics of the campaign.[23]

The era of good feelings between O'Kelly and the Methodist leadership ended in 1787 when O'Kelly blocked Wesley's appointment of Richard Whatcoat as bishop in America. As O'Kelly later told the story, he resisted the appointment of Whatcoat, a British Methodist, because "the free people of America were exceeding jealous of the growing body of Methodists, because of the European heads."[24] Maybe O'Kelly had heard proslavery Virginians malign Methodists as "Tools of the British Administration" because of their role in the petition campaign. Maybe he had heard Coke and Asbury, the only bishops in America, branded as "contemptible Emissaries and Hirelings of Britain."[25] The lingering stigma of Loyalism helps to explain O'Kelly's eagerness to sever all connections with the "European" branch of the Methodist family. But there was more to O'Kelly's opposition to the appointment. The former Fluvanna dissident continued to chafe under ecclesiastical domination; only in 1787, it was not Anglicanism, but British Methodism that kept American Methodists in a subordinate position. In a letter written to an American preacher in 1787, O'Kelly compared the imperious attitude of the brethren "beyond the water" to a master's dominion over the slave: "for our consolation they may say by us as the oppressors do by the slaves, 'They have nothing to do but work eat and sleep. We take care.'"[26] In O'Kelly's mind, slavery and ecclesiastical dominion were beginning to coalesce into a configuration of oppressive authority.

After blocking Whatcoat's appointment, O'Kelly turned his attention from the struggle for home rule to the conflict over who would rule at home. O'Kelly grew progressively disenchanted with the government of the American Methodist Church in the late 1780s. For one thing, he frowned upon Asbury's plan for a governing council comprised of bishops and presiding elders and, for another, he objected to the bishops' authority to appoint preachers to their circuits. To O'Kelly's way of thinking, it was no mistake that the architects of American Methodist polity, Coke and Asbury, hailed from "the land of Kings and Bishops."[27] More and more, O'Kelly's quarrel with the Methodist leadership came to focus on the power of the bishops.

Amid the debates about Methodist polity, and in the context of a heightened anxiety about worldliness, O'Kelly published his *Essay on Negro Slavery* in 1789. The Word of the Lord burned "like fire in my bones," O'Kelly testified, compelling him to bear witness against the sin of slavery.[28] The prophet in O'Kelly got the better of the pamphleteer, for in the second half of the *Essay*, his indignation gathered force as his argument lost direction. But throughout the work—sustaining it and lending it coherence in the absence of a clearly defined structure—ran a conviction that the success of the new Church and the new nation depended on the emancipation of the slave.

America's prospects looked bleak to O'Kelly in 1789. "Clouds are gathering at a distance: thunders not yet discharged, rumbling, roar from Sinai and Zion! Arbitrary power over the unalienable rights of thousands prevails!"[29] Both the Methodist Church and the nation had earned God's wrath, for by defiling themselves with slavery they more closely resembled mystical Babylon, Mother of Harlots and Abominations, than the New Jerusalem. O'Kelly referred to St. John's prophecy of the downfall of Babylon—an event which Protestant commentators had long associated with the decline of the papacy—and highlighted slavery as one of the sins that brought on the destruction of the city. "Is not America in this respect a sister to Babylon and Rome there spoken of?" he asked. And, he continued, addressing his Methodist brethren, "When shall our church be purified from spiritual whoredom, and this species of antichrist?"[30]

By playing the harlot with slavery, America fostered luxury, idleness, and greed, vices which undermined the health of religion and the republic. "And will ye live after the flesh and die? or, through the Spirit mortify the deeds of the body, and live?" he inquired of his readers.[31] Slavery afflicted the body politic as well as the Body of Christ, for "so far as slavery prevails, so far is the community defective in answering the noble purposes of society."[32] Several pages later, O'Kelly elaborated on this idea, stressing that slavery was "by no means conducive to the improvement of manufactures and commerce; or in any ways serviceable to a virtuous and free people."[33] Piety and national prosperity would languish so long as Americans continued to indulge the lusts of the flesh through the use of slave labor.

Although America's sins were manifold, O'Kelly believed that the nation might yet find forgiveness and enjoy the Lord's favor. Let gradual emancipation begin, O'Kelly declared, and

> there will be less perhaps of the luxurious weed tobacco, and more of the blessed grain which is the staff of human life: there will be no slaves, but many good servants: more farmers, and fewer speculators: more agriculture and less idleness: cow-hide whips will be converted into shoes, and upstart slave-drivers will grasp the handle of the plough: manufactures will be carried on to perfection: every man will then be bound to his own country by the ties of interest and gratitude: and our nation will become the mart of nations and the garden of the Lord. Then the hands of faithful ministers . . . will be lifted up, while they cry, "Arise, shine, for thy light is come, and the glory of the Lord is risen upon thee."[34]

Virtuous freeholders tilling the soil, vicious overseers rehabilitated through hard work, instruments of cruelty rendered beneficial to man, flourishing trade, thriving religion—here was the perfect Christian commonwealth, the republican City of God, a picture of millennial felicity that drew inspiration from Isaiah's vision of the messianic kingdom as well as the Whig tradition.

O'Kelly encouraged Americans to realize this glorious destiny by throwing off the trammels of vice and by freeing their slaves. "Climb this one mountain, brethren, and perhaps you may never meet with so great a one, between this and the Holy Land," he wrote his fellow Methodists. He urged the civil powers to "assist us in carrying on this labour of justice and love."[35] Together they might still redeem the republic from the debilitating sin of slavery.

Having borne his witness against this one species of oppression, O'Kelly once again turned his attention to its ecclesiastical counterpart, the authority of the bishops. Episcopacy, O'Kelly contended, "rivits the oppressive chains, and promotes tyranny while we write, and preach against slavery."[36] The rule of the bishops was a "tyrannical and unscriptural form of government," a betrayal of both the Revolution and Christ's order for the primitive Church.[37] At the General Conference of 1792, O'Kelly rallied the "free citizens of Zion" to a defense of their gospel liberties against the encroaching power of the bishops. After he opened a spirited debate by challenging the bishops' right to appoint preachers to their circuits, anti-British and antislavery rhetoric surfaced in a manner reminiscent of the Whatcoat affair. One of O'Kelly's supporters cried out, "Did not our fathers bleed to free their sons from the British yoke? and shall we be slaves to ecclesiastical oppression?"[38] O'Kelly reported that his followers were "too sensible of the *sweets* of liberty, to be content any longer under British chains!"[39] When the majority of delegates to the Conference made it clear that they did not share O'Kelly's distrust of the bishops, O'Kelly and his supporters proclaimed their liberty by withdrawing from the meeting.

They never returned. At a meeting held in Manakin Town, Virginia, almost on the ninth anniversary of the Christmas Conference, O'Kelly's followers considered their alternatives and concluded, "a separation, or slavish submission was unavoidable. And we unanimously chose the former."[40] The man who had abetted the Fluvanna insurgents in 1779 presided over the founding of a new denomination in 1793. They called it "The Republican Methodist Church," and O'Kelly hoped that it would be "a republican, no slavery, glorious Church!"[41] The movement grew rapidly, especially in southern Virginia and North Carolina, where O'Kelly had been ministering for about sixteen years. Sometimes a whole body of Methodists went over to join the new Church. By 1809, the denomination numbered twenty thousand in the southern and western states; eventually, it would link up with disaffected Presbyterians in Kentucky and wayward Baptists in New England. The subsequent history of the denomination lies outside this study, but an ironic footnote might be added: in 1854, after the founder's death and several mergers, the denomination split along sectional lines over the issue of slavery.[42]

Shortly after the schism in 1792, O'Kelly clarified the nature of his protest for friends who remained within the Methodist fold. "I cordially despise slavery in every sense of the word: but thee I love," he assured them.[43] Monarchy, episcopacy, and slavery were all of a piece for O'Kelly; the work of liberation had to proceed at many levels. O'Kelly never lived to see America become the garden of the Lord, but he continued his labors as a faithful husbandman.

III

LIKE BARROW AND O'KELLY, DAVID RICE OWED allegiance to the Kingdom of God and the American republic. As a subject in the Kingdom, the Presbyterian minister obeyed the commandments of the Lord, preached the gospel, and engaged in benevolent activity. As a citizen of the republic, Rice safeguarded the virtue and stability of America. These two loyalties always overlapped in Rice's life, but for a brief moment in 1792, they merged completely as Rice attempted to practice the politics of benevolence.

Rice's family background and religious training prepared him for a career as an antislavery Presbyterian. He was born in 1733 in Hanover County, the cradle of Virginia Presbyterianism, to parents who held strong convictions against keeping blacks in slavery. His father regarded slaves as "more plague than profit" on the farm, while his mother had more principled objections to "traffic in human flesh."[44] The young Rice eventually came into contact with Samuel Davies, and during the years when Davies was expanding his ministry to the slaves, contending with their masters, and soliciting funds from abroad, Rice attended his meetings and was converted. When Davies left Virginia in 1759 to become president of the College of New Jersey, Rice followed his spiritual father to pursue advanced theological studies. Rice graduated in 1761, the year that Davies died.[45]

The years of contact with Davies left an enduring imprint on Rice's life, especially on his doctrine of benevolence. Through personal example and frequent exhortation, Davies had taught the necessity of combining piety with public service, neither of which, by itself, demonstrated a love for God. Benevolence without piety, Davies instructed his students, was only "a warm Affection for the Subjects, to the Neglect of their Sovereign," while piety without social concern amounted to nothing more than a "sour and malignant Humour."[46] Davies held out the ideal of "the truly good and useful Man" for his students to emulate,[47] and Rice incorporated that ideal into his own life and thought. The more we honor the Lord, Rice told his listeners on one occasion, "the more good we do in the world; the more we contribute to the happiness of rational intelligent being; the more we promote the interest of civil and religious society; the temporary and eternal interests of men." The truly good, truly useful Christian scorned the "vanities, pageantries and pomps of life" and used his resources instead to secure "the relief of the miserable," he stated.[48]

By engaging in antislavery activity, Rice pursued the implications of benevolence down an avenue that Davies never chose to explore. At some point in the 1750s, probably before he left for the College of New Jersey, Rice discovered an "honest SOMETHING" in his breast that bore witness against slavery, and this conviction remained with him through the rest of his life.[49] Rice thought of it as "a law of my nature; a law of more ancient date than any act of parliament; and which no human legislature can ever repeal." Other people could read this law inscribed on their hearts, he believed, "unless it is blotted by vice, or the eye of the mind blinded by interest." For his own part, Rice felt compelled to obey the dictates of his spiritual constitution, even though human governments might sanction slavery. "Should I do anything to countenance this evil, I should fight against my own heart: should I not use my influence to annihilate it, my own conscience would condemn me," he wrote years later.[50] Rather than war against his own heart, Rice sought the annihilation of slavery and other social evils. In 1763, he selected II Timothy 2:3 as an appropriate text to inaugurate his ministry in Hanover County: "Thou therefore endure hardness, as a good soldier of Jesus Christ."[51]

For the duration of his twenty-year ministry in Virginia, the moody, sometimes irritable, clergyman implemented his doctrine of benevolence by serving his fellow men in a variety of capacities. He immersed himself in the work of evangelizing the slaves of the county, a ministry in which he excelled. What precisely he did about slavery itself at this time is unclear. He joined with other members of the Hanover Presbytery in petitioning the Virginia legislature for relief from the burden of supporting the Anglican

Church. After removing to the Peaks of Otter region of Bedford County, Rice shepherded a mixed flock of Episcopalians, Baptists, Presbyterians, and Methodists. As the imperial crisis deepened, Rice appeared before the county's Committee of Public Safety and announced that if King George extended his prerogative beyond its constitutional limits, "the compact between king and the people would then be broken; . . . resistance would not only be lawful, but an indispensable duty; it would be resisting a tyrant, not a king."[52] The Presbyterian minister remained in Bedford County throughout the Revolution, undisturbed by the southern campaigns that ultimately led to victory at Yorktown.

At the conclusion of the war, Rice accepted a call from some settlers in Kentucky and moved his family to Danville. Appalled by the ignorance of religion, the drinking, and the quarrelling that he found on the frontier, Rice longed to impose the doctrinal and ethical rigors of New Side Presbyterianism on the inhabitants. "O for the Tennents, the Blairs, and the Daviesses, to come and preach to us in Kentucky!" he cried.[53] But slavery was one feature of life back east that Rice did not wish to see duplicated in Kentucky. When delegates to Kentucky's first constitutional convention assembled at Danville in 1792, one of the items under consideration was whether slavery would be permitted in the new state. Reverend Rice was on hand to deliver one of the most lucid and forceful antislavery appeals of the eighteenth century.

The Presbyterian minister entered the political arena to make certain that the new laws of Kentucky conformed to the dictates of heaven. Human legislators, he warned the delegates, cannot absolve individuals from their allegiance to the King of heaven. And yet, by keeping slaves, Americans ruined "God's creatures whom he has made free moral agents, and accountable beings; creatures who still belong to him, and are not left to us to ruin at our pleasure."[54] The fact that whites enslaved blacks to cater to their "ease, luxury, lust, pride, or avarice" only deepened his conviction that there was nothing benevolent about the practice.[55] Rice caricatured the slaveholding gentry's objections to emancipation as the prating of an indolent coxcomb. "What,—must young master saddle his own horse?" Rice mimicked. "Must pretty little miss sweep the house and wash the dishes?—and these black devils be free!"[56] As the truly vicious, truly useless man, the slaveholding gentleman loomed before Rice as the perfect antithesis of Davies' ideal.

By denying slaves the liberty to obey God, Rice maintained, white Americans undermined the stability and moral vigor of the commonwealth. Rice would have agreed with John Locke's definition of slavery as the "*state of War continued*" between a conqueror and a captive,[57] but Rice would have denied the lawfulness of the conquest. "The master is the enemy of the Slave; he has made open war against him, and is daily carrying it on in unremitted efforts," Rice asserted. "Can anyone then imagine, that the Slave is indebted to his master, and bound to serve him?"[58] Rice went beyond portraying the slave as an enemy to his master and the state and championed the cause of blacks who waged an outright war for their liberties. In the West Indies, he declared, "you may see the sable, let me say, the brave sons of Africa engaged in a noble conflict with their inveterate foes. There you may see thousands fired with a generous resentment of the greatest injuries, and bravely sacrificing their lives on the altar of liberty."[59] Although white American opinion about the uprising on St. Domingo had not yet crystallized in 1792, and although Americans had recently completed a revolution of their own, few Kentucky slaveholders could muster Rice's enthusiasm for a black insurrection.[60] In a less visible way, Rice told them, slavery subverted the political order by corrupting the manners of the master, a belief which he held in common with Barrow and O'Kelly. "A vicious commonwealth is a building erected on quick-sand, the inhabitants of which can never abide in safety," he warned.[61] Revelation, republicanism, and common sense spoke with a single voice with regard to slavery, Rice argued; Kentucky would not prosper if slavery were allowed.

By prohibiting slavery, however, the delegates would attract "five useful citizens" to the state for every slaveholder that they turned away, "and who would not rejoice in the happy exchange?"[62] By enacting a plan of gradual emancipation for blacks already in slavery, the leaders of Kentucky would increase the number of industrious inhabitants even more. The delegates had the unique opportunity of presiding over the inception of a state, Rice declared in his concluding remarks. "As a separate state, we are just now come to the birth; and it depends upon our free choice, whether we shall be born in this sin, or innocent of it."[63] Despite the forcefulness of Rice's appeal, and the support of the other six ministers in attendance, the antislavery delegates failed in their attempt to eliminate an article of the constitution that recognized slavery in Kentucky.[64]

In the aftermath of the convention, Rice transferred his hopes for an end to slavery from the political arena to the realm of the heart. If people could be led to discover that "honest SOMETHING" that the youthful Rice had found in his breast years before, then perhaps they would voluntarily emancipate their slaves. In 1794, Rice wrote the Pennsylvania Abolition Society about his efforts to "communicate light" on the evil of slavery, but admitted that many still refused to read the law of the heart. "Interest, all powerful Interest, closes the eyes and hardens the heart to a great degree, . . ." he complained. Not surprisingly, Rice singled out rich slave-holders and other "weighty, influential Characters" as the most recalcitrant citizens of Kentucky.[65] Although the winning of individual hearts and minds proved a difficult task, Rice decided that this approach resembled the one taken by the early Christians. "I think the christian religion abolished slavery in the roman Empire; not by producing laws for its abolition, but by its effects on the hearts of christians[,] disposing them to justice and mercy," he explained to one of his correspondents. Rice expressed his desire to see a similar process occur in the United States as a testimony to "the benignity of the religion of Jesus."[66] Rice was certain that, given enough time, benevolence would triumph over mere politics, and that a constituency of loyalists to the kingdom of God would accomplish what legislators had failed to do. He had great faith.

IV

SAMUEL HOPKINS HAD A WRETCHED PULPIT STYLE, and he knew it. But whenever he discoursed on the millennium, his face brightened, his words flowed more easily, his phrases acquired an uncharacteristic elegance, and his gestures grew more animated and expressive. Hopkins' vision of the millennium comforted him in a troubled world that seemed unresponsive to Christian and republican remedies. It was an intensely personal vision, one which compensated him for disappointments accumulated in his careers as preacher, patriot, and antislavery advocate.

Like many Americans of the Revolutionary era, Hopkins embraced republican ideals in response to some unsettling changes which took place in eighteenth-century society, but few of his contemporaries experienced those changes as abruptly as Hopkins did. Raised on a farm in Waterbury, Connecticut, Hopkins took his first pastorate in Great Barrington, Massachusetts, a rough frontier town where men still came to church with guns on their shoulders. There Hopkins reduced people to blinking stupefaction with his abstract sermon topics, while his monotonous voice, halting syntax, and wooden gestures did nothing to enhance his preaching.[67] The uncomplicated world of western Massachusetts presented many challenges to Hopkins, the New Divinity theologian, but, on the whole, rural life agreed with the son of a New England farmer. Hopkins kept his hand in farming by cultivating some land near the meetinghouse. In the late 1750s, a trustee from the College of New Jersey deleted Hopkins' name from a list of candidates for president of the school after observing "the country style in which Mr. H. lived, and the correspondence of his manners to such a state."[68] None of this would last for Hopkins, however, because in 1769, members of his congregation decided that they had tolerated his strict communion policy and his theological wranglings long enough, and they dismissed him after twenty-five years of service.

After Hopkins accepted a call from the First Congregational Church of Newport, Rhode Island, he entered a social world quite different from that of Waterbury or Great Barrington. In Newport, Hopkins suddenly confronted a pluralistic, cosmopolitan, competitive world dominated by a merchant elite, many of whom had erected their magnificent estates on wealth derived from the slave trade.[69] The countrified pastor did not adjust well to his new surroundings. At a time when other rural New Englanders sensed that their homogeneous, unified world of the past was breaking up under the impact of dimly perceived forces, Hopkins had been thrust into the kind of society that they despised and feared. Hopkins joined those Americans, rationalists and evangelicals

kins then added a remark which indicated that his mood of disappointment had deepened into one of resignation. "I must leave
it with the Supreme Ruler of the universe, who will do right, and
knows what to do with these States, to answer his own infinitely
wise purposes; and will vindicate the oppressed, and break the
arm of the oppressor, in his own way and time, and cause the
wrath of man to praise him."[79] In another letter to Levi Hart,
Hopkins blamed all the controversy about slavery and the constitution on demonic forces whose release had been foretold in
the sixteenth chapter of St. John's Revelation. "Ah! these unclean
spirits, like frogs," he lamented. "They . . . are spreading discord
and exciting men to contention and war, wherever they go; and
they can spoil the best constitution that can be formed."[80] These
two letters, written within about three months of each other, suggest that Hopkins' acquiescence to the existence of slavery had
something to do with his reading of the prophetic signs of the
times.

The relationship between Hopkins' interest in eschatology and
his passivity became apparent in 1793. In that year, he published
A Treatise on the Millennium, a product of his reflections on current
events and years of study of the Bible and Protestant commentators. William Ellery Channing, the nineteenth-century Unitarian
leader, had sat in Hopkins' congregation as a boy, and he recol-
lected that for Hopkins, the millennium was more than a belief.
"It had the freshness of visible things," Channing remarked. "He
was at home in it." Channing went on to observe that Hopkins'
Treatise had "an air of reality, as if written from observation."[81] In
his doctrine of the millennium, Hopkins created an idealized version of the home that he lost when he left Great Barrington and
that he had never been able to recover; his treatise actually was
written from observation in the sense that he had lived it as a boy
and as a young pastor in western Massachusetts. The millennium,
Hopkins declared "will be a time of universal peace, love, and
general and cordial friendship."[82] No extravagance in food or rai-
ment would be found. The "art of husbandry" would be "greatly
advanced" as people would discover ways to increase the yield of
the land.[83] There would be no slavery: "there will be no unrighteous persons, who shall be disposed to invade the rights and

property of others, . . . but every one shall securely sit under his own vine and fig-tree, and there shall be none to make him afraid."[84] In short, agrarian simplicity would be restored on earth.

After describing the splendors of the future, Hopkins cautioned his readers to expect many hardships before things got better. As a postmillennialist, Hopkins believed that Christ would return to earth after the thousand year reign of the saints, but contrary to a shopworn interpretive device used by historians, this belief did not make Hopkins optimistic, nor did it spur him on to social activism. According to Hopkins' reading of prophecy and history, the sixth vial of Revelation 16 was being poured out on the earth in preparation for the overthrow of "spiritual Babylon." The pouring of the vial began an era when the "three spirits like frogs" went abroad spreading discord, impiety, and a spirit of worldliness.[85] Even as he wrote, this prophecy was being fulfilled, Hopkins believed, and the pouring of the vial would continue until sometime in the nineteenth century.[86] Hopkins declared that none of his contemporaries would live to see the millennium. So what could believers of Hopkins' day do to prepare for the great day? Go and make converts to ensure a continuity of believers through the period of tribulation, came the answer. Evangelicals had "work enough to do" in preaching the gospel and in reforming the churches.[87] Hopkins made no mention of any programs for social reform that might hasten the arrival of the millennium.

The implications that Hopkins' millennial outlook had for his antislavery activity also became evident in 1793, the year when he published the *Treatise*. In *A Discourse Upon the Slave Trade and the Slavery of the Africans,* delivered before the Providence Society for Abolishing the Slave Trade, a nearly seventy-two-year-old Hopkins stood before his listeners and informed them that the commerce in slaves was proof that the sixth vial was running. But, he assured them, someday both slavery and the slave trade would be abolished, and "all men shall be united into one family and kingdom under Christ. . . ."[88] In the meantime, he said, benevolent individuals should preach the gospel and thereby subdue the pride and greed that caused slavery in the first place. "The gospel is suited to root these evils out of the world, and wholly abolish slavery; and will have this effect where it is fully and faithfully preached, and cordially received and obeyed."[89] This counsel may have seemed less than helpful for a group dedicated to direct attacks on the slave trade, but it was the same advice that Hopkins had offered to readers of the *Treatise.*

Dismayed by the durability of evil, Hopkins took refuge in an idealized version of a vanishing past. "Whilst to the multitude he seemed a hard, dry theologian, feeding on the thorns of controversy," Channing wrote, "he was living in a region of imagination, feeding on visions of a holiness and a happiness which are to make earth all but heaven."[90] In that fair region, the unlovely features of this world lost their vividness and immediacy.

Taken as a whole, the beliefs of these antislavery figures amounted to a fourfold variation on a common theme: to be strong, the republic must be pure, and slavery corrupted purity. This might be regarded as a secularized version of the message that antislavery evangelicals delivered to the churches in the 1780s and 1790s. But republicanism did not serve these evangelicals merely as a lexicon of secular equivalents for religious ideas; it imparted a freshness to their understanding of such doctrines as sin, redemption, Christian liberty, and the millennium, enabling them to speak a timely word to their contemporaries in a period of intense political debate.

The thought and work of these four individuals show that the term "republican religion" can mean something quite different from the unwritten creed of a few deists and free-thinkers.[91] Republicanism gave the faith of these evangelicals a political dimension, while their religious convictions imbued their political outlook with a deep tinge of millennialism. The political ideas of the day activated a component of evangelicalism that might otherwise have remained dormant. All evangelicals believed that God had rescued them from the personal tyranny of sin and granted them a freedom which could be maintained through rigorous self-discipline. This Christian freedom, however, had no overtly political meaning. But republican ideology invited evangelical patriots to contribute to the strength, liberty, and prosperity of the new nation by living up to their religious ideals. Evangelicals did so in an enthusiastic and diligent manner, viewing holiness, in part, as a political obligation. This consciousness of political responsibility led O'Kelly and Rice to seek a more direct way to influence governmental policy on slavery. Evangelicals ventured into the political arena tentatively, always mindful that meekness and humility were not highly prized by the other participants. Yet they retained the belief that the nature of politics would be transformed if all the participants were born anew in Christ. Indeed, in the millennial views of Barrow, O'Kelly, and Hopkins, the need for human governments disappears as men and women dwell in agrarian simplicity and respond directly to God.

If republicanism expanded the evangelical sphere of responsibility, it also gave some believers a deeper insight into the political consequences of sin. Not only did these four individuals strive against the evil within, but they also contended with institutionalized forms of iniquity. From personal experience, they knew that sin could exercise a tyrannous influence over the self. But sin could tyrannize over whole peoples when it achieved institutional form in oppressive systems of government such as monarchy, slavery, or, as in O'Kelly's case, episcopacy. Republicanism taught evangelicals to think of these oppressive systems as more than just reflections of individual wickedness: these systems were active sources of evil, fouling the political and social environment with corruption, and multiplying threats to the spiritual liberty of the self-disciplined believer. When these four men attacked oppressive forms of government, they struck at systems at war with the self. They warned that so long as Americans tolerated slavery in the republic, they would experience a freedom that was deficient and spiritually impoverishing.

When governments refused to yield on the question of slavery, these four evangelicals responded in various ways. Barrow removed himself physically from a world the slaveholders made and emigrated to a land which conformed more closely to his vision of a Christian republic. O'Kelly demanded a tightening of communal discipline to provide a model of republican piety, even though this path led to schism. Rice turned to the approach of persuading individual consciences of the need for emancipation. Hopkins settled in for a long wait and listed conversion of the world as his chief concern. Emigration, schism, reliance on moral suasion, faith in conversionism—in many ways these four men defined the options available to other antislavery evangelicals at the turn of the century.

V

A

RELIQUE
OF
OPPRESSION

WHILE HOPKINS ENTERTAINED VISIONS OF the millennium, his evangelical colleagues in Connecticut flocked to endorse the aims of the local abolition society. The Connecticut Society for the Promotion of Freedom and the Relief of Persons Unlawfully Holden in Bondage was founded in 1790, and during the five uneventful years of its existence, the evangelical wing of the Congregational clergy—comprised mainly of New Divinity men—gave its support to the organization. The Society also included moderate Calvinists like Yale's Ezra Stiles, unrepentant liberals like James Dana, prominent laymen of a pious disposition, and prominent laymen of an irreverent disposition. When the Society's work is compared to the ambitious programs of sister organizations in New York and Pennsylvania,[1] it appears that the Connecticut Society did not do much more than enlist the support of almost every religious and political leader in the state.

Evangelical participation in the Society raises questions about the antislavery commitment of ministers who, far from being outcasts or mistreated dissidents, held reputable positions in the religious establishment of Connecticut. Did the privileged status of evangelical Congregationalists produce antislavery sentiment at all different from that of less favored evangelicals? What was there about organized antislavery work that drew the evangelical members of the Congregational clergy into alliance with ministers and laymen who might not have shared their religious outlook? These questions lead one beyond the fragmentary records of the Society, but the answers suggest that the Society promoted something more

than antislavery sentiment and provided relief for persons other
than those held in bondage.

I

TWO OF THE REGION'S MORE ENERGETIC spokesmen shed light on
the character of antislavery sentiment among Connecticut's Congregational ministers. Jedidiah Morse and Timothy Dwight had
several things in common. To begin with, both grew up in New
England, and both received their advanced education at Yale College. Unlike leaders of other denominations, these two Congregational ministers enjoyed the sanction of the civil authorities and
the awareness that men in their position had taken an active part
in New England affairs for generations. Neither of them subscribed to the hyper-Calvinism of the New Divinity, but because
they rejected the genial rationalism of the liberals and used revivals to foster evangelical piety, they were mistaken for "Hop-
kintonians" by their theological opponents.[2] In the late 1790s,
Morse and Dwight would achieve notoriety by championing Christian orthodoxy against an array of real and imaginary foes. But, at
an earlier stage of their careers, slavery occupied their attention as
an embarrassing blemish on the American landscape. Their antislavery sentiment was not, as it was for a Barrow or a Hopkins, an
expression of the conflict between evangelicalism and the dominant culture of the area; instead, Morse and Dwight pitted New
England's Christ against southern culture.

Morse interspersed his antislavery ideas through the pages of a
best-selling book on geography. While he was a student at Yale,
the Connecticut youth delivered a series of lectures on American geography to a school of young girls in New Haven and, in
1784, Morse published these lectures in a book entitled *Geography
Made Easy*. Anxious to broaden his knowledge of the country,
Morse jumped at the chance to serve as the pastor of a Congregational church in Midway, Georgia.[3] After he moved there in 1786,
he eagerly gathered information and cultivated friendships that
would help him in the preparation of a revised, enlarged edition
of his book. The Yankee minister also made his first direct acquaintance with the southern slave system in the course of his

travels, and his reaction to the encounter became part of the revised text.[4] In 1789, after he assumed pastoral duties at the Congregational church in Charlestown, Massachusetts, Morse published the results of his work as *The American Universal Geography.*

As in the earlier work, Morse included remarks on the manners and customs of people in each state along with a description of mountains, rivers, and other characteristics of the land. The New England states provided Morse with a standard of spiritual health and material prosperity. Here, he asserted, dwelled a freedom-loving people, who were pious, industrious, and happy.[5] Morse allowed that similar virtues abounded in New York, New Jersey, Pennsylvania, and Delaware,[6] but his charity extended no further south.

In Morse's estimation, slavery prevented the southern states from attaining the level of Christian civilization enjoyed by their northern sisters. Slavery left masters in Maryland to "saunter away life in sloth, and too often in ignorance," he stated.[7] After reluctantly acknowledging that "a few eminent men" from Virginia made contributions to the new nation, Morse declared that a prevailing "spirit of gaming and barbarous sports" militated against literary and scientific inquiry.[8] "This dissipation of manners is the fruit of indolence and luxury, which are the fruit of the African slavery," he concluded.[9] In North Carolina, the "indolent minds of people at large" ruled out serious political and philosophical discussion. Whereas "most civilized countries" observed the Sabbath, Morse stated, the whites in North Carolina desecrated the day with their "convivial visitings," while the blacks disturbed the peace with their "noisy diversions."[10] Because slavery exempted many inhabitants of South Carolina from labor, they "too generally want that enterprize and perseverance, which are necessary for the highest attainments in the arts and sciences." The haughty South Carolinians also neglected to obey the well-known biblical injunction to "do to others as we would that others should do unto us."[11] Southern evangelicals had voiced many of the same sentiments about the moral effects of slavery, but where southern believers tended to associate these vices with a particular class, Morse regarded them as attributes of a region sinking into bar-

barism.[12] The spectacle of southern slavery revolted Morse, not because it entailed the misery and degradation of blacks, but because the system generated a host of unsavory cultural by-products.

From his parish in Greenfield, Connecticut, Timothy Dwight echoed Morse's praise for the unique virtues of New England. Dwight's situation, however, presented him with a paradox that was not as immediate for his counterpart in Charlestown. In Massachusetts, a series of court decisions led to the extinction of slavery by 1790, while in Connecticut, the legislature passed a law in 1784 declaring that only slaves born after March 1 would be free, and only when they reached the age of twenty-five.[13] Dwight was troubled by the prolonged existence of slavery in a state so highly favored by the Lord. In *Greenfield Hill,* a versified celebration of rural Connecticut life that he published in 1794, Dwight shifted uneasily between attempting to resolve the paradox and distracting attention from it.

Dwight began the poem with a survey of the tranquil beauty of the landscape that stretched before him. In the vicinity of Greenfield Hill, "every swain" lived "free, happy, his own lord," patiently farming the land and delighting in the pleasures of his pastoral surroundings.[14] Unlike Europe, land of "lordly churches" and "wealth enormous and enormous want," Connecticut offered its inhabitants the blessings of pure religion, mild government, and an equitable distribution of property:

> in every village, smil'd
> The heav'n-inviting church, and every town
> A world within itself, with order peace,
> And harmony, adjusted all its weal.[15]

Dwight believed that anyone who wished to promote the happiness of mankind would benefit more from studying Connecticut than all the empty theories dreamed up by philosophers.[16]

In Part II of the poem, slavery intruded upon this bucolic scene, not with the sound of the lash or with cries of anguish, but with the strains of a cheerful melody. "But hark!" Dwight wrote, "what voice so gaily fills the wind?/Of care oblivious, whose that laughing mind?/'Tis yon poor black."[17] What made the black so oblivious to his situation? The Connecticut slave, Dwight reported, never

wore burdensome chains or endured any of the physical hardships usually associated with bondage, for "here mild manners
good to all impart,/And stamp with infamy th' unfeeling heart."[18]
However much Dwight tried to minimize the severity of slavery in
Connecticut, he still had to reconcile the presence of the bondsman with his assertion that "every swain" lived as "his own lord."
To sustain the picture of a community of independent farmers,
Dwight portrayed the slave as the master's working partner, someone who received a reward for his labor just like any other industrious yeoman:

> He toils, 'tis true; but shares his master's toil;
> With him, he feeds the herd, and trims the soil;
> Helps to sustain the house, with clothes and food,
> And takes his portion of the common good.[19]

Dwight's well-fed, well-clad slave, like the Sambo figure of antebellum literature, "slides on, thro' life, with more than common
glee."[20]

After struggling to make slavery conform to a vision of rural felicity, Dwight admitted that servitude impaired the black's
moral and intellectual faculties, reducing him to a status below
that of whites. "Thus slavery's blast bids sense and virtue die;
/Thus lower'd to dust the sons of Afric lie," he wrote.[21] This admission led Dwight to issue the most unequivocal statement on slavery that appeared in the poem:

> O thou chief curse, since curses here began;
> First guilt, first woe, first infamy of man;
> Thou spot of hell, deep smirch'd on human kind,
> The uncur'd gangrene of the reasoning mind;
> Alike in church, in state, and household all,
> Supreme memorial of the world's dread fall;
> O slavery! laurel of the Infernal mind,
> Proud Satan's triumph over lost mankind![22]

By issuing such a declaration, Dwight inadvertently magnified the
"spot of hell" that marred his portrait of Connecticut.

Rather than attempt to deal once again with the problem of
slavery in Connecticut, Dwight abruptly shifted the scene to the

West Indies. The poet, "wing'd by thought," imagined himself walking through fields "as Eden gay," inhaling the fragrance of flowers that grew there in abundance.[23] The shrieks of tormented slaves, however, destroyed the appearance of Edenic beauty and exposed to Dwight the hellish realities of the place. "Illusions all!" he wrote, "'tis Tartarus round me spreads / His dismal screams, and melancholy shades. / The damned, sure, here clank th' eternal chain."[24] Dwight employed excessive amounts of gore to depict the cruelties of West Indian slavery, almost as if he were trying to dwarf the magnitude of slavery in Connecticut by placing it against a backdrop of unalleviated horror. Indeed, after the West Indian vision had been dispelled in the silvery dawn of a New England Sabbath, Dwight no longer felt obliged to make any mention of the issue. As the sun played upon the scene, shining in Connecticut, not the West Indies, as "Eden's seventh-day light,"[25] neither church, state, nor household appeared even faintly "smirch'd" with the stain of slavery.

Even though Dwight did not deal with southern slavery in the poem, he was not indifferent to its existence. By choosing the West Indies instead of the American South as the scene of his reverie, Dwight attempted to fix the blame for the worst aspects of slavery on France or Great Britain, heighten the contrast between the Old and New World, and thus fulfill one of the larger purposes of the poem.[26] With regard to the United States, Dwight shared Morse's conviction that slavery accounted for the differences between the manners of New England and the South, but while Morse described a region devoid of civilizing influences, Dwight saw the manners of New England spreading gradually to all of the less fortunate states. "When the enterprize, industry, economy, morals, and happiness, of New England, especially of Connecticut, are attentively considered, the patriotic mind will perhaps find much more reason to rejoice in this prospect, than to regret it," Dwight announced grandly.[27] For Dwight, Greenfield stood as the model of what all of America could be.

Taken together, the ideas of Morse and Dwight offer clues to the way in which regional pride, ambivalence, and defensiveness colored the antislavery sentiment of evangelical Congregationalists in Connecticut. Slavery was at once the labor system of a backward, languishing region, and a flaw on an idyllic landscape; slavery was evil, but not nearly so evil in Connecticut as it was in other places. If anyone doubted that the "mild manners" of Connecticut rendered the plight of the slave less onerous there, Dwight could point proudly to some "interesting and respectable efforts . . . for the purpose of freeing the Negroes."[28] He was referring to the activities of the Society for the Promotion of Freedom.

II

SECTIONAL LOYALTY HELPS TO EXPLAIN why evangelical ministers disliked slavery, but to understand why so many volunteered for organized antislavery work, one must survey the problems which confronted Congregational ministers at this time. By the early 1790s, the active years of the Society, popular support for the Congregational clergy of Connecticut had eroded to a point where ministers found themselves presiding over a body of sullen, unappreciative laymen, clients who had grown dissatisfied with the performance of the religious professionals. This problem would subside later in the decade as the Second Great Awakening brought a renewed appreciation for the clergyman's evangelistic abilities, but while it persisted, organized benevolent activity offered Congregational ministers in Connecticut an alternative to ineffectiveness.[29]

The estrangement between pulpit and pew in Congregational churches had been developing for some time. Throughout the 1770s, clergymen deplored the failure of some laymen to attend church and the behavior of others who, when they did come to church, would "turn their Backs upon the holy Ordinance of the Lord's Supper."[30] In their struggle to gain the attention of the people, ministers faced stiff competition from political affairs during these years, but the clergymen also had themselves to blame for the laity's unresponsiveness. In many respects, the laymen were the real losers in the "paper war" that raged between New Divinity and Old Light ministers after the death of the elder Edwards. The message of the new birth became less distinct, less compelling as Edwards' disciples quarreled with their enemies over qualifications for church communion and the nature of regeneration. One Connecticut layman pleaded with the ministers to stop their polemical debates and manifest a more tolerant spirit toward one another:

> Would God that all Christ's ministers would cease
> Their paper war, follow the prince of peace,
> Forbear to wrangle with their scribling pens,
> And show the world that christians can be friends.[31]

But the war continued, and by the 1780s, many laymen had either lost interest in the contest, acquired a distaste for clergymen of any kind, or departed to find spiritual sustenance elsewhere.

Religious apathy was the most immediate problem confronting Congregational ministers after the Revolution. The ministers at the General Association's meeting of 1783 discussed the problem of churches which had no settled pastor. To generate lay concern on the matter, the ministers warned of the "awful danger" to which people were exposed while living "destitute of a settled gospel ministry and ordinances."[32] The laymen of those churches, however, failed to respond with the proper sense of urgency about the vacant pulpits and, in 1784, the General Association had to issue a more severe statement on the problem.[33] As the 1780s wore on, the ministers realized that even those laymen who could avail themselves of a settled pastor treated the privilege with nonchalance. Gravely noting the "great, general, and increasing neglect there is in attending to the public Worship of God," the Association of 1788 drafted an admonition to the churches on the subject of religious duty.[34]

When this admonition appeared in the newspaper, some laymen responded by venting anticlerical attitudes that had been building since the 1770s. "We have heard your animadversion upon our absence from Sabbath meetings," one "Populus" replied in *The New Haven Gazette*, "and humbly conceive if you wish our attendance there, you would make it worth our while to give it." Missing a sermon would be the same thing as missing an opiate, he continued, "and can the loss of a nap expose our souls to eternal perdition?"[35] Another writer, who had evidently been subjected to a stiff dose of the New Divinity, wondered what the clergymen were so upset about. After all, the Calvinist ministers taught that since God had chosen the elect long ago, "We have nothing to do in the affair of our salvation." And if the recipients of grace had already been selected, "disobedience to the gospel cannot aggravate our doom, nor obedience promote our felicity." Furthermore, he stated, the clergy depicted people as so corrupt that "our very prayers are abominable to God." The empty pews merely indicated that the ministers had been successful in communicating their doctrines, the writer concluded sarcastically.[36]

For those who nurtured a hatred of Calvinism and the clergy, deism often provided a way to retain a belief in God and a meaningful universe without recourse to creeds, churches, or ministers.[37] Just how many Connecticut laymen took this route in the 1780s is difficult to determine, but there were lawyers who indulged a fashionable skepticism toward orthodox Christianity and, in 1784, Ethan Allen's *Reason the Only Oracle of Man* alerted clergymen throughout New England to the dangers of deism. As a token of the Connecticut clergy's edginess about religious infidelity, the General Association of 1786 opened a discussion on the way in which miracles confirmed the validity of the Bible.[38]

Rather than embrace deism, a larger number of disgruntled laymen in Connecticut found Baptist and Methodist fellowships to be attractive alternatives to the church of their ancestors. The continuing growth of the Separate Baptists, firm predestinarians in theological outlook, demonstrated that not everyone who left Congregationalism had become disenchanted with Calvinism. By 1790, the Baptists could count fifty-five churches in the state.[39] On June 17, 1789, Methodism arrived in Norwalk in the person of Jesse Lee and, in 1791, Asbury himself stood on the doorstep of Yale College. The Methodists gathered recruits slowly, but by 1795 the New England Conference numbered more than two thousand members.[40] The Congregational clergy's influence over the laity diminished with every desertion.

On the political front, Congregational ministers saw a faction of anticlerical lawyers growing restless with the clergy's control of Yale College. This faction, named "The Nocturnal Society of Stelligeri" by its opponents, included such men as Zephaniah Swift, David Daggett, and Uriah Tracy. Yale's president Ezra Stiles

feared that the Stelligeri would persuade Connecticut's legislature
to seize control of the corporation and thoroughly secularize the
curriculum of the institution.[41]

The clergy's lack of rapport with Connecticut's laymen was a
symptom of a more serious malady which afflicted the New England social order, a symptom of what Richard D. Birdsall described as "the dissociation between the purposes of the society
and the real beliefs of individuals that had come to pass by the
end of the eighteenth century."[42] Birdsall argued that the Second
Great Awakening revitalized the New England social order by
ending the "crisis of faith," and by enlarging the individual's sense
of participation in community life. But the Second Awakening
was not to occur in New England until the late 1790s and, in the
meantime, Connecticut's Congregational ministers had to cope with
the difficulties before them. The strategies which they pursued
suggest that they recognized the need to articulate a set of over-
arching beliefs and the desirability of enlarging their own participation in community life.

The ministers addressed the problems facing them in several
ways. To prepare ministers for the battle with doubters and deists, the General Association of 1791 instituted a lecture series
on the "Evidences of Christianity." The clergymen designated
the day before commencement at Yale College as the time when
each lecture would be delivered.[43] Ministers of differing sentiments
gathered on these occasions to hear a defense of the faith which
they held in common. The fact that these exercises in consensus
were a product of external pressures rather than mutual affection
did not render them any less significant. Also during these years,
Jonathan Edwards the younger prescribed benevolent activity as
the remedy for anyone suffering from doubts about the truth of
Christianity. The practice of "benevolence, justice, truth, faithful-
ness and beneficence" provided "a plain and sure way to the solution of all such doubts, . . ." he said. Let a person be disposed to
show piety toward God and "true virtue toward men," and "he
shall know whether the gospel be a revelation from God, or a
mere human invention. . . ."[44] In two ordination sermons, Benjamin Trumbull told ministers to "form connections with men of
piety, ingenuity and sentiment; and derive from this source, as

well as from reading, every advantage of which you are capable."[45] Trumbull offered his associates good advice: connections with the right kind of people, lay or clerical, gave coherence to the minister's changing world; connections provided a sense of pertinence when many laymen had made it clear that they could get along without the Congregational ministry.

Consensus, benevolence, connections—by emphasizing such themes, Congregational clergymen made a working alliance for benevolent ends possible in the 1790s. The consensus may have been fragile, and the connections may have been uneasy ones, but antislavery sentiment in Connecticut acted as a strong adhesive.

III

LATE IN THE SUMMER OF 1790, a small group of ministers and laymen drew up a constitution for the Connecticut Society for the Promotion of Freedom and the Relief of Persons Unlawfully Holden in Bondage. They pledged not only to work for the abolition of slavery, but also to "enlighten the minds and correct the morals of Negroes, to render them industrious, and furnish them with the means of honest Employments." To fulfill these purposes, they decided to hold regular meetings on the day following the Yale commencement and on the annual election day in May.[46] On paper, at least, the Society resembled the largely Quaker organizations in New York and Pennsylvania, but the Connecticut Society quickly took on a character of its own.

Who joined the Connecticut Society? Of the clergymen involved, the New Divinity men formed the largest identifiable group. Jonathan Edwards, Jr., Benjamin Trumbull, Levi Hart, Medad Rogers, Samuel Nott, Nathan Perkins, Allen Olcott, Ammi R. Robbins, Aaron Kinne, Jeremiah Day, and Nathan Strong all subscribed to the aims of the Society by signing the constitution or by attending the meetings. Timothy Dwight, evangelical poet and companion of the New Divinity men, also supported the organization, as did James Dana, the pastor of New Haven's Center Church who despised everything about the New Divinity.[47] By serving as the first president of the organization, Ezra Stiles took time from his duties at Yale to exert a conciliatory influence over the proceedings. Edwards and Trumbull also played an active role—both served on the Committee of Correspondence—and Edwards was vice-president.[48] All of the ministers involved were Congregationalists. Although few of them attended every meeting, many would have been on hand anyway for the Yale commencement or the annual election at Hartford.

The Society was by no means an exclusively clerical affair, for eminent laymen swelled the ranks of the organization. First, there were the "men of piety, ingenuity and sentiment" who figured so prominently in Trumbull's counsel. As members of the Society, lawyers such as Tapping Reeve, Timothy Dwight's brother Theodore, Simeon Baldwin, and Chauncey Goodrich gained experience in benevolent work that prepared them for leadership roles in the evangelical organizations of the early nineteenth century. Theodore Dwight and Goodrich would later serve as lay directors of the Connecticut Bible Society, and Reeve and Baldwin as officers of the Moral Society.[49] The clergymen could count on these men to lend a sympathetic ear. In addition to this retinue of pious laymen, several of the Stelligeri made their appearance at the Society's meetings. Men like Zephaniah Swift, David Daggett, and Uriah Tracy managed to lay aside their anticlericalism to work for antislavery goals. And if they could not embrace the religious convictions of other laymen in the Society, the Stelligeri could appreciate their devotion to the principles of Federalism and their interest in state and national politics.[50] The Stelligeri knew how to make connections just as well as the clergymen.

Beyond signing the constitution and attending the meetings, what did the members do to promote freedom in Connecticut? The constitution itself offered few hints as to specific measures that the members might undertake. One member read the document and decided: "It does not appear that the Society is of much importance as it respects its influence in this State, as there is here scarcely a claim for its exertions." Little appears to have transpired at the meetings. At one, for instance, those present admitted new members, voted to publish a full membership list, and then adjourned. None of the surviving minutes suggest that the Society actually trained blacks for "honest Employments," as the constitution had announced. From reading the constitution and minutes, one would have to conclude, as a member did, that the

Society existed only to lend moral support to similar organizations in other states.[51]

The minutes reveal little about the Society's activity because most of the work done by the members took place outside of the regularly scheduled meetings. The members offered free blacks a valuable service by providing them with legal aid and protection against unscrupulous whites. In the wake of the gradual abolition law of 1784, some whites in the state engaged in the cruel but lucrative business of kidnapping free blacks and selling them into slavery in the southern states or the West Indies. In 1788, the Connecticut General Assembly enacted a law forbidding residents to kidnap blacks or participate in the slave trade, but both practices continued. To monitor violations of the law, the Society's Committee of Correspondence relied on information transmitted by individual members, who acted as a Committee's eyes and ears in every locality. The Committee received reports of blacks being abducted by armed men, complaints that whites were participating in the slave trade, and requests for aid and advice.[52] In response, members of the Committee threatened to prosecute whites who were suspected of holding blacks illegally. Committee members also asked prominent individuals in the state to use their influence to help blacks held as slaves in the South; for instance, Governor Huntington was asked to write the governor of North Carolina and intercede on behalf of a black in bondage there.[53] The correspondence of the Committee does not indicate how successful its efforts actually were.

With a major portion of the business transacted by the Committee beforehand, the members who attended the regular meeting could concentrate on the oration that one of their number had prepared for the occasion. The oration occupied an important place on the Society's agenda for two reasons. First of all, it performed an educational function by disseminating information on the political and moral evils of slavery. The orators armed the members with facts and figures on the history of the slave trade, trained them to refute Scriptural arguments in support of slavery, and kept them abreast of antislavery activity in other countries. In so doing, the speakers endeavored to "increase and disperse the light of truth with respect to the subject of African slavery, and so prepare the way for its total abolition," as the younger Edwards put it. By publishing the speech, moreover, the Society could distribute it to a wider audience and "diffuse thro the State much striking and useful information and . . . raise the feelings of many, who do not yet feel as they ought, upon the Subject."[54] More importantly, however, the oration served as the means by which ministers and laymen affirmed common values, loyalties, and animosities.

With esteem for the Congregational ministry in short supply, the affirmation of the clergy's importance provided ministers with a particularly welcome source of encouragement. The ministers achieved recognition for their service as officers of the Society and as members of the Committee of Correspondence, but they must have been more deeply gratified to hear their efforts being acclaimed from the lectern. They also must have been slightly startled to see who was offering the kind words on their behalf. Zephaniah Swift, a free-thinking lawyer with a reputation for anti-clericalism, went out of his way to heap praise upon the ministers for their progressive attitudes and their willingness to stand in the forefront of benevolent causes. "It is a truth which ought not to be omitted," he stated with reference to Christianity, "that the ambassadors of this holy religion . . . have taken an active and decided part in favour of the defenceless tribes of Africa." The clergy's usefulness extended beyond antislavery work, Swift told the members. "What benefits may not civil society expect from the generous exertions of a class of men who labour to restore mankind to their natural rights in this world, in order to prepare them for eternal felicity in the world to come," he asked.[55] By attempting to deepen everyone's appreciation for the clergy, Swift showed that an atmosphere of congeniality surrounded the proceedings of the Society, inspiring the participants to sometimes unusual displays of harmony and good feeling.

The orators also used the antislavery discourse as an opportunity to affirm the peculiar blessings of Connecticut life. After surveying the history of the slave trade, Swift turned his attention from "such dreary objects" to a consideration of slavery in Connecticut. "Here," he promised, "a very different scene will be exhibited." The treatment of slaves in the state "was always distinguished by that mildness and clemency which accorded with the characters of their masters," he averred.[56] In his oration of 1794, Theodore Dwight voiced sentiments identical to those which his brother had expressed in *Greenfield Hill.* The evangelical layman viewed the situation of Connecticut slaves as "flourishing and happy" due to "the advancement of civilization, and the diffusion of a liberal policy. . . ." And yet, like his brother, Theodore Dwight regarded the presence of this "relique of oppression" as an uncomfortable reminder that civilization had not advanced far enough in Connecticut. After all, "Why should a countenance in this happy land, be saddened with the melancholy evil!"[57] Swift and Theodore Dwight betrayed the same ambivalence toward slavery as Timothy Dwight: the existence of slavery was distasteful, even embarrassing, for these individuals, but not really alarming; slaves were sad to be in bondage, they said, but happy to be in Connecticut. Such attitudes could hardly incite the members to wage an uncompromising war on slavery in Connecticut.

While spokesmen for the Society maintained their equanimity about slavery in the state, they could scarcely suppress a shudder at what was in store for the South. Jonathan Edwards, Jr., for example, contemplated the prospects of southern whites with horror. In an appendix to the published version of his discourse, the New Divinity minister declared that unless southern masters abandoned their plantations to the blacks and emigrated to the North, God would certainly reduce them to "a mungrel breed" through racial intermixture. Either way, southern whites would suffer the wrath of the Almighty, Edwards argued; the loss of their lands would be grievous, but if they did not evacuate, Providence would force them to make a "much dearer settlement" with the blacks, "and one attended with a circumstance inconceivably more mortifying, than the loss of their real estates, I mean the mixture of their blood with that of the Negroes into one common posterity." Providence would compensate the blacks, on the other hand, either by providing them with their masters' land, or by "raising their color to a partial whiteness," Edwards believed. He expressed relief that in the northern states, where blacks were less numerous, intermixture would not produce "any sensible diversity of colour."[58] Theodore Dwight also saw calamities coming upon the southern states. The Federalist in Dwight took pleasure in pointing up the hypocrisy of southern Jeffersonians who, while holding slaves, portrayed New England leaders as aristocrats and cryptomonarchists. "Let them visit New-England, and learn the rudiments of freedom," Dwight retorted. In his mind, the slave insurrection on St. Domingo portended a similar upheaval in the American South, but when that bloodbath began, Dwight stated flatly, no self-respecting New Englander would lift a hand to help beleagured southern whites: "Surely, no friend to freedom and justice will dare to lend him his aid."[59] The misfortunes that befell the South were simply none of Connecticut's affair, according to Dwight and Edwards.

From the orations and sketchy minutes of the proceedings, it is evident that the Society's regular meeting fulfilled objectives other than those in the Constitution. Through the meetings, Congregational clergymen discovered a ministry which did not make too many demands upon their time, but which led them beyond the often discouraging confines of the church. At the meetings, they could encourage benevolence, the antidote to infidelity, while cultivating the friendship of Connecticut's best and brightest. At the same time, the laymen—if they were so inclined—could consult with the clergy on religious and political matters, or they could use the gathering as an occasion to develop contacts with each other.[60] The lecturers, for their part, conducted exercises in mutual admiration, performed rites of absolution, and pronounced a benediction upon Connecticut's elite. Everyone participated in an international crusade designed to benefit the slave. For most members, supporting the antislavery cause must have been a wholly agreeable task.

IV

THE SOCIETY MOUNTED ONE INEFFECTIVE assault on slavery in Connecticut and then faded from view. After petitioning the legislature for total abolition in 1792, the Society mobilized its forces to elicit a response from the legislative session of May 1794. Partly as a result of the Society's urging, the Assembly passed a bill that would have freed all slaves on April 1, 1795, made provisions for the education of black children, and compelled masters to care for infirm and elderly blacks. The Council, however, declined to give its consent to the bill, and with that rebuff the campaign for total abolition lost momentum.[61] The Society itself did not survive much longer. In 1795, Edwards and Uriah Tracy attended the second convention of abolition societies in Philadelphia, but in succeeding years, no delegates from Connecticut appeared at the conventions.[62] No records of the Society's activity exist for the years following 1796. If any evangelical Congregationalist still had misgivings about slavery in the state, he could remember that this was Connecticut, and that the gradual emancipation law of 1784 had put slavery on the road to extinction; time and mortality would eradicate the last vestiges of the system.

Although the evangelical Congregationalists of Connecticut resembled other believers in their emphasis on the new birth, they had little in common with a great many evangelicals when it came to social experience. Connecticut's Congregational ministers rarely had to endure the contempt of the better sorts, and they never faced persecution at the hands of the governing authorities. The Congregational ministers of Connecticut simply had no serious quarrel with a social and political order which granted them a privileged status and a more or less steady income. Their quarrel with slavery, therefore, took on a character quite different from that of a Barrow, a Hopkins, or a Rice; it lacked a cutting edge, a focus of animosity, and a sense of urgency. Elsewhere in the United States, antislavery work earned evangelicals the wrath of the local elites, not their blessing. When compared to antislavery evangelicals in other areas, the Connecticut ministers look like relaxed members of an exclusive club. Only to the extent that the South symbolized depravity could their antislavery work be described as part of a struggle against the "world."

In spite of its distinctive features, the Connecticut Society had one characteristic in common with other antislavery organizations in the 1790s: an inability to devise a strategy for influencing federal policy on the slavery question. The demise of the Connecticut Society occurred shortly before a decline in organized antislavery activity in the United States. The movement for national antislavery conventions ran out of steam as member societies lost interest or simply disappeared from sight. By the early 1800s, even the

New York and Philadelphia Societies, which had attracted the support of a few urban evangelicals, were showing signs of lethargy.[63] Evidently the organized movement was uncertain as to how to proceed toward the goal of total abolition. Many societies concentrated their fire on the slave trade in the belief that once this vital artery had been cut, the domestic institution would die a natural death. In the North, the achievement of local victories against the trade, together with a confidence that Congress would outlaw all slave imports after 1808, contributed to a sense that the major battles had been won.[64] Aside from an occasional petition to Congress, the antislavery societies saw little need for sustained political activity at a national level. The Quaker-dominated groups in New York and Philadelphia continued their efforts to educate freemen, but many members drifted away. Members of the Connecticut Society were hardly in a position to make any suggestions about a national antislavery program; they had failed to formulate a successful strategy on a state level. When abolitionists of the antebellum period wrestled with the problem of political action, they would find little to guide them in the work of eighteenth-century organizations.

In the years after 1795, Connecticut's Congregationalists retained their contempt for southern culture and their pride in the New England heritage. These convictions contributed to the deepening of the sectional crisis in the years leading up to the Civil War. By then, slavery in Connecticut was dead, and the ministers could be wholly uninhibited about calling down God's wrath upon slaveholders.

VI

FAITH
WITHOUT
WORKS

INCE THE 1770S, ANTISLAVERY EVANGELICALS had strug-
gled to make opposition to human bondage a part of
the Christian witness. Playing upon the white evangelical
sensibility and fears about worldliness, they had managed to obtain a hearing before informal gatherings of believers,
church councils, and the nation at large. If they had not cleansed
the churches or the republic of slavery, they had provoked debate by issuing a vigorous challenge to the evangelical strategy of
Christianizing the master-slave relationship. They had effected
some private manumissions, and they had persuaded ecclesiastical
bodies to declare their approval of broad antislavery principles.

In the latter years of the eighteenth century, however, the subject of emancipation receded from prominence in evangelical circles. Many evangelicals defaulted on their commitment to abolish
slavery, while ecclesiastical bodies expressed a willingness to post-
pone action on their antislavery principles until some more favorable day. Proponents of an older viewpoint forcefully reasserted
the argument that conversion of the master and the slave provided a sane and acceptable solution to the problems of slavery.
Several factors contributed to the decline of interest in emancipation—the threat of repression, concern about subversives, the start
of a revival, and enthusiasm for overseas missions—but, at the
turn of the century, staunch antislavery evangelicals began to find
themselves isolated, their entreaties unwelcome, and their activities suspect.

I

ANTISLAVERY EVANGELICALS IN THE SOUTH had always encountered
opposition to their activities, but their situation in the late 1790s
gave them additional reasons to walk circumspectly.

On the whole, the status of evangelicals in the region had im-
proved immensely since the time when their preachers had been
beaten up by mobs. Religious persecution was a thing of the past,
although memories of the heroic days filled older evangelicals
with nostalgia. When they contemplated the numerical growth
achieved over those same years, southern evangelicals paused
sometimes to give thanks, other times to wonder whether they had
conceded too much to the world in their quest for converts.[1] As a
token of their success, evangelicals had made progress in over-
coming planter resistance to slave evangelism. Commenting on
the number of slave converts in the South, one correspondent
noted: "their owners begin to discover that their slaves are of
increasing value to them when they become religious."[2] But success
removed the circumstances which had helped to make antislavery
commitment possible: with the end of religious persecution and
the softening of opposition to slave evangelism, white evangelicals
no longer endured the experiences which had enabled them to
identify with the black victims of oppression.

Success also brought an awareness that all of the gains could be
swept away if evangelicals attempted to define emancipation as a
binding duty for all Christians. The Methodists had learned this
in 1784, and ten years later the Presbyterian Synod of the Carolinas reviewed the lesson by attributing Methodist weakness in
North Carolina to "their doctrine of the emancipation of slaves, a
doctrine very unpopular in that country."[3] Southern evangelicals—
no longer at open war with the dominant culture, and well on
their way to becoming representatives of a new dominant culture—began to shoulder responsibility for the maintenance of social stability in the region.

That stability was apparently threatened by the tumultuous
events on St. Domingo. Tales of the slaughter and destruction
that took place on the island filtered into the South, fraying the
nerves of masters and creating a climate of opinion that was inhos-
pitable to criticism of slavery. Masters heard, or thought that they

heard, slaves whispering about occurrences on the "French Island"; slaveholders detected, or thought that they detected, an increase of slave unrest after the outbreak of violence on St. Domingo.[4] Under the circumstances, many southern evangelicals found it advisable to heed the voice of prudence and discourage agitation on slavery.

To avoid discussions that might imperil Christian unity or social stability, ecclesiastical councils fixed upon the strategy of relegating the problem of slavery to the political sphere. When the Virginia Baptist General Committee defined slavery as a legislative problem, for example, it handed Baptists an excuse for inaction.[5] If slavery was a legislative problem, a believer might reason, then responsibility for emancipation fell upon the lawmakers. Until such time as they saw fit to act, Baptist churches should withhold comment and tend to their spiritual affairs, among which slavery no longer had a place. John Leland recognized the readiness of Virginia Baptists to dissociate slavery from the legitimate concerns of the church. In his valedictory address, he had to preface his remarks on slavery with the assurance that he did not intend to "drop the ministerial vest, and assume the politican's garb to-day. . . ."[6] In 1796, the Ketocton Association confirmed a tendency of Virginia Baptists to excuse themselves from responsibility on the grounds that it was none of their business. When the Happy Creek Church sent the Association an inquiry on the righteousness of slaveholding, the Association refused to give an answer, "considering it an improper subject of investigation in a Baptist Association, whose only business is to give advice to the Churches respecting religious matters; and considering the subject of this query to be the business of government. . . ."[7] As a political problem, slaveholding simply did not constitute a soul-endangering sin.

Presbyterian bodies in the South also employed this strategy to deflect the entreaties of antislavery evangelicals. Evidently, the General Assembly's carefully worded letter of 1795 had failed to pacify dissidents in Kentucky's Transylvania Presbytery for, in 1796, the Presbytery entertained a series of questions, petitions, and remonstrances on slavery. Leaders of the Presbytery answered one such remonstrance by affirming that, although they

were "fully convinced" of slavery's evil, "they view the final remedy as alone belonging to the civil powers. . . ."[8] This formulation could not have pleased David Rice. In a similar fashion, the
Synod of the Carolinas dismissed an overture requesting Presbyterian churches to petition state legislatures for a gradual emancipation law. Members of the committee which drafted a reply declared that it was their "ardent wish" to see slavery abolished, but,
they said, discussion of the matter should be deferred until the
time "when such shall be contemplated by the Legislatures of our
Southern States."[9] Emancipation was a commendable goal, the committee stated, but the initiative to realize that goal would not come
from the Synod.

These equivocations did not dissuade antislavery Presbyterians
in Kentucky. Despite the frustrations of working through ecclesiastical channels, the dissidents of Transylvania Presbytery urged
their local judicatory to clarify its position on the evil of slavery.
At a meeting of the Presbytery's leaders in 1797, those present
first took up the question, "Is slavery a moral evil?" They agreed
that it was. Next they considered the question, "Are all persons
who hold slaves guilty of all moral evil?" and "it was voted in the
negative." Thus far, the participants had decided that slavery was
sinful, but that not everyone who held slaves committed sin. Quite
naturally, they then tried to answer the question, "Who are not
guilty of a moral evil in holding slaves?" At that point the assembly demurred: "Resolved that the question now before presbytery
is of so much importance that the consideration of it be put off till
a future day."[10] Realizing that they had ventured onto a dangerous
area of discussion, a majority of participants drew up sharply and
backed away from the issue.

Other Kentucky Presbyterians ruffled their superiors by ignor-
ing ecclesiastical channels and embarking on a course of action all
their own. At some point in the late 1790s, the united congregations of Cane Ridge and Concord took it upon themselves to
exclude slaveholders from communion. In 1800, the Synod of
Virginia reasserted its authority over the offending churches. Before it reprimanded the united congregations, the Synod emphasized that the thought of so many blacks living in slavery was "a
reflection to us peculiarly afflictive." But the trouble with the

congregations of Concord and Cane Ridge, the Synod went on, was that they represented slaveholding to be a "known sin"; they wrongly assumed that everyone who owned slaves knew slaveholding to be a sin, when in fact their consciences may not have been convicted of the evil. Only those who held slaves "at the same time that they consider it their duty to emancipate them immediately" deserved to be excommunicated. This, however, was "a charge which ought not to be advanced without sufficient evidence to support it."[11] But how could antislavery Presbyterians distinguish the unpersuaded conscience from the disobedient conscience, the apparent sinner from the real? And what reply could they give to the slaveholder who insisted that his conscience was clear? The Synod provided no answers and, aside from reiterating the General Assembly's pronouncement of 1795, it offered no guidance on how to facilitate the "good work" of freeing the slaves.[12]

Elsewhere in the South, Presbyterian clergymen discovered that they could not even mention the subject of emancipation in public without incurring the displeasure of church officials. In July of 1796, the Presbytery of South Carolina summoned a young antislavery minister named James Gilleland to give an account of his activities. After Gilleland denied that he had ever preached "anything against the government," the Presbytery enjoined him to be silent in the pulpit when it came to emancipation.[13] Since he regarded this judgment as a contradiction to his understanding of God's Word, Gilleland appealed his case to the Synod of the Carolinas. The Synod, however, upheld the Presbytery's decision, concluding that "to preach publicly against slavery in present circumstances, and to lay it down as the duty of every one to liberate those who are under their care, is that which would lead to disorder, and open the way to great confusion." The Synod allowed Gilleland the freedom to use his "utmost endeavors in private" if he desired to help slaves.[14] Robert Wilson, another Presbyterian clergyman in South Carolina, thought about leaving either the state or the ministry rather than submitting to enforced silence on slavery. In 1798, Jonathan Edwards the younger encouraged Wilson to remain in his office, for in private he could still assist like-minded brethren and perhaps lead younger ministers to his way of thinking.[15] Neither Wilson nor Gilleland could live within a restricted sphere of activity: Gilleland left for Ohio in 1804, and Wilson followed him in 1805.[16]

The Methodist Church withdrew from active antislavery work more slowly and painfully than any other denomination with roots in the South. By 1796, the antislavery pronouncements of the General Conference had taken on a strained quality, almost as if the Methodists felt compelled to remind themselves and the world of their good intentions. "We declare that we are more than ever convinced of the great evil of African slavery, . . ." the Conference announced in a preface to a section of the *Discipline*. In that section, the General Conference declared that anyone who sold a slave would be expelled, and that anyone who purchased a slave was required to set a date for his or her manumission. The local conferences of Virginia, Baltimore, and South Carolina treated the General Conference's recommendations with studied neglect and, in 1804, the General Conference dropped the section on slavery from copies of the *Discipline* sent to states south of Virginia.[17]

While others equivocated or engaged in acts of collective handwringing, at least one denominational body in the South took a firm, authoritative, and quite unapologetic stand in favor of slavery. In 1800, Wood Furman drafted the circular letter on behalf of the Charleston Association of South Carolina Baptists. "The scripture doctrine on the station and duties of servants, is clear and decided," Furman stated confidently. "Rather, therefore, than advocate the speculative, abstract opinions, or attempt the innovations of practice, which on this subject have been advanced and planned by others; let us adhere to these scriptural principles . . . so clearly laid down in the volume of inspiration," he declared. "On these we may and ought to insist."[18] Furman's straightforward biblicism was rare among southern evangelicals at this time, but it demonstrates that long before the agitation of the antebellum years, a few evangelicals in the region styled themselves as champions of the revealed Word against the heterodox abolitionists. The Charleston Baptists permitted no tampering with the Holy Scriptures or divinely-sanctioned institutions like slavery.

Southern evangelicals had good reason to be sensitive to public opinion when they treated the issue of slavery, as reaction to

Gabriel Prosser's conspiracy made clear. In the summer of 1800, white Virginians uncovered a plot which, had it been carried out, would have resulted in an assault on Richmond by two hundred slaves. At the center of the conspiracy stood Gabriel Prosser, an enigmatic slave artisan who went to the gallows without uttering a word in the way of a confession. But as details of the plot emerged from the testimony of other conspirators, evangelicals—especially Methodists—unexpectedly found themselves enmeshed in a web of implication. Gabriel and his lieutenants hung on the periphery of religious meetings to gather recruits, the conspirators said. The slaves used Scripture texts to bolster their courage; at one planning session, a slave remembered reading in the Bible that if they worshiped God, "five of you shall conquer an hundred & a hundred a thousand of our enemies."[19] If the insurrection had taken place, a conspirator stated, "all the whites were to be massacred, except the Quakers, the Methodists, and the Frenchmen, and they were to be spared on account as they conceived of their being friendly to liberty. . . ."[20] After the plot had been uncovered, a white Methodist shipmaster named Taylor allowed the fugitive Gabriel to remain onboard, although Taylor later professed ignorance as to his passenger's true identity.[21]

In the minds of southern leaders, Gabriel's conspiracy awakened old fears about the relationship between religion and slave insubordination. One prominent aristocrat in Virginia regarded the fellowship of white and black evangelicals as a source of future unrest:

> Fanaticism is spreading fast among the Negroes of this country, and may form in time the connecting link between the black religionists and the white. Do you not, already, sir, discover something like a sympathy between them? It certainly would not be a novelty, in the history of the world, if Religion were made to sanctify plots and conspiracies.[22]

The lesson was not lost on other leaders. The mayor of Richmond prohibited blacks from attending the night meetings of Methodist ministers while, in 1800, the South Carolina legislature banned blacks from gathering for religious instruction, even in the com-

pany of whites, after sundown and before sunrise. Unlawful meetings were to be dispersed by sheriffs or militia officers, the legislature declared. The spread of revivals in North Carolina fired
rumors of slave conspiracies there as well.[23]

In view of the turmoil created by the Gabriel conspiracy, the
Methodist General Conference could scarcely have chosen a worse
time to circulate an address on slavery. Signed by Coke, Asbury,
and Whatcoat, the address asserted that "the whole spirit of the
New Testament militates in the strongest manner against the practice of slavery. . . ." The signers exhorted their Methodist brethren to petition state legislatures for gradual emancipation and
thereby "hasten to the utmost of our power the universal extirpa-
tion of this crying sin."[24] Having failed to extirpate the evil from
their church, Methodist leaders hoped to direct antislavery energies into political action, but they succeeded only in substantiating
the fears of those who saw them as meddlesome fanatics.

No one realized this better than Methodist ministers in Charleston, South Carolina, for a storm of violence broke over their
heads as a result of the address. In early September of 1800, a
Methodist minister named John Harper discovered copies of the
broadside in an otherwise innocuous box of books. After showing
the address to a few persons of "prudence," Harper allowed a
local magistrate to burn all remaining copies of the document. In
spite of these precautionary measures, word of the broadside's
contents leaked out, inciting the citizens of Charleston to take to
the streets. A mob of two hundred people, led by "a lawyer of
note," laid seige to Harper's house and hurled threats in its direction. On a separate occasion, a crowd surrounded Harper as he
emerged from a Sunday night preaching service but, as he grate-
fully acknowledged, he was "defended from the effects of their
rage by some friends, who now bear the marks of hard blows as
the effect of their interposition." One of Harper's clerical associates did not escape injury. The next evening, a mob seized George
Dougharty after a prayer meeting, beat him, and dragged him to
a pump. A reprint of David Rice's speech to the Kentucky convention only aggravated the situation, Harper reported. Harper's
friends begged him to leave the city, and he warned Ezekiel Cooper

that Asbury would visit Charleston at the peril of his life. "Some magistrates of the highest respectability have given it as their opinion," Harper informed Cooper gravely, "that we need not expect peace in this State unless we abjure our principles respecting slavery contained in the form of Discipline."[25] At its next meeting the General Conference did just that.

Rather than alienate their followers or risk precipitating storms of popular outrage, evangelical leaders in the South reverted to an old formula: they attempted to eliminate the overt cruelties of slavery by Christianizing the master-slave relationship. This approach had been vigorously advocated even during the most intense period of evangelical debate on slavery. In 1787, Henry Pattillo published *The Plain Planter's Family Assistant*. The Presbyterian clergyman, who was a former student of Samuel Davies, followed the master's teaching on slavery more closely than another student named Rice.

Like Rice, Barrow, and O'Kelly, Pattillo was disturbed by the corrupting effects of slavery, but his resemblance to the antislavery evangelicals ended there. In a message ostensibly addressed to his readers in bondage, Pattillo signaled masters that he was no firebrand: "I wish them to know, that they are by no means their friends, who put freedom into their heads." He expressed confidence, however, that Providence would effect emancipation for the slaves "in due time."[26] With regard to present realities, Pattillo freely admitted that wickedness often flourished on the plantation, but he ascribed this situation to "the influence of heathen slaves over the inhabitants in their younger days."[27] If masters took responsibility for the conversion of their slaves, he said, righteousness and prosperity would reign over the plantations. To win adherents to his point of view, the minister played upon the master's self-image as patriarch of his plantation "family": your slaves, he told them, "have so often fed from your hand; played at your door, and shown such a willingness to please and oblige you, that you consider them as your *humble friends*. . . ."[28] By providing slaves with religious instruction, masters would demonstrate a paternalistic regard for the welfare of their servants. For those more concerned about managing a labor force than fulfilling patriarchal obligations, Pattillo showed that converted slaves were obedient workers, indifferent to their status, and prayerful about their master's well-being.[29]

The passage of years only deepened Pattillo's conviction that he had advocated the correct approach to slavery in 1787. "The subject of manumission will greatly injure our interest as a church," he instructed a friend in 1799. "I once touched it with caution: it offended some, and pleased none; tho' I mentioned it as a very distant object."[30] It is somewhat surprising that Pattillo brought up the subject at all, since in 1787 he had assigned "the slaves of my *Plain Planter*" a place among "the happiest of human beings."[31] If the abuses of the system could be regulated under the watchful eye of the church, Pattillo believed, the qualitative difference between freedom and slavery would be neglible enough to render antislavery work unnecessary.

Other evangelicals came to see the wisdom of such an approach. At the same meeting that dealt with Gilleland's appeal, the Synod of the Carolinas ordered heads of families under its jurisdiction to instruct slaves in religion.[32] Although the Dover Association of Virginia Baptists encouraged individual members to petition the legislature for emancipation, it also began to offer advice on how to discipline "believing masters" who treated their slaves with cruelty.[33] An association of back-country Baptists in South Carolina sought to eliminate "oppression," which they defined as a display of excessive cruelty.[34] This usage departed from that of antislavery evangelicals who defined "oppression" as a synonym for slavery itself. Some Baptists recommended an amelioration of the slave's plight as a form of Christian humanitarianism. A spokesman for South Carolina Baptists argued that evangelicals should conscientiously engage in the slave trade to deliver blacks from less benevolent hands: "Humanity then may dictate to Christians . . . to purchase as many as they can of these poor people, with an honest intention to render them as happy as circumstances will admit."[35] One Baptist historian reasoned that slavery could awaken altruistic impulses in whites, for "those who are inclined to tenderness and compassion, may always find occasions for displaying these noble virtues."[36] By supplying believers with a variety of options short of emancipation, southern evangelical leaders granted that slavery and piety could coexist, and that antislavery evangelicals had no monopoly on benevolence.

The trend toward accommodation is dramatically illustrated in the thinking of Thomas Coke and Francis Asbury. In the 1780s, Coke had faced down mobs which had assembled in reaction to his antislavery pronouncements but, in 1795, he minimized the importance of the slave's temporal status. "My dear brother," he wrote Ezekiel Cooper, "have great compassion for the poor Negroes, and do all you can to convert them. If they have religious liberty their temporal slavery will be comparatively but a small thing."[37] Asbury's change of heart can be better documented. In 1797, he told a Methodist in South Carolina: "It is of great consequence to us to have proper access to the masters and slaves." He then included an example from his own experience to drive the point home:

> I had a case, a family I visited more than a year ago, a
> tyrannical old Welshman. I saw there he was cruel,
> his people were wicked, and treated like dogs. "Well,"
> say you, "I would not go near such a man's house."
> That would be just as the devil would have it. In one
> year I saw that man much softened, his people ad-
> mitted into the house of prayer, the whole plantation,
> forty or fifty singing and praising God.[38]

Through the grace of God, Asbury discovered, the plantation could be changed from a nursery of sin to a showcase of godliness. By the early 1800s, Asbury could seriously entertain a question that had previously been unthinkable: "Would not an *amelioration* in the condition and treatment of slaves have produced more practical good to the poor Africans, than any attempt at their *emancipation*?"[39] Years of strife and personal frustration lay behind that question, but the man who had once tied Methodist fortunes to active opposition to slavery had learned to accept a good deal less.

Without sanctioning the existence of slavery, most evangelicals in the South attempted to transform the character of the institution by transforming the hearts of the people involved. Saving souls, after all, had always been their primary objective. To state their position in terms set forth by Freeborn Garrettson, if evangelicals in the South had to choose between antislavery activity and "plain christian experience," then they preferred to delay action on slavery and return their attention to the less problematic doctrines of the gospel. The advent of the Second Great Awakening reinforced that choice. Before examining the impact of the revival, however, we must turn briefly to developments in New England, where a different kind of conspiracy absorbed the interest of antislavery evangelicals.

II

On May 9, 1798, Jedidiah Morse electrified scores of worshipers by disclosing the existence of a plot to overthrow the government and Christianity. Members of the audience had gathered in compliance with President Adams' Fast Day Proclamation, but from the pulpit they heard something wholly unlike the usual exhortations to repent and reform. Morse told them that agents of a secret organization known as the Order of Illuminati had infiltrated the United States to spread atheism, anarchy, and immorality. Drawing heavily from John Robison's colorful but unreliable *Proofs of a Conspiracy*, Morse outlined the strategy of the Illuminists: they attempted to undermine faith in the Bible; they insinuated their members into key positions in schools and literary societies; and they endeavored to weaken the authority of ministers and political leaders through slander and misrepresentation. Already, Morse declared, the Illuminati had executed their dark designs on France; now French agents and their American collaborators were active in the United States. He summoned the faithful to stand up and be counted in the fight against the insidious forces at work within American society.[40]

Although Morse offered his audience no concrete evidence of such a plot, he succeeded in striking a responsive chord among New Englanders. Federalists in the region still remembered the intrigues of Citizen Genet, the overzealous French diplomat who nearly compromised American neutrality by using the United States as a base in France's war with Great Britain. Reports of the Jacobin Reign of Terror and the exaltation of the Goddess of

Reason had drifted across the Atlantic. Tom Paine's *Age of Reason*, with its contemptuous treatment of revealed religion, had created a furor in orthodox circles, while the spread of "French" infidelity provoked Timothy Dwight—who became president of Yale in 1795—to launch a vigorous counterattack. France's high-handed treatment of American diplomats in the XYZ Affair had recently burst into public view, kindling a militant patriotism throughout the new nation. Conservative New Englanders eyed the growth of Democratic Societies with suspicion. The idea that a sinister organization lurked behind these seemingly unrelated developments had a strong appeal for New Englanders in the late 1790s.[41] For evangelical Congregationalists, whose interest in antislavery work had been flagging for several years, the Illuminati posed a far greater menace to Christian civilization than the slaveholder.

Illuminism commanded the attention of almost every antislavery spokesman among the evangelical Congregationalists. On July 4, 1798, the Dwight brothers sallied forth to arouse the citizens of Connecticut to an awareness of their peril. At Hartford, Federalist Theodore Dwight portrayed Thomas Jefferson as a fellow traveler of the Illuminati, if not an actual member of the Order.[42] At New Haven, Timothy Dwight startled his audience with the question, "Shall our sons become the disciples of Voltaire, and the dragoons of Marat; or our daughters the concubines of the Illuminati?"[43] These were momentous times, Dwight stated, and as proof he listed the progress of efforts to abolish slavery, "which," he was certain, "will within a moderate period bring it to an end."[44] Although the aging Hopkins did not participate actively in the Illuminist scare, he described Robison's *Proofs of a Conspiracy* as a "well supported" book, and he pronounced Timothy Dwight's oration "a masterly performance."[45] Almost a year after he unveiled the existence of the conspiracy, Morse was on hand to defend the reputation of the clergy, who were unfairly regarded as "an expensive, useless, nay even, noxious body of men." To prove that France had hostile designs on the United States, he disclosed that the French radicals had tried to recruit a black legion on St. Domingo, one which would have invaded the American South and incited slaves to revolt.[46] Morse conjured up the specter of servile insurrection to instill a fear of the godless French, not, as other antislavery evangelicals had attempted, to underscore the inescapable dangers of keeping blacks in bondage.

By the fall of 1799, the Illuminist controversy had sputtered out amid ridicule, insistent but unanswered demands for proof, and charges that the Federalists and their clerical allies had exploited the issue for partisan purposes. For the evangelical Congregationalists who participated in the crusade, anti-Illuminism performed some of the same functions as antislavery work: the affirmation of traditional values, the defense of New England culture, and the assertion of clerical authority.[47] The anxiety which fed both movements, however, began to diminish with scattered reports of a revival.

III

"O LORD, REVIVE THY WORK IN THE MIDST of the years." The prophet Habakkuk's prayer expressed the sentiments of countless American evangelicals who yearned for a fresh outpouring of the Holy Spirit. A half century had elapsed since the Great Awakening and, although evangelicals had witnessed a few localized revivals, no major outbreak of religious fervor had taken place since the 1740s. But as evangelicals later recounted, just when the infidels seemed ready to triumph, just when the church appeared ready to expire from the listlessness of its members, the Lord visited the land with a revival so glorious and extensive that it eventually came to be known as the Second Great Awakening.[48] The revival had a number of far-reaching consequences for evangelicalism and American culture, but as one of its short-term effects, the revival accelerated the decline of evangelical opposition to slavery.

The Awakening began at different times in different places, and with varying degrees of intensity. Gentle showers of religious blessing fell across New England in the late 1790s, commencing an era which slightly overlapped the period of the Illuminist scare. Congregationalists in the region rejoiced that no incidents of unseemly emotionalism marred the revival as in the First Great Awakening. "God was emphatically in the still small voice, . . ." a Massachusetts evangelical pointed out. "No extravagance, either in gestures or outcries, appeared."[49] The still small voice proved to be an effective means of reformation, for as New England clergymen told it, the revival routed the forces of infidelity and provided a *"death-wound* to the vain amusements of the young people."[50] By 1802, Connecticut evangelicals could allow themselves to exult over the religious situation, a luxury that they had not been able to afford for decades. "Never, perhaps, since the apostolic age," a Connecticut evangelical stated, "has there been among Christians so general a zeal, such spiritual and generous exertions to advance the kingdom of Jesus, and to bring all nations to an acknowledgment of the truth as it is in him."[51] This was heady stuff for ministers who had recently been forecasting dark days for the church.

Out on the Kentucky frontier, the revival erupted with a force that would have scandalized evangelicals in New England. As McKendree, Asbury, and Whatcoat rode toward Nashville, Tennessee, in October of 1800, they heard a "strange report" about religion. "We were told," Whatcoat said, "that the Presbyterians work by new rules; that they make the people cry and fall down, and profess to be converted."[52] The three Methodists probably had heard news of the sacramental meetings held at the Gasper River Church in Kentucky. Under the direction of Presbyterian ministers such as James McGready, John Rankin, and William Hodge, a new revival experience known as the camp meeting had evolved. Thousands of people, sometimes whole congregations, camped outdoors for the duration of the revival meeting, which often lasted several days. People did indeed "cry and fall down" when they were convicted of sin.[53] In early August of 1801, a crowd numbering between twelve and twenty-five thousand converged on Cane Ridge, Kentucky, for what was to be the most memorable and most flamboyant camp meeting of them all. Baptist, Methodist, and Presbyterian ministers shared preaching duties and circulated among the crowds to console afflicted sinners. The Cane Ridge revival also featured such bizarre physical manifestations as the jerks, the barks, and the laughing exercise. As the participants broke camp and left for home, they were convinced that they had seen a mighty demonstration of God's power.[54]

Not all evangelical ministers condoned the excess of emotionalism. Only a month after the Cane Ridge outburst, David Rice observed one scene of pandemonium, strode to the pulpit, and bellowed, "Holy! Holy! Holy! Is the Lord God Almighty!" Stunned into silence, the crowd listened to Rice deliver an admonition on "noise and false exercise."[55] It was a futile effort on Rice's part for, in little more than a year, Kentucky's brand of revivalism had swept across the South to the seaboard areas.

As the revival progressed, evangelicals collected and reprinted first-hand accounts of the work for the edification of believers throughout the country. Other evangelicals launched periodicals which included narratives of the revival, sermons, poems, and biographical sketches of exceptionally pious believers. The inspirational literature of the Awakening reveals that evangelicals had lost none of their admiration for the long-suffering slave, and none of their distaste for the godless master, but most of them had lost interest in attacking the evils of slavery.

A procession of noteworthy converts marched through the pages of this literature: reclaimed backsliders, contrite infidels, and repentant libertines, for example. Along with them, exciting the wonder of white believers, came born-again masters and slaves. A minister from North Carolina recorded a dramatic reconciliation between a slave and her mistress as a testimony to the power of the gospel. As he told the story, a converted black woman seized her owner's hand and cried, "O mistress you prayed for me when I wanted a heart to pray for myself. Now thank God he has given me a heart to pray for you and every body else."[56] God could also reduce the haughty slaveholder to repentance. The same minister reported how, at one service, "three young men were struck down in the act of cutting whips to correct some poor negroes who were crying for mercy. . . ."[57] These remarkable providences supplied readers with heartening evidence that the master-slave relationship could be sanctified in the eyes of the Almighty.

Occasionally, a vignette of the brutal realities of the slave system appeared in the periodicals, but evangelical treatment of slavery's horrors had become mannered, self-indulgent, and wholly divorced from any call for antislavery commitment. When a contributor to the *Virginia Religious Magazine* submitted "The Negro's Complaint" for publication, he clearly had more interest in the emotional response of the reader than in the plight of the slave.

"The mind that does not vibrate to the following delicate strokes of nature, must be divested of taste, or frozen to the feelings of humanity!" he wrote fervidly. "The genuine effusions of the soul, rising in the language of compassion, should start the tear of pity, and awake the sympathetic glow of the heart!"[58] In 1803, the *Massachusetts Missionary Magazine* reprinted St. John de Crèvecoeur's ghastly account of a slave suspended in a cage, but the editors furnished no comment or explanation for its appearance in the issue: the story simply confronted the reader, detached from the surrounding copy and an explicitly antislavery context.[59] The appeal to sensibility, which had been a weapon in the antislavery evangelical's arsenal, had become a sterile exercise in sentimentality.

For the most part, evangelicals chose to focus on an image of the slave as a beneficiary of the gospel rather than as victim of oppression. The *Massachusetts Missionary Magazine* printed a "Prayer of an African" in 1803, a prayer allegedly overheard by a gentleman from South Carolina. Even though he wore the "soften'd chain" of slavery in America, the African thanked God that he had been taken from a land of heathen darkness:

> Blest be the day that bro't me thence,
> To this enlighten'd shore,
> Where, loos'd from bonds of ignorance,
> I'm taught my God t' adore.[60]

The *General Assembly Missionary Magazine,* a Presbyterian concern, carried the story of a slave named Dinah, who had once been owned by Gilbert Tennent. She also expressed gratitude that God had brought her from Africa to a Christian land. Not wishing to suggest that the end justified the means in God's sight, the writer promptly added, "she seldom failed to remark that it was no excuse for those who had unjustly taken her from her country and parents, that God over-ruled it for good." Did Dinah's conversion excuse those who held her as a slave in America? The writer remained silent on that question. Instead he remarked: "How careful should all masters and heads of families be to use their best endeavours to save the souls committed to their care."[61] Like Davies, the Presbyterian writer believed that the higher freedom of Christianity provided slaves with a generous compensation for their temporal sufferings.

When they were not thanking God for bringing them from heathen Africa, the slaves of evangelical periodicals offered whites instruction in humility and contentment. The Presbyterian who wrote the feature on Dinah observed that one day this lowly servant of God would receive a heavenly reward. "How many who have governed and tyrannized over the world will then wish that their lot had been that of this pious African?"[62] A white believer was refreshed by the "artless, savoury, solid, unaffected experience" of a religious slave in New York.[63] The editors added the finishing touches to a portrait of a humble but happy bondsman: "His mind was reconciled to his station, and he lived contented in the lowest state of servitude."[64] Black "outcasts of men" had long fascinated white evangelicals, of course, but in the era of the Second Awakening, stories of slaves reconciled to God, their master, and their station helped while believers become reconciled to the existence of slavery; the stories made it easier for whites to lay aside residual doubts and delay action on the matter indefinitely.

White evangelicals could also use the pious slave to disarm the few remaining opponents of slave evangelism. In the early 1800s, a South Carolina preacher named Edmund Botsford penned a tract entitled *Sambo and Toney: A Dialogue Between Two Servants.* Known as "the flying preacher" for the speed with which he performed his duties, the white Baptist minister regarded speaking to blacks as his specialty. Two purposes guided Botsford in writing the tract. On the one hand, he wanted to provide "serious blacks" with a source of instruction, and on the other, he hoped to allay the fears of suspicious masters. "The Dialogues will show to the master what we wish to inculcate, and may be the means of removing prejudice from his mind, . . ," he wrote.[65] What Botsford wished to inculcate was a gospel made safe for the plantation.

As the title suggested, the argument of the tract took the form of a dialogue between Sambo, a religious slave, and Toney, an unregenerate slave. Botsford demonstrated his fondness for entering into the slave's "views of things" by having Sambo compare the wayward sinner to a runaway slave.[66] Eventually Toney experiences conversion and goes to ask his master's forgiveness for being a bad servant. "He talked so good," Toney reports, "it made me love him more than ever."[67] Uncle Davy, an elderly slave, arrives on the scene to offer advice on the importance of good Christian conduct: "If a master is a bad man, what so likely to make him better as to see his servants faithful and honest, and living peaceable among themselves?"[68] Here were no blacks like David, the preacher who told slaves in South Carolina that God would deliver them as He had delivered the Israelites; here were no potential recruits for a Gabriel Prosser, quoting Scripture to steel their resolution to revolt. Instead, Botsford showed the slaveholder model servants who would enhance the plantation environment by cheerfully discharging their duties.

A truly well-ordered plantation required a godly master as well as godly slaves, evangelicals believed, a master who would lead his slaves in the paths of righteousness. The *Virginia Religious Magazine* afforded its readers a glimpse of such a plantation in an interview with Mr. Jervas. A firm believer in the superior performance of Christian slaves, Mr. Jervas took it upon himself to watch over the spiritual welfare of his people. As a result of his ministrations, piety and industry increased among his slaves.[69] Neither Whitefield, Davies, Morgan Edwards, nor Pattillo could have asked anything more of the master.

Only one type of slaveholder invited censure from the *Virginia Religious Magazine,* and that was a type despised by southern evangelicals for many years: the worldly, dissolute planter. Even here the *Magazine* advanced its criticism with caution, fearful that its remarks might be interpreted as an attack on slaveholding. Masters who took sexual liberties with their slaves came under fire in one issue, for example, but the writer of the article first assured his readers that he would not "pour a torrent of crocodile tears" over the slaves, nor would he plead for emancipation.[70] And yet the gentleman who "rides in state, and revels in luxury," who fathered children in the slave quarters and then sold them to support his profligate habits, obviously failed to measure up to a planter like Mr. Jervas.[71] The mere fact that corrupt masters existed, however, implied nothing about the inherent righteousness of slaveholding.

The Second Great Awakening hastened the decline of antislav-

ery work by demonstrating, to the satisfaction of most white believers at least, the compatibility of slaveholding and godliness.
Pious masters instructing their slaves in righteousness, pious slaves
serving their masters with Christian humility—in the warm glow
of such a vision, the former associations between slaveholding,
persecution, and a sinful lifestyle melted away. Southern evangelicals had not yet developed this line of thought into a defense of
slavery as a positive good, but they anticipated a later generation's view of the plantation as a school where benighted heathens
learned rudiments of Christianity and civilization. Northern evangelicals, for the most part, still opposed slavery in sentiment, even
if they felt little compulsion to translate that sentiment into antislavery activity.

The Awakening dealt a more serious blow to the fortunes of
antislavery evangelicals by dispelling the mood of apprehension
that had sustained a concern about the issue. With grace abounding, how could they assert that God was judging America for the
sin of slavery? As Richard Furman stated forthrightly, "the blessing of God has been bestowed abundantly by effusions of Grace
on both masters & servants in our churches. This could hardly be
expected to be bestowed on persons living in the unrepented sin
of Man Stealing. . . ."[72] As the winter of their discontents passed
into a vernal season of reassurance and renewal, most white evangelicals discarded a concern about slaveholding along with doubts
about their collective purity.

IV

IN NORTHERN EVANGELICAL CIRCLES, the revival weakened opposition to domestic slavery by channeling antislavery sentiment toward a seemingly unrelated enterprise. The Awakening spawned
an intense interest in home and foreign missions. Denominational
bodies rededicated themselves to the task of converting Indians
and whites on the frontier, while local missionary societies raised
money for such projects and avidly corresponded with similar
organizations in the United States and Great Britain. In their
coverage of missionary endeavors, the religious magazines combined inspirational value with the color and excitement of a trav-
elogue. Readers followed the exploits of missionaries to Africa,

India, and the South Sea Islands, as well as less exotic places like Vermont and western New York. As their interest in attacking domestic slavery subsided, northern evangelicals turned their attention to the injured continent of Africa.

As early as 1773, Hopkins set forth the idea that America had contracted a moral debt with Africa by engaging in the slave trade, and that this debt could only be discharged if Americans provided Africa with the gospel. At that time, Hopkins called upon Christians to show their opposition to slavery by contributing money to prepare two black preachers as missionaries.[73] In the 1790s, the desire to repay Africans began to overshadow the commitment to free their relations in America. William Patten, minister of Newport's Second Congregational Church, delivered a sermon on the slave trade in 1792, and in it he vividly described a raid on an unsuspecting African community. Patten acknowledged that captured Africans would be transported as slaves to America, but the minister was not overly concerned with their fate. "These let us leave, and attend to those who remain in the country," he stated.[74] By concentrating on the destruction that slave traders inflicted on Africa's coast, Patten directed the sympathies of his audience away from American slaves to the wretchedness of blacks left behind.

The distant shores of Africa also began to absorb the attention of Patten's distinguished colleague at Newport's First Church. Hopkins appeared before the Providence Society for Abolishing the Slave Trade in 1793, and urged members to throw their support behind an African mission as evidence of their antislavery commitment. Over the years, Hopkins had become convinced that, due to the prejudice of white Americans, free blacks could never enjoy happiness in the United States. He therefore saw the mission as part of an effort to colonize Africa with emancipated slaves.[75] But the mission had a more cosmic significance for Hopkins: it would vindicate the wisdom of God in the permission of sin. Hopkins informed members of the Providence Society that God probably had allowed the slave trade so that blacks could embrace the gospel in the New World and then bear the glad tidings back to Africa. Thus "all this past and present evil, which the Africans have suffered . . . may be the occasion of an overbalancing good. . . ."[76] Even before the Second Great Awakening,

then, antislavery evangelicals in the North labored under a sense
of obligation to the blacks of Africa.

After the start of the Awakening, northern religious magazines
popularized the idea that the Christianization of Africa would
atone for the accumulated sins of slavery and the slave trade.
The *New York Missionary Magazine* published "A Dialogue between
Africanus, Americanus, and Benevolus" in 1801 to enlist support for an African mission. After noting the progress of efforts
to convert whites and Indians in the United States, Africanus
chides Americanus for his inattention to the heathen of Africa.
The United States has "peculiar obligations" to the blacks because
of slavery, Africanus reminds his companion. "And now," Africanus inquires, "what restitution can be made for the wrongs we
have done to the Africans?" The burden of guilt is heavy, he
declares solemnly. "But blessed be God! we have a rich treasure
which we can send to them, with a little cost and pains, which will
do more towards compensating them for the injuries we have
done them, than if we could give them mountains of silver and
gold."[77] By exporting the treasures of the gospel to Africa, the
writer suggested, America might correct the imbalance of trade
that had developed between the two continents.

A similar logic informed the argument of "The Pilgrims," which
appeared in the *Massachuesets Missionary Magazine* in 1804. Representatives from four continents gather in this article to hold a
conference on missions: Primus hails from Europe, Secundus
speaks for Asia, Tertius reports on African affairs, and Quartus is
an American. Tertius uses the occasion to point up America's
indebtedness to Africa:

> We really owe Africa many informed guides, because
> we have deprived her of many ignorant inhabitants.
> For every slave we are deeply in debt; and God will not
> make peace with us; if we refuse ample restoration;
> and all the negroes bought from Africa will be swift
> witnesses against us at the great day.[78]

In response, Quartus confesses that "the importation of slaves is
one of the crying sins of this land," and he unfolds a plan to make

restitution: American masters must treat their slaves with kindness, expose them to the gospel, and prepare some of them to return to Africa as ambassadors for Christ. After all, "what can rich planters do more pleasing to God, than to qualify some of their more promising negro-lads for missionaries among their ignorant relations in Africa?"[79] Quartus' proposal contains no hint that rich planters would please God more by emancipating their slaves. Primus thrills at the prospect of slave ships fitted out for a holier purpose, plying their way toward Africa with willing passengers: "Soon let the merchants, who buy and sell the souls of men, throw overboard the manacles for slaves, and cleanse their ships from the blood of slaves, and prepare them for African missionaries."[80]

Northern evangelicals had difficulty finding ways to realize such a vision. Complaining that no missionary society in America had paid sufficient attention to Africans, believers in Rhode Island formed their own society in 1803. William Patten acted as secretary of the organization, and Samuel Hopkins, with a scant six months to live, overcame the disabling effects of a stroke to serve as the first president. Members of the society assigned themselves two tasks: first, to promote the gospel in Rhode Island, and second, "to assist Africans in coming to a knowledge of the truth," whether they lived in Africa, America, or the West Indies.[81] A year later, however, the members were still casting about for something to do. "With respect to Africans," they were forced to admit, "the Society has no particular plan: nor is there any other than a general prospect of being useful to them." But they expressed a hope that somebody in the United States would do something for "the spiritual interests of this description of men."[82] Hopkins had gone to his grave without seeing one black preacher return to Africa to fulfill his dream. Whether for want of imagination, financial resources, or missionary-minded blacks, the Rhode Island Society never carried out one of its central tasks.

In Connecticut, antislavery evangelicals contented themselves with sending "best wishes and most earnest prayers" to their counterparts in Great Britain. On behalf of the General Association—soon to become the core of the Connecticut Missionary Society—Timothy Dwight and Benjamin Trumbull wrote to congratulate Granville Sharp on his role in promoting the Christianization and colonization of Africa. Sharp was a prominent British abolitionist who helped to found the Sierra Leone colony. His admirers in Connecticut conveyed their eager anticipation of the day when Africa "shall stretch forth her hands to God." After describing evangelistic work among the Indians, the ministers dutifully reported to Sharp that Americans had not been "wholly inattentive to the emancipation and happiness of the black People." Many blacks had been liberated and educated, they said, while the evils of slavery itself were "in many respects greatly lessened." In their minds, however, the "glorious design of Christianizing the Heathen" promised to provide the greatest benefit to mankind.[83] Evidently, the Connecticut ministers thought that British evangelicals had things in Africa well in hand, for they offered no missionaries and initiated no evangelistic scheme of their own.

The Christianization of Africa remained a comforting vision rather than a workable program for northern evangelicals. It satisfied the demand for a theodicy of the slave trade, the need to explain why a just God had allowed the enslavement of blacks in the first place. At the same time, the vision encouraged white evangelicals to think that their unfinished business with domestic slavery could be settled by donating the gospel to a far-off land. But by 1803, the year of Hopkins' death, the grandiose vision had not yet materialized, and northern evangelicals had nothing to show for their fitful exertions. Perhaps all the talking and planning had created an illusion that they actually had discharged their debt to black people. Perhaps sincere prayers and an occasional contribution to the London Missionary Society's work in Africa were enough to salve the consciences of other white believers. At any rate, the vision survived Hopkins and his generation and, in 1817, it helped to guide the founders of the American Colonization Society.

By the early years of the nineteenth century, respected individuals, members of denominational councils, and magazine editors had indicated that they did not view slavery as an insurmountable obstacle to the pursuit of righteousness. Indeed, many of these same figures regarded antislavery agitation as the chief threat to the peace and prosperity of the church. The evil of slaveholding had become a closed subject, an extraneous issue, a highly sensitive matter, anything but a pressing concern. Yet, in face of official disapproval and lay opposition, there were those evangelicals who continued to remind their white brothers and sisters of an unfulfilled commitment.

VII
PROPHETS
WITHOUT
HONOR

A HANDFUL OF PERSISTENT EVANGELICALS never surrendered their belief that slaveholding was an irredeemably wicked practice. In the ten years between 1798 and 1808, however, they were forced to abandon hope that universal emancipation would be achieved in the very near future. Having seen their antislavery initiatives become mired in the bogs of casuistry or relegated to the equally unpromising realm of politics, they realized that in the minds of most white believers, emancipation had been banished to the periphery of concern. Much the same could be said about the antislavery evangelicals themselves during this period. The unfulfilled quest for purity led antislavery evangelicals along several paths in the decade before 1808, and most of those paths carried them to marginal positions on the religious landscape.

I

THE ANTISLAVERY EVANGELICALS APPEAR conspicuously at odds with fellow believers when their remarks are placed against the backdrop of the Second Great Awakening. Slavery clouded their perspective on contemporary religious events and denied them a share in the jubilation that swept through evangelical camps with the onset of the revival.

A few evangelicals dared to inject the slavery issue into the otherwise congenial narratives of the revival. At the end of his report on the Awakening in Kentucky, Methodist William McKendree appended a remark which deviated from the usual expressions of unrestrained enthusiasm. "There is one thing more which I think deserves a thought," he began. "According to the reports, there is a great revival of religion in this country: and we are very sincere republicans: but alas! as yet their united strength is utterly too weak to abolish slavery in Kentucky and Cumberland."[1] McKendree would not content himself with lamentations in the next several years, but would use his newly acquired position as presiding elder of the Kentucky District to implement antislavery reforms. After reporting that people under his care had been "completely methodized" by the revival, Thomas Ware recorded a wistful afterthought: "what would they not have been, had slavery never been introduced amongst them?"[2] Both McKendree and Ware acknowledged that the revival had invigorated evangelicalism, but they qualified this admission with regret that slavery hindered believers from realizing their full spiritual potential.

The persistence of slavery also highlighted the limitations of the revival for David Rice, who had given up full-time pastoral work because of a head ailment. In 1803, Rice stood before leaders of the Synod of Kentucky and announced that, contrary to widespread belief, the millennium was not an imminent possibility. He knew that the spectacle of mass conversions had kindled hope of an impending triumph of Christian principles in the world, but the Presbyterian minister observed certain evils which led him to doubt that the latter-day glory was at hand. After listing several reasons for his pessimism, he devoted his attention exclusively to the problem of slavery. So long as "professors of christianity are not rightly disposed to 'break every yoke and let the oppressed go free,'" he told leaders of the Synod, the "bright beams" of the millennial dawn would never play upon the earth. The existence of slavery showed Rice that Christians had not yet yielded their hearts to the Lord of benevolence: "They are so attached to the idol, interest, that they do not find it in their hearts to do justice in this respect, to 'do as they would be done by.'"[3] Rice's attempt to dampen millennial expectations probably won him few friends on that day, and his emphasis on the failures of the revival stood in contrast to the appraisals offered by other evangelical leaders.

As one of Rice's distant admirers, Methodist William Colbert remained oblivious to the fact that the religious situation had taken on a more auspicious character since the turn of the century. Colbert read a reprint of Rice's speech to the Kentucky convention and saluted the Presbyterian from afar as a true "Lover of freedom."[4] Waging a lonely battle against slaveholders in the upper South, Colbert seized opportunities to "Scorge" the "infernal drovers of the human race." After one such performance, Colbert entered a comment into his journal which revealed how radically his perception of current events differed from that of other believers: "May we not suppose that cloud[s] of vengeance are collecting over the heads of the inhabitants of this country, for their cruelty [to] the poore distressed Africans[?]"[5] If Colbert gave voice to these sentiments, his listeners may well have dismissed him as a doomsayer whose prophecies had grown tediously familiar over the years.

White evangelicals could not so easily dismiss those slaves who belied the fiction, promoted fondly in religious literature, that Christianity always made slaves more tractable and less concerned with their temporal status. In 1807, for example, a Baptist church in Kentucky heard a complaint brought against a slave known only as "Esther Boulware's Winney." Winney had offended her white brothers and sisters by expressing two convictions. First of all, she stated that "she once thought it her duty to serve her Master & Mistress but since the lord had converted her, she had never believed that any Christian kept Negroes or Slaves." What was worse, she gave out that "she believed there was Thousands of white people Wallowing in Hell for their treatment to Negroes —and she did not care if there was as many more." Unrepentant before her accusers, Winney was excluded from church fellowship until she learned to display more charity toward other Christians.[6] There were certainly other slaves who felt as Winney did, but most of them either kept their ideas to themselves or chose more subtle ways to express their hatred of the system.[7] Needless to say, the testimony of slaves like Winney never became part of the revival narratives.

Amid the prevailing chorus of praise and self-congratulation, antislavery evangelicals sounded a discordant note by raising an unpleasant, unwelcome issue. They measured the success of the revival, not by the emotional intensity of the camp meetings or by the number of converted infidels, but by the progress of work to eliminate slavery. Some evangelicals in Kentucky went beyond criticism and set out to purify their local fellowships from slaveholders.

II

KENTUCKY REMAINED A HOTBED OF ANTISLAVERY agitation after the stir about emancipation had died down among evangelicals elsewhere in the South. In contrast to the situation in Virginia and South Carolina, Kentucky's relatively low density of slave population enabled civil authorities there to take a more relaxed attitude toward antislavery activity.[8] Patterns of migration also contributed to the vitality of antislavery work in Kentucky. So many Baptist ministers had moved from Virginia to the new state that Robert Semple designated Kentucky as "the cemetery of Virginia Baptist preachers,"[9] and other Virginia evangelicals were to find their final resting place in Kentucky as well. Many of the emigrants carried a hatred of slavery across the Appalachian Mountains with their material possessions. The names of David Barrow, David Rice, and William McKendree come to mind in this regard, but less illustrious figures such as William Hickman and Carter Tarrant also hailed from Virginia. When delegates to Kentucky's second constitutional convention of 1799 left the proslavery article substantially intact,[10] antislavery evangelicals turned their attention once more to the churches. For many of these believers, who were still devoted to the ideal of a church cleansed from slavery, background and circumstances produced a determination to succeed where evangelicals before them had failed.

Antislavery Presbyterians in Kentucky made only a few sporadic attempts to expel slaveholders from their churches. In 1796, dissidents in Transylvania Presbytery received word from their superiors that there was not "sufficient authority from the word of God" to deny slaveholders communion and, in 1799, it will be remembered, the united congregations of Concord and Cane Ridge experimented briefly with such a policy before being reined in by the Synod of Virginia.[11] David Rice took a pragmatic view, and frowned on this policy because he realized that no ecclesiastical council higher than the local church would sanction it.[12]

When William McKendree supported local antislavery efforts, however, he acted within guidelines explicitly endorsed by the General Conference of the Methodist Church. The *Discipline* of 1796 urged local lay officials to manumit their slaves; they authorized yearly conferences and quarterly meetings to formulate their

own rules concerning those officials.[13] In 1806, McKendree super-
vised some "purifying work" among the lay officials of Kentucky's
Livingston Circuit and recorded each manumission as a divinely-
approved act of self-sacrifice: one white brother made a "free
offering" of thirteen slaves; another "offered up six on the altar
of love"; still another gave one slave, which, like the widow's mites
in the gospel account, was significant because the single slave represented "his all." After one last brother freed his slaves at the next
quarterly meeting, McKendree reported enthusiastically: "We
shall . . . be free from the stain of blood in our official department. Glory, Hallelujah! Praise ye the Lord!"[14] McKendree then
proposed that the whole Western Conference prohibit Methodists
from buying and selling slaves and that it require future members
to fix a date for the manumission of their servants. These two
rules had been enacted, but not enforced by the General Conference in 1796.[15]

Only the first of McKendree's proposals would be enacted in
the Western Conference. In the fall of 1808, McKendree attended
the yearly conference held at Liberty Hill, Tennessee, having just
recently been ordained a bishop in the Methodist Church. At this
time, the geographical boundaries of the Western Conference extended from Ohio to the Mississippi Territory. On the last day of
the Conference meeting, the delegates considered petitions from
two Kentucky circuits asking for a decisive rule on slavery.[16] Bishop
Asbury, who attended the Western Conference with McKendree,
rose and read a statement counseling caution and moderation on
the subject, but some of the delegates greeted his remarks with
hisses of disapproval. Flustered by the reception accorded his
statement, Asbury stammered something to the effect of "O well!
I can tear it up." At that point, McKendree read a statement of his
own which suggested a rule similar to the one in the *Discipline* of
1796.[17] A committee comprised of three Kentucky Methodists was
appointed to draft a rule, and the resulting formulation shows
that the committee members took McKendree's proposal seriously.
Any member who bought or sold a slave from "speculative motives," the rule stated, would be expelled from fellowship by the
local quarterly meeting. The delegates to the Conference voted to
adopt the committee's rule.[18] To be sure, the determination of an

individual's motives could be a nearly impossible task, and the exemption of sales "in a case of mercy or humanity" provided a loophole for imaginative slaveholders, but the Western Conference had taken a step toward reducing the problem of slavery to manageable proportions. Although antislavery Methodists in Kentucky looked back on this rule with pride, it did not affect the General Conference's decision, reached in 1808, to abandon the rule of 1796 and allow yearly conferences to make their own rules on the buying and selling of slaves.[19] Asbury, for his part, entered the proceedings of the Liberty Hill Conference into his journal without comment.[20]

A small group of Kentucky Baptists adopted a more thoroughgoing plan of reformation and separated themselves completely from the evils of slavery, but they did so only by separating themselves from a majority of their white brethren. Unlike their Presbyterian and Methodist counterparts, individual Baptist congregations acknowledged no higher ecclesiastical authority than the local church, although they set up advisory councils known as associations. Antislavery agitation shattered the unity of the Salem Association in 1789, when the Association declined to offer advice on the righteousness of slaveholding. The Rolling Fork Church responded to the Association's silence by withdrawing its membership.[21] In 1794, Joshua Carman and Josiah Dodge led the Mill Creek Church out of the Salem Association when fellow Baptists again turned a deaf ear to their antislavery proposals.[22]

These early schisms served as a mere prelude to the events of 1805, for in that year a series of unrelated developments culminated in a wave of disaffection. To stifle discussion on slavery, the Elkhorn Association invoked a well-worn formula at its meeting in 1805, judging it "improper" for churches or ministers to "meddle with emancipation from Slavery or any other political Subject."[23] Soon after this decision, William Hickman abruptly terminated a nineteen-year pastorate at the Elkhorn Church by announcing that he could no longer tolerate the presence of slaveholders in the congregation. Following a sermon on Isaiah 58:6, that text revered by antislavery evangelicals, Hickman declared himself "no more in Union" with the Elkhorn Church or the Elkhorn Association.[24] Also in 1805, Carter Tarrant and John Sutton led off a faction of the Hillsboro Church and the Clear Creek Church to found an antislavery church at New Hope in Woodford County, and the Bracken Association lost members in another controversy over slavery.[25]

These splinter groups acquired a gifted spokesman and organizer with the separation of David Barrow from the North District Association. In its circular letter of 1805, the North District included a thinly-disguised attack on the work of Barrow and his antislavery cohorts. "Some are so far deluded," the Association stated, "that their printing, preaching & private conversation, go to encourage disobedience in servants, & a revolution in our civil government."[26] The North District expelled Barrow from his seat in the Association in 1806 and then attempted to have his Mt. Sterling Church discipline him further; this was an extraordinary step for a Baptist association to take.[27] The North District later repented of its severity, but by then it was too late for conciliatory gestures: Barrow and Tarrant had forged an antislavery association from unchurched dissidents and the separatist congregations of Bracken, Elkhorn, Salem, and North District.

In August of 1807, eleven ministers and nineteen laymen gathered at New Hope to lay the foundations for the Baptized Licking-Locust Association, Friends of Humanity. They set forth their terms for fellowship in a format which resembled an antislavery catechism. "Can any person be admitted a member of this meeting, whose practice appears friendly to perpetual slavery?" one rule read. "Answer. We think not." The evangelical Friends of Humanity also decided that all slaveholders were to be denied communion in their churches, but they exempted masters with young or infirm slaves and widows who possessed no legal power to manumit their slaves.[28] After discussing qualifications for fellowship, the Friends of Humanity felt obliged to insert a statement which underscored their commitment to orthodox Christianity: "Have our ideas of slavery occasioned any alteration in our views of the doctrine of the gospel? Answer. No."[29] This declaration suggests that nonseparating Baptists thought otherwise, but the Friends of Humanity maintained that theirs was a reformation without innovation, a return to apostolic practice rather than a departure from New Testament doctrine.

A roster of the leading emancipators, as the evangelical Friends were also called, reveals that the movement attracted both respectable and unbalanced types of Baptists. Barrow, Tarrant, and George Smith had all achieved eminence as preachers in Virginia before they moved to Kentucky.[30] Donald Holmes and Jacob Grigg, on the other hand, appear to have been among the more erratic members of the circle. Holmes, a native of Scotland, was expelled from a church in Virginia for flirting with Elhanan Winchester's doctrine of universal restoration.[31] After graduating from the Baptist Academy in Bristol, England, Jacob Grigg managed to make a nuisance of himself wherever he went. His ministry in Sierra Leone was cut short when he created a "disturbance" which upset the governor of the colony. Grigg then emigrated to the United States and lived successively in Virginia, North Carolina, Kentucky, and Ohio before he settled back in Virginia, where he took to drinking heavily.[32] The Baptized Licking-Locust Association was, therefore, a collection of misfits and exemplars of the faith, momentarily united by a common hatred of slavery.

The founding of the new association did not mean that slave-holding Baptists had heard the last from the emancipators. Barrow and Tarrant laid bare the evasions and inconsistencies in the Baptist position on slaveholding, and they did so with a discernment acquired from their experience in Virginia. Refusing to regard slaveholding as a political problem, Barrow continued to denounce it as a "fashionable" sin: "I believe, the main objections against emancipation are never brought in sight—which I presume are the following, viz. 'The love of money,' which is covetousness, self-aggrandizement, and self-ease."[33] Tarrant also blamed worldliness for the defective moral vision of the Baptists. "Blinded by covetousness and intoxication with the cup of Babylon, they call evil good and good evil," he declared.[34] As for the excuse that the civil government allowed Baptists to keep slaves, "What is this in fact," Barrow asked, "but saying, the policy of a nation supercedes the law of God?"[35] Tarrant scored a direct hit when he jeered, "Some will plead our civil government, as if the church was beholden to the world for assistance in matters of religion, and had no king nor constitution of her own. . . ."[36] In their stance against worldliness and their refusal to let civil authorities determine mat-

ters of conscience, Barrow and Tarrant faithfully preserved two
hallmarks of Baptist spirituality but, on the subject of slavery, they
spoke as prophets without honor among southern Baptists.

Tarrant's hope that God had forever separated the Friends of
Humanity from the "friends of oppression"[37] began to fade with
the passage of years. In its heyday, the antislavery association
numbered twelve churches, twelve ministers, and three hundred
members, but support for the organization dwindled as individuals like Joshua Carman emigrated to Ohio or, like William Hickman, drifted back into fellowship with slaveholding Baptists.[38] The
Friends of Humanity organized themselves as the Kentucky Abolition Society in 1808, a move which probably reflected the leadership's decision to broaden their base of support by opening
membership to non-Baptists. The Kentucky Friends of Humanity
carried on a separate and feeble existence in the coming years,
and the leaders divided their time between the Association and
the Abolition Society.[39] Perhaps it was this overlap of personnel
which led critics to complain that the emancipators were "blend-
ing the church and world together."[40] At any rate, both the Association and the Abolition Society died out around the year 1820,
soon after Barrow's death in 1819.

The emancipators were maligned as "a dangerous body of citizens" who formed "combinations against the government" and
who uttered subversive ideas in the company of slaves.[41] Older
Baptists like Barrow and Tarrant had been charged with similar
offenses at an earlier stage of their preaching careers. It was ironic that they closed out their ministries with those charges still
ringing in their ears, and that many of their fellow Baptists now
stood with the accusers.

III

THE FERTILE SOIL OF OHIO BECKONED OTHER evangelicals besides
Joshua Carman in the decade before 1808. By enacting the Northwest Ordinance in 1787, Congress prohibited the extension of
slavery into territories north of the Ohio River and east of the
Mississippi River.[42] In so doing, members of Congress unknowingly
created a preserve for southern evangelicals who could not reconcile themselves to a social order based on slavery. Harried by

church officials, discouraged by their failure to eliminate slavery in the South, antislavery evangelicals made their way toward Ohio in search of a pure fellowship and a virtuous commonwealth.

As the reflections of two antislavery Methodists indicate, emigration to Ohio meant something more than simply moving from one state to another. In the late 1790s, Philip Gatch and his brother-in-law James Smith beheld clouds of judgment gathering over their native Virginia because of slavery. Smith, a minister in O'Kelly's Republican Methodist Church and half-brother of emancipator George Smith, identified with the prophet who cried, "O that I had in the wilderness a lodging place, that I might rest in the day of trouble, when the Lord cometh up to invade the people with his troops."[43] By 1795, Smith had decided to seek out that hiding place in the wilderness, and just as Barrow did in the same year, he explored the regions of Kentucky and Ohio.

Upon setting foot in Ohio, Smith rejoiced that the Lord had brought him at last to "a land of sacred liberty / and joyous rest." The inhabitants of this happy land lived a life of republican simplicity, he observed: the industrious farmer relied on no one's labor but his own, and the "ruddy damsel" performed her household duties by herself, far removed from the atrocities perpetrated by slaveholders.[44] Smith described Ohio's future in terms reminiscent of O'Kelly's vision for a Christian commonwealth:

> O, what a country this will be at a future day!
> What [a] field of delights! What a garden of
> spices! What a paradise of pleasures! when
> these forests shall be cultivated and the gospel
> of Christ spread through this rising republic,
> unshackled by the power of kings and religious
> oppression on the one hand and slavery, that
> bane of true Godliness, on the other.[45]

In Ohio, Smith discovered not only a repository of virtue, but a sanctuary for all the afflicted and dispossessed of the earth who, like himself, sought a haven from the approaching storms of divine wrath. When "an incensed Deity" brought judgment upon Virginia, he wrote in his journal, "may it be, when I or those that pertain unto me have found an asylum in thy peaceful borders."[46]

Convinced that God's controversy with Virginia had already entered its final stages, Smith and Gatch gathered their families, two of Smith's freed slaves, and all the possessions that could be loaded onto wagons and left for Ohio in 1798, the same year that Barrow departed for Kentucky. Gatch entered some lines into his journal to mark the event:

> For fertile field and pleasant plains,
> Where liberty and freedom reigns [sic],
> We left our native land.[47]

By early November, the emigrants had left the evils of slavery behind them for good.

In the late 1790s and early 1800s, a number of antislavery evangelicals decided that the time had come to make a geographical separation from slavery. On one of his preliminary tours of Ohio, Smith met the godly Mr. Talbert, a man whose hatred of slavery led him to "take sanctuary" in Ohio. An elderly Baptist named Dunham left Kentucky because he feared that God would withdraw His Spirit from lands which resisted His dictates on slavery.[48] Presbyterian William Dunlop came from Kentucky and helped his freed slaves to set up a farm in Ohio. Both James Gilleland and Robert Wilson arrived from South Carolina in the early 1800s. Gilleland presided over an Ohio church largely comprised of exslaveholders, many of whom had come from South Carolina.[49] When William Williamson emigrated from South Carolina in 1805, he brought his slaves with him and freed them upon his arrival. "I have moved to a Gospel-Land," he wrote one of his friends back home, "a Land of light and liberty."[50] By such means, individual evangelicals attempted to cleanse themselves from guilt and escape the wrath to come.

The dread of further contamination compelled some Ohio Baptists to insulate themselves from contact with any religious body which had anything to do with slaveholders. When the Miami Association of Ohio Baptists was founded in 1797, Joshua Carman and Josiah Dodge crossed over from Kentucky to offer the hand of fellowship. The presence of the two emancipators, shortly after their separation from the Salem Association, served as more

than a symbolic gesture, for in the coming years the Miami Association refused to correspond with any of the slaveholding associations in Kentucky. Miami even declined to have dealings with
Pennsylvania's Redstone Association because some of Redstone's
member churches were located in Virginia.[51] On the question
of whether Miami's member churches might allow visiting slaveholders to take communion, the Association adopted a flexible,
yet guarded attitude. "We advise that caution be used by the
churches that they do not admit among them those who hold the
sentiment and use the practice of hereditary slavery; but that
that occasional communion from time to time be permitted, as
brethren feel freedom."[52] Miami's efforts to close off all avenues
of moral pollution failed to satisfy one of its member churches.
Purists in that church voted to withdraw from the Association,
protesting that Miami corresponded with the Philadelphia Association, and that the Philadelphia Association, in turn, corresponded
with slaveholders of the Charleston Association.[53] The taint of evil
could be contracted indirectly, the purists believed, and the southern emigrants among them had not come all that distance just to
renew fellowship with slaveholders.

Emigration drained the South of veteran antislavery activists,
but it also strengthened the forces of abolitionism in the Old
Northwest. Many transplanted southerners continued the struggle
against slavery from their newly established homes in Ohio, and
some of them acted as living links to the antebellum era. James
Gilleland, for example, was one of the Ohio Anti-Slavery Society's
vice-presidents, and Thomas Morris, a Presbyterian from Virginia,
took an active part in the affairs of the Liberty Party.[54] The emigration of antislavery figures did no irreparable damage to southern
evangelicalism; if anything, the departure of a few malcontents
enhanced each denomination's prospects for internal harmony on
slaveholding. But for the emigrants themselves, removal served as
one final witness to southern believers. Unable to cleanse their
region from slaveholding, unwilling to assist in the work of Christianizing the practice, these evangelicals preferred self-exile to
further complicity with sin.

IV

AT A TIME WHEN MANY ANTISLAVERY evangelicals were falling silent or carrying on with diminished force, a new figure burst upon the American religious scene, filled with zeal and a holy indignation at the wrongs inflicted upon the African people. A God-intoxicated man named Thomas Branagan arrived in Philadelphia in the late 1790s, and almost immediately he began to pour forth a torrent of antislavery verse. As one of evangelicalism's free spirits, Branagan was deliberately vague about his denominational preferences, and it is therefore impossible to associate him exclusively with any one sect. Despite the problem of classification, a figure so colorful, prolific, and downright irrepressible merits consideration apart from evangelicals with definite institutional commitments. Thomas Branagan, converted slavetrader and self-proclaimed poet of the common man, combined an intense hatred of slavery with a disdain for its victims in America.[55]

One of the most distressing things about Branagan from a historian's perspective is that we know little more about him than what he chose to tell his readers, and he displayed a tendency to embellish the truth. The basic outlines of his career seem plausible enough. Born in Ireland of Roman Catholic parents, Branagan signed aboard an English slaver in 1790, when he was about sixteen years old. When not engaged in the business of enslaving blacks, he explored the interior of Africa and enjoyed, so he said, the hospitality and natural generosity of the inhabitants. After these adventures, Branagan set sail for the West Indies, where he served as the overseer of a sugar plantation on Antigua.[56] Whether or not he could have advanced from this station to "what the world calls a gentleman" remains uncertain, but during his stay on Antigua he underwent an experience which led him to choose "virtue clothed in rags" over "vice arrayed in costly apparel."[57] At the age of twenty-one, he testified, the "gracious Redeemer had compassion on me and blessed me with a sense of his pardoning love and regenerating grace. . . ."[58] It was then that he resigned his position as overseer, even though some of his Methodist acquaintances on the island advised him to continue in that line of work. But Branagan now believed that those who had anything to do with slavery "were guilty of oppression in the sight of God."[59] After a brief and unhappy visit to Ireland, he booked passage on a ship bound for Philadelphia.

Following his arrival in the city, the new convert volunteered for service as a preacher in "one of the most pious sects in America," which probably meant that he served as an itinerant for the Methodist Church. Branagan also took it upon himself to visit such longstanding objects of Methodist charity as the sick and the needy.[60] A steady stream of antislavery publications came from his pen during these early years in Philadelphia. *A Preliminary Essay, on the Oppression of the Exiled Sons of Africa* appeared in 1804 as Branagan's attempt to promote interest in a forthcoming epic poem on the slave trade. That poem came out in 1805 under the title of *Avenia: or, A Tragical Poem, on the Oppression of the Human Species, and Infringement on the Rights of Man.* In the same year he came out with *Serious Remonstrances Addressed to the Citizens of the Northern States.* This was followed in 1807 by a more confessional piece of poetry which Branagan entitled *The Penitential Tyrant.*

Though the overwrought style of his poetry may distract the modern reader from the fact, Branagan carried a heavy load of guilt for his participation in the slave trade. In *The Penitential Tyrant,* specters of murdered blacks point accusing fingers and implore him to publish the horrors which he has witnessed.[61] Branagan concluded both *Avenia* and *The Penitential Tyrant* with a hymn to the redeeming love that saved a wretch like himself:

> His Son, amazing thought! Oh, boundless love!
> To save lost man, flew from realms above,
> *And died that we might live!*[62]

Poetry thus served Branagan as the means to dispel those haunting visions and to reaffirm the forgiveness of God.

But Branagan also hoped that his poetry would help to impress white Americans with the enormity of their crimes against black people. By juxtaposing the treachery, avarice, and ruthlessness of the Christian slave traders against the unspoiled simplicity, dignity, and bravery of the primitive Africans, he followed the conventions of the eighteenth-century literature of sensibility. Africa loomed in his imagination as a land which bore a closer resemblance to Eden than any place on earth. In *A Preliminary Essay,* he described Africa's "vernal groves, fragrant flowers, dewy lawns, limpid streams, enchanting landscapes; and a thousand other beauties," and he noted that the sight of the inhabitants reminded him of "the first human pair in their paradisical residence."[63] As products of these recollections, Branagan's fictional Africans emerge from his verse as models of moral purity: there is the lovely and virtuous Avenia. friend of the friendless; her lover Angola longs for her with chaste affection; and her brother Louverture, named after the black revolutionary on St. Domingo, is a valiant African prince who exemplifies the martial virtues. In *Avenia,* Branagan portrayed the destruction of their blessed realm by a horde of "baptiz'd ruffians."[64]

In the promotional work which came out before the poem, Branagan professed to scorn "the foolish dreams of the romance or the novel," with their rapid succession of "adventures, intrigues, rapes, duels, elopements, darts, sighs, groans, armies, murders."[65] And yet the plot of *Avenia* largely consists of such devices. Before the arrival of the slave traders, Avenia and Angola frolic together on Africa's "lawns," while other black couples play innocently at their "rural games."[66] Then the cruel white Christians invade and take Avenia and Angola captive. A large-scale battle between the slave traders and an African army ensues, with the conflict surging back and forth across the plain. Black warriors strike noble poses and deliver lengthy monologues in the heat of the fighting. Blood and gore flow plentifully. After Louverture is slain in combat, the archangel Gabriel ushers the fallen warrior into the presence of the Almighty, and a heavenly host which includes George Whitefield, John Wesley, and, somewhat incongruously, George Washington sings praises to the Lamb of God.[67] Avenia, never rescued by the black army, throws herself off a precipice after being violated by her captor. At the end of the poem, Africa's original innocence, tranquility, and Edenic splendor lay among the casualties, victims of white exploitation and a superior technology.

For their despoilation of Africa, Branagan warned, white Americans stood condemned before the God of the oppressed. "Repent, confess your sins, lie low in dust, / Sons of Columbia, and forsake your lust," he enjoined them in *The Penitential Tyrant.* As

other evangelicals in the past had done, Branagan invited white
believers to extend a benevolent hand to the downtrodden:

> You, whom kind Heav'n with copious wealth has blest,
> Lend back to Heav'n, by aiding the distrest;
> 'Tis yours the sons of anguish to relieve,
> To cheer the poor, nor let affliction grieve;
> To sympathize and melt at human wo,
> Is what the wealthy to th' unhappy owe.[68]

Only hardened tyrants would fail to respond with a show of tender
feeling, he believed, for "hell and avarice never, never melt."[69]

From lines such as these, one might expect Branagan to have
been in the forefront of efforts to help free blacks in the Quaker
City, but the man who expressed outrage at the degradation of
Africans regarded blacks closer at hand as detestable carriers of
vice. In *Serious Remonstrances Addressed to the Citizens of the Northern
States,* Branagan dealt with this issue and proposed a solution.
As blacks migrated or escaped to the North, he explained, they
brought with them the "accumulated depravity" of slavery, a condition which rendered them unfit for membership in a free society. Once they were emancipated, blacks would almost certainly
give themselves over to a life of dissipation and become a public
burden, he contended.[70] Using horticultural metaphors, Branagan
compared southern slavery to a tree whose limbs overshadowed
the northern states. The "poisonous fruit of that tree when ripe
falls upon these states," he wrote, "to the annoyance of the inhabitants, and the contamination of the land which is sacred to liberty."[71] Moreover, he said, the presence of blacks discouraged industrious whites from emigrating to America: "how must it damp
their spirits when they come and have to associate with negroes,
take them for companions, and what is much worse, be thrown
out of work and precluded from getting employ to keep vacancies
for blacks."[72] Branagan would not be the last northerner to base
his hatred of slavery on a hatred of blacks and a defense of the
white laborer; both the Free Soil movement and the Republican
Party would combine the same ingredients in their antislavery
ideologies.

Branagan advised citizens of the North to lop off the overhanging branches of slavery and transplant them to some distant part of the national domain—presumably the more distant, the better. He called upon white Americans to make blacks "free and happy in every sense of the word, in a republic of their own" somewhere beyond the western frontier. Moral purity and racial homogeneity went hand in hand in Branagan's scheme, for by removing blacks to the West, American whites would "shake their blood from our garments" once and for all.[73] This was indeed benevolence without tears.

Having delivered his testimony on the evils of slavery, Branagan devoted his energy to other causes in the coming years. Although *The Penitential Tyrant* of 1807 proved to be his last versified protest against slavery, his list of publications on various subjects lengthened to include more than twenty volumes. When he observed how members of the "clerical tribe" neglected their duties to the poor, Branagan set off in 1811 to preach salvation to the victims of misfortune in "their wretched lanes and alleys."[74] Somewhere in those wretched lanes and alleys, the figure of Thomas Branagan disappears from the historian's view and, except for an occasional pamphlet or book, very little is known of his whereabouts or his activities. The records of St. George's Methodist Episcopal Church reveal, however, that he died in Philadelphia in 1843.[75]

Antislavery poet, self-ordained apostle to the poor, exponent of white nationalism—these labels designate facets of Branagan's varied career, but they hardly summarize the man. He is not remembered in denominational histories, nor are his works listed in the annals of early American literature. Nevertheless, Branagan earned himself a distinctive place among antislavery evangelicals through the sheer bulk of his writing and the fervor with which he proclaimed his message.

Antislavery evangelicals of the early nineteenth century dissented sharply from the prevailing view that emancipation was extraneous to the evangelical mission. They welcomed the revivals, but refused to identify numerical strength with spiritual health, for popularity could be interpreted as evidence that the movement had surrendered too much to the world. These veterans of eighteenth-century evangelicalism lived to see the advent of a new world created largely by younger believers, a world of rising evangelical influence and responsibility for maintaining the social order. This world was serviced by religious academies, seminaries, missionary boards, benevolent societies, and publishing houses. Many aging veterans, especially those in the South, might have felt uncomfortable in such a world. Their opposition to slavery would have allowed them to continue a more familiar role as prophet on the edge of respectable society.

For all their warnings of divine retribution, antislavery evangelicals failed to generate a sense of urgency among white believers because a plausible connection between slaveholding and godlessness could no longer be made. The social context which had fostered that association was disappearing. Connecticut's Congregationalists had shown that slaveholding and sin could be associated with an entire region, but it would be left to a later generation to develop this view into a compelling antislavery argument. Many southern evangelicals of the early nineteenth century admitted failure by withdrawing from their denominations or from the region, thus sacrificing any influence they may have had for the sake of purity. But because of the work of isolated individuals, a discernible strain of criticism persisted in all the major denominations in the early 1800s.

EPILOGUE

IN THE SAME YEAR THAT BRANAGAN PUBLISHED *The Penitential Tyrant,* President Jefferson signed a bill forbidding American participation in the Atlantic slave trade. The bill stipulated that after January 1, 1808, any American citizen found guilty of transporting enslaved Africans to the United States would forfeit the ship and its human cargo and pay a fine of $5,000. Anyone convicted of selling the Africans upon their arrival would face a prison term of five to ten years. Decades of petitioning and lobbying had preceded enactment of the bill, and antislavery figures everywhere, whether they were evangelicals, Quakers, or philosophes, enjoyed the long-sought moment of triumph. Many of these same individuals could point to solid achievements in the North, for by 1808 slavery was either dead or on the way to extinction in every state above the Mason-Dixon line.

With the enactment of the bill, however, the American antislavery movement as a whole began to lose momentum and direction. One reason for the lull in activity was that the larger movement had exhausted its energies in a concentrated assault on the slave trade. More significantly, many antislavery figures suffered a misapprehension that the United States government had cut the vital artery of domestic slavery when the trade was abolished.[1] In the wake of the bill's enactment, two prominent evangelicals reflected on the meaning of past antislavery work. Although they represented differing viewpoints, both reached the premature conclusion that the evangelical attack on slavery had come to an end.

At a celebration marking the abolition of the slave trade, Jedidiah Morse attempted to bring the curtain down on nearly forty years of evangelical agitation on slavery. Two hundred blacks marched through the streets of Boston on that day and filed into the African Meeting House for a service of thanksgiving. There Morse ascended the pulpit to preach a sermon on John 8:36: "If the Son therefore shall make you free, ye shall be free indeed." While Africa lay in "heathenish and Mahometan darkness," Morse told them, God allowed white men to capture those blacks who were to be made free in Christ. "But since the blessed gospel now sheds its genial influence on Africa, by the preaching of the missionaries of the cross," he contended, "its natives have no need to be carried to foreign lands, in order to enjoy its light; and God hath shut the door against their further transportation." In addition to setting forth the evangelical theodicy of the slave trade, Morse expressed hope that its abolition would open the way for the spread of the gospel in Africa.[2]

As for the blacks remaining in bondage in the United States, Morse predicted that the abolition of the trade would lead to an amelioration of their plight. A direct and immediate assault on domestic slavery was unnecessary, he believed, for it would be abolished gradually by the diffusion of gospel principles through America. In the meantime, Christian duty required that believers treat slaves as the apostles did: "Let them remain as they are, and make their condition in that state as comfortable and happy, as possible."[3] In his enthusiasm for African missions, his stress on evangelism at home, and his acquiescence to the prolonged existence of slavery in America, Morse accurately mirrored attitudes that prevailed among white evangelicals in the North.

Writing a few months after Jefferson signed the abolition bill, Richard Furman held up the Methodist attack on slavery as a case study in the foolishness of antislavery agitation. Furman, a leading spokesman for the South Carolina Baptists, addressed his remarks to a correspondent who requested advice on whether an association should discuss the matter of slavery. So long as the association confined its discussion to the treatment of slaves, Furman had no objections. But he warned that any hint that slaveholding was a sin would ruin the effectiveness of the association. A "certain denomination of professing Christians" had once formulated rules against slaveholding because its leaders viewed it as contrary to the law of God, he wrote, alluding to the Methodist rules of 1784. But now that denomination had fallen silent on the issue and made no attempt to enforce the rules. "And," Furman gloated, "when called upon to explain this mysterious business, they said— 'These rules did not suit the country'; and 'That they had agreed to suspend their operation' for the present." With obvious delight, he continued: "That is, to suspend in effect, the operation of the law of God, on which hang all the law & the prophets!" Furman was confident that the Methodists, having learned their lesson, would not repeat this rash and wholly unnecessary performance. "Their own respectability, comfort, and usefulness require it, . . ." he added, disclosing some very unspiritual concerns.[4]

By their uninterrupted labors, a few evangelicals served notice that they did not regard the abolition of the overseas trade as a mortal blow to domestic slavery, and that they would not shrink from antislavery work because it might jeopardize their respectability. In the same year that the ban went into effect, Baptist emancipators founded the Kentucky Abolition Society, Methodists at Liberty Hill enacted their rule on slavery, and the Baltimore Conference required masters to file deeds for the eventual manumission of their slaves. The next year James Lemen, who was baptized by the ubiquitous Josiah Dodge, established a branch of the Friends of Humanity in Illinois.[5] These actions ranked among the more visible antislavery endeavors, and they indicate that although evangelical opposition to slavery had subsided in strength, it was by no means dead. Through intermittent, mostly uncoordinated activities, these and other unknown evangelicals helped to keep a concern about slavery alive during the so-called "neglected period of antislavery."[6] This period extended roughly from the abolition of the slave trade to the emergence of immediate abolition in the 1830s.

It would take a separate study to determine precisely what influence eighteenth-century evangelicals had on a later generation of abolitionists. Very briefly, however, it can be noted that the immediatist viewpoint owed much to earlier evangelicals in its uncompromising moral fervor, its warning of divine retribution, and its insistence that slavery be regarded as an expression of inner corruption rather than as a social or economic system.[7] But by the antebellum era, the antislavery argument had become freighted with concepts and slogans which showed that the problem of slavery had taken on an entirely sectional character: "the slave power," "free soil," and "irrepressible conflict," for instance. Sectional consciousness was certainly not unknown among eighteenth-century evangelicals, and the possibility of a civil war worried individuals such as Samuel Hopkins. Unlike later abolitionists, however, most eighteenth-century evangelicals could not regard slaveholding as a distinctively southern iniquity.

Recent historians of antebellum America have correctly asserted that there was no necessary connection between evangelicalism and social reform. Evangelicals could overcome the world through personal holiness and revivalism rather than by direct attacks on social evil. In the antebellum period, many white evangelicals still believed that there was nothing intrinsically evil about slaveholding, and that the more repugnant aspects of the practice would fade from view with the conversion of masters and slaves.[8] These evangelicals maintained a tradition which dated back to the days of Whitefield and Davies. Southern white evangelicals continued to portray slaveholding as a form of Christian stewardship, and they carried on their efforts to reconcile slaves to their status through Christianization. For those northern and southern evangelicals who still had qualms about slavery, the colonization movement offered a gradualistic, wholly inoffensive program of voluntary emancipation and removal of slaves. When immediate abolitionism reared its head in the major denominations in the 1830s and 1840s, moderate and conservative leaders in the North joined southerners in reaffirming that emancipation was not an essential part of the Christian gospel. Northern church leaders balked, however, when southerners demanded an explicit sanction of slaveholding, a demand which contributed to the sectional division of the Methodist and Baptist denominations.[9] Down to the eve of the Civil War, a number of northern evangelicals remained wedded to the idea that slavery would disappear as an indirect result of revivalism.[10]

The evangelicals who embraced immediatism posed another alternative and exemplified what may be regarded as a recessive trait within the movement. Abolitionism of the 1830s grew out of an entirely different social setting than its eighteenth-century predecessor. Nevertheless, there are similarities between the experiences and attitudes of antislavery evangelicals in both eras. Many believers in the antebellum North felt a profound sense of alienation from the social order in which they matured. In their eyes, the North's rapid commercial and industrial development was creating a society which encouraged greed, materialism, drunkenness, sexual license, and crudity. Restraints on individual conduct appeared to be weakening in a rootless, expanding environment where taverns, brothels, and cheap theaters seemed to multiply faster than schools and churches, and where a lack of community surveillance removed inhibitions which had promoted good behavior in more settled times.[11]

Thrust into a world teeming with temptation, evangelicals of the antebellum era gave renewed stress to the theme of self-control. Mastery over the self, they declared, provided the key to victory over the world; only by exercising a relentless discipline over the desires within could they hope to escape from the wickedness around them. Fears about the spiritual consequences of "luxurious living" surfaced once again in evangelical circles, prompting believers to reject the glitter of fashionable society in favor of a more austere lifestyle.[12] The mere possession of wealth was not evil, so long as it was channeled into God's work. Preaching before middle-class Protestants who had tasted prosperity, but who perhaps felt guilty about desiring more of the good life, revivalists like Charles Finney condemned those desires and called upon people to dedicate their lives and wealth to the service of God.[13] Hundreds of middle-class converts answered this "call to seriousness"[14] and went forth to do battle against the enemies of the self: strong drink, prostitution, gambling, and desecration of the Sabbath.

For some of these evangelical crusaders, slavery became a highly-charged symbol of corruption, just as it had for emancipators in the eighteenth century. The slaveholder represented irresponsible wealth, unbridled lust, a frivolous lifestyle, damnable arrogance—everything that the self-disciplined believer despised. The slave stood exposed to this wickedness in a system which, according to some Northern evangelicals, denied him the ability to attain true self-mastery.[15] Some evangelicals of the antebellum years regarded slavery as an insurmountable obstacle to the progress of the Kingdom; they attacked it and demanded immediate repentance from the slaveholder.

As they carried their message throughout the North, these evangelicals often faced persecution, not from slaveholding gentlemen, but from Northern "gentlemen of property and standing."

Evangelical abolitionists were convinced that these worldly Northern aristocrats were in league with their southern counterparts to suppress the truth. As in the case of eighteenth-century evangelicals, the experience of persecution reinforced their antislavery commitment and deepened their sympathy with the slave.[16]

Evangelicalism did not lead inevitably to antislavery commitment in the antebellum period any more than it did in the eighteenth century. But in both eras, a feeling of social alienation and a heightened sense of vulnerability to the world helped to draw out the antislavery potential in the evangelical experience.

In various ways, antebellum believers demonstrated that they remembered an earlier period of evangelical opposition to slavery. Sometimes eighteenth-century evangelicals received an oblique recognition of their labors, as when a southern Baptist historian deleted all strictures on slavery from one of Barrow's letters, or when editors of Asbury's journal expunged some antislavery remarks from the text.[17] When they could not hide the antislavery activities of their forebears, other writers attempted to explain it away; writing after the Civil War, McKendree's biographer apologized for the Bishop's excess of antislavery zeal and soberly instructed his readers that the good man lived to change his mind.[18]

Evangelical abolitionists, on the other hand, lauded and magnified the work of their predecessors in an effort to deny their southern opponents the sanction of history. The colonization movement rightly claimed Samuel Hopkins as an early advocate of its views. For Methodist Hiram Mattison, the antislavery deeds of the founders comprised a "golden epoch" in the history of the denomination, a glorious era before minions of the slave power plunged the church into a period of declension.[19] Presbyterian John Robinson included the work of David Rice and the Transylvania Presbytery in his chronicle of abolitionism. Rice's speech to Kentucky's constitutional convention saw publication once again during the Civil War. William Birney compiled a list of Presbyterian worthies who emigrated from the South in the 1790s and early 1800s.[20] The apotheosis of eighteenth-century evangelicals continued in the work of historians who saw them as heroic forebears in the struggle for freedom. In these accounts, antislavery figures appear to have set off a chain of events that would lead inevitably

to the founding of the Republican Party and victory over southern arms.[21]

The antislavery evangelicals of this study, of course, knew nothing of these later events. No premonitions of Sumter, Appomat-
tox, or the Emancipation Proclamation informed their perspective
on their own endeavors. They did not see themselves as the heroic
vanguard of an antislavery host, nor did they believe that they
had sounded the tocsin in a campaign whose outcome was assured
from the beginning. They met with too many disappointments to
take such a lofty view of their work. In groping toward a definition of themselves and their faith in an often troubled world, they
encountered a form of servitude which objectified aspects of their
personal war against sin. The slave's cause thus became, in a sense,
their own cause. What is more, these believers opened a debate on
questions which are still very much alive in evangelical circles:
whether the church should take a stand on potentially divisive
social issues, or whether it should tend to "spiritual" matters;
whether the experience of the new birth entailed a responsibility
to abolish existing forms of oppression, or whether the gift of the
gospel was itself an adequate compensation for whatever hardships the victims of injustice had to endure on earth.

All too often, the antislavery evangelicals displayed more interest in their own righteousness than in the welfare of the oppressed. They consistently underestimated the durability of the
slave system, the tenacity of their opponents, and the indifference
of most white believers. But by fashioning the first evangelical
critique of slaveholding, and by helping to lay foundations for
later abolitionist work, these individuals built better than they
knew.

NOTES

PREFACE

1. See, for instance, Bernard Bailyn, *The Ideological Origins of the American Revolution* (Cambridge, Mass.: Harvard University Press, 1967), pp. 232–46; Arthur Zilversmit, *The First Emancipation: The Abolition of Slavery in the North* (Chicago: University of Chicago Press, 1967), pp. 227–28; and, to a lesser extent, Duncan J. MacLeod, *Slavery, Race and the American Revolution* (London: Cambridge University Press, 1974), pp. 22–26.

2. Irving S. Kull, "Presbyterian Attitudes Toward Slavery," *Church History* 7 (June 1938): 101–14; Walter B. Posey, "The Baptists and Slavery in the Lower Mississippi Valley," *Journal of Negro History* 41 (April 1956): 117–30; Conrad James Engelder, "The Churches and Slavery: A Study of the Attitudes Toward Slavery of the Major Protestant Denominations" (Ph.D. diss., University of Michigan, 1964); W. Harrison Daniel, "Virginia Baptists and the Negro in the Early Republic," *Virginia Magazine of History and Biography* 80 (January 1972): 60–69; W. Harrison Daniel, "The Methodist Episcopal Church and the Negro in the Early National Period," *Methodist History* 11 (January 1973): 40–53. The best of all the denominational studies is Donald G. Mathews, *Slavery and Methodism: A Chapter in American Morality, 1780–1845* (Princeton: Princeton University Press, 1965).

3. Reuben E. Alley, *A History of Baptists in Virginia* (Richmond: Virginia Baptist General Board, [1973]), pp. 125–27; Garnett Ryland, *The Baptists of Virginia, 1699–1926* (Richmond: Virginia Baptist Board of Missions and Education, 1955), pp. 150–55.

4. David Brion Davis, *The Problem of Slavery in Western Culture* (Ithaca: Cornell University Press, 1966), pp. 385–90, and *The Problem of Slavery in the Age of Revolution, 1770–1823* (Ithaca: Cornell University Press, 1975), pp. 201–7, 286–96; Winthrop D. Jordan, *White Over Black: American Attitudes Toward the Negro, 1550–1812* (Chapel Hill: University of North Carolina Press, 1968), pp. 190–93, 361–65.

5. Perry Miller, "From the Covenant to the Revival," in *The Shaping of American Religion,* ed. James Ward Smith and A. Leland Jamison (Princeton: Princeton University Press, 1961), vol. I, p. 336n.

CHAPTER I

1. George Whitefield, *The Two First Parts of His Life with His Journals* (London: W. Strahan, 1756), pp. 295–96.

2. Ibid., p. 296.

3. For various appraisals of the Awakening, see William G. McLoughlin, *Isaac Backus and the American Pietistic Tradition* (Boston: Little, Brown, 1967); Edwin S. Gaustad, *The Great Awakening in New England* (New York: Harper and Row, 1957); Richard Hofstader, *Anti-Intellectualism in American Life* (New York: Alfred A. Knopf, 1962), pp. 64–69; Perry Miller, *Jonathan Edwards* (New York: Sloan Associates, 1949); Alan Heimert, *Religion and the American Mind* (Cambridge, Mass.: Harvard University Press, 1966); J. M. Bumsted and John E. Van de Wetering, *What Must I Do to Be Saved? The Great Awakening in Colonial America* (Hinsdale, Ill.: Dryden Press, 1976); Richard L. Bushman, *From Puritan to Yankee: Character and the Social Order in Connecticut, 1690–1765* (Cambridge, Mass.: Harvard University Press, 1967); Edmund S. Morgan, "The Three Temperaments," *New York Review of Books,* February 23, 1978, pp. 8–9.

4. For background on the origins of the Awakening, see Gaustad, *Great Awakening*; Bushman, *From Puritan to Yankee*; Charles H. Maxson, *The Great Awakening in the Middle Colonies* (Chicago: University of Chicago Press, 1920); James R. Tanis, *Dutch Calvinistic Pietism in the Middle Colonies: A Study in the Life and Theology of Theodorus Jacobus Frelinghuysen* (S-Gravenhage: Nijhoff, 1967).

5. Gaustad, *Great Awakening*, p. 100; Tanis, *Frelinghuysen*, p. 105.

6. The story of the split between Calvinists and Wesleyans can be found in nearly every account of revivalism in eighteenth-century England, but for a detailed examination of Wesley's theology, see Harald Lindström, *Wesley and Sanctification* (Nashville: Abingdon Press, 1946).

7. Frank Baker, *From Wesley to Asbury: Studies in Early American Methodism* (Durham: Duke University Press, 1976), pp. 23, 71.

8. Elmer T. Clark et al., eds., *The Journal and Letters of Francis Asbury* (Nashville: Abingdon Press, 1958), vol. I, pp. 300, 682, vol. II, p. 35; hereafter known as Asbury, *Journal.*

9. Baker, *From Wesley to Asbury*, p. 23.

10. Gaustad, *Great Awakening*, p. 28; Baker, *From Wesley to Asbury,* p. 86.

11. My understanding of evangelicalism has benefited from Donald G. Mathews, *Religion in the Old South* (Chicago: University of Chicago Press, 1977). See also F. Ernest Stoeffler, "Pietism, the Wesleys, and the Methodist Beginnings in America," in *Continental Pietism and Early*

American Christianity, ed. F. Ernest Stoeffler (Grand Rapids, Mich.: Eerdmans, 1976), pp. 184–221. In *The Protestant Temperament: Patterns of Child-Rearing, Religious Experience, and the Self in Early America* (New York: Alfred A. Knopf, 1977), Philip Greven emphasizes the element of self-denial in the evangelical experience, but his neglect of the evangelical sense of joyous liberation leads to a flawed portrait of the movement. In *The Urban Crucible* (Cambridge: Harvard University Press, 1979), Gary Nash uses "Evangelical" as a label for radical artisans, reform-minded professionals, as well as the "dispossessed" of the cities who were affected by the Awakening (pp. 342–45).

12. See Frederick B. Tolles, "Quietism versus Enthusiasm: The Philadelphia Quakers and the Great Awakening," in Tolles, *Quakers and Atlantic Culture* (New York: MacMillan, 1947), pp. 91–113, especially pp. 97, 109.

13. Mathews, *Religion in the Old South,* pp. 42–46; Gaustad, *Great Awakening,* p. 106.

14. Tanis, *Frelinghuysen,* pp. 130–31; Heimert, *Religion and the American Mind,* pp. 32, 33, 306, 381.

15. Heimert traces the outlines of this millennial vision, but vastly overrates its potential for social and political radicalism. See chap. 2 of *Religion and the American Mind.*

16. George Whitefield, *Three Letters from the Reverend George Whitefield* (Philadelphia: B. Franklin, 1740), p. 13.

17. William Stevens Perry, ed., *Historical Collections Relating to the American Colonial Church* (Hartford, Conn.: Church Press, 1870–1878), vol. IV, pp. 304–5.

18. [Charles F. Pascoe, comp.], *Classified Digest of the Records of the Society for the Propagation of the Gospel in Foreign Parts, 1701–1892* (London: The Society, 1893), p. 15.

19. For early evangelistic work among slaves, see Marcus W. Jernegan, "Slavery and Conversion in the American Colonies," *American Historical Review* 21 (April 1916): 504–27; Faith Vibert, "The Society for the Propagation of the Gospel in Foreign Parts: Its Work for the Negroes in North America Before 1783," *Journal of Negro History* 18 (April 1933): 171–212; and Frank J. Klingberg, *An Appraisal of the Negro in Colonial South Carolina* (Washington, D.C.: Associated Publishers, 1941).

20. Whitefield, *Three Letters,* p. 15.

21. Ibid., pp. 14, 16.

22. Samuel Davies, *Letters from the Rev. Samuel Davies, Shewing the State of Religion in Virginia, Particularly Among the Negroes,* 2nd ed. (London, 1757), pp. 10, 16.

23. Ibid., p. 10. See also George William Pilcher, "Samuel Davies and the Instruction of Negroes in Virginia," *Virginia Magazine of History and Biography* 74 (July 1966): 293–300.

24. Col. James Gordon, "Journal of Col. James Gordon, of Lancaster County, Va.," *William and Mary Quarterly* 11 (January 1903): 199.

25. Davies, *Letters*, p. 21.

26. Samuel Davies, *The Duty of Christians to Propagate Their Faith Among Heathens, Earnestly Recommended to the Masters of Negro Slaves in Virginia* (London: J. Oliver, 1758), p. 27.

27. Ibid., p. 23.

28. Ibid., pp. 21, 27.

29. Samuel Davies, *Virginia's Danger and Remedy* (Williamsburg, Va.: William Hunter, 1756), p. 26.

30. Quoted in Frank J. Klingberg, "The S.P.G. Program for Negroes in Colonial New York," *Historical Magazine of the Protestant Episcopal Church* 8 (December 1939): 330.

31. Patrick Henry et al., "Letters of Patrick Henry, Sr. Samuel Davies, James Maury, Edwin Conway and George Trask," *William and Mary Quarterly* 2nd series 1 (October 1921): 280.

32. George Whitefield, *The Works of the Reverend George Whitefield* (London: J. Gillies, 1771), vol. II, pp. 208–9.

33. Perry, *American Colonial Church*, vol. I, p. 369.

34. Edwards A. Park, ed., *The Works of Samuel Hopkins, D.D. With A Memoir of His Life and Character* (Boston: Doctrinal Tract and Book Society, 1852), "Memoir," vol. I, p. 114; hereafter referred to as Hopkins, *Works; General Assembly Missionary Magazine* n.s. 1 (July 1807): 46.

35. See, for example, Herbert W. Schneider, *The Puritan Mind* (Ann Arbor: University of Michigan Press, 1958), p. 208; Joseph Haroutunian, *Piety Versus Moralism* (New York: Henry Holt, 1932); and Edmund S. Morgan, "The American Revolution Considered as an Intellectual Movement," in *Paths of American Thought*, ed. Arthur M. Schlesinger, Jr., and Morton White (Boston: Houghton Mifflin, 1970; originally published 1963), pp. 18–22.

36. Park, "Memoir," in Hopkins, *Works*, vol. I, p. 22.

37. Ibid., vol. I, pp. 132f; "A Narrative of the rise & progress of a proposal and attempt to send the gospel to Guinea," Case 8, Box 23, Gratz Collection (Historical Society of Pennsylvania, Philadelphia).

38. David Austin to Roger Sherman, February 20, 1790, Hist. mss. (Manuscripts and Archives Room, Sterling Library, Yale University); William B. Sprague, *Annals of the American Pulpit* (New York: Robert Carter, 1859), vol. I, p. 659.

39. Jonathan Edwards, Jr., to Ebenezer Baldwin, January 17, 1774 (Beinecke Library, Yale University).

40. Sprague, *Annals*, vol. I, p. 638. These unsigned articles appeared in the *Connecticut Journal and New Haven Post-Boy* from October 1773 to March 1774.

41. C. C. Goen, *Revivalism and Separatism in New England, 1740–1800* (New Haven: Yale University Press, 1962); McLoughlin, *Backus.*

42. William G. McLoughlin, *New England Dissent, 1630–1833* (Cambridge: Harvard University Press, 1971), vol. I, p. 438.

43. Ibid., vol. II, p. 768; Thomas B. Maston, "The Ethical and Social Attitudes of Isaac Backus" (Ph.D. diss., Yale University, 1939), p. 137.

44. William L. Lumpkin, *Baptist Foundations in the South: Tracing Through the Separates the Influence of the Great Awakening, 1754–1787* (Nashville: Broadman Press, 1961), pp. 105–13.

45. David Thomas, *The Virginia Baptist* (Baltimore: Enoch Shay, 1774), p. 6; George W. Paschal, *History of the North Carolina Baptists* (Raleigh: North Carolina State Convention, 1930), vol. I, pp. 346–47.

46. Robert H. Bishop, *An Outline of the History of the Church in Kentucky . . . Containing the Memoirs of Rev. David Rice* (Lexington: T. T. Skillman, 1824), p. 57. See also John Opie, "The Melancholy Career of 'Father' David Rice," *Journal of Presbyterian History* 47 (December 1969): 295–319.

47. Donald J. D'Elia, *Benjamin Rush: Philosopher of the American Revolution,* Transactions of the American Philosophical Society 64 (Philadelphia: American Philosophical Society, 1974), p. 84.

48. Joseph F. Tuttle, "Rev. Jacob Green, of Hanover, N.J., As an Author, Statesman, and Patriot," *Proceedings of the New Jersey Historical Society* 2nd series. 12 (1893): 189–241.

49. Baker, *From Wesley to Asbury;* Frank Baker, *Methodism and the Love Feast* (London: Epworth Press, 1957).

50. Asbury, *Journal,* vol. I, p. 4; vol. III, p. 62.

51. Frank E. Maser, ed., "Discovery," *Methodist History* 9 (January 1971): p. 35.

52. Joshua Coffin, *A Sketch of the History of Newbury, Newburyport, and West Newbury* (Boston: S. G. Drake, 1845), pp. 339–40.

53. Perry Miller, "From the Covenant to the Revival," in *The Shaping of American Religion,* ed. James Ward Smith and A. Leland Jamison (Princeton: Princeton University Press, 1961), vol. I.

54. Gordon S. Wood, *The Creation of the American Republic, 1776–1787* (Chapel Hill: University of North Carolina Press, 1969), pp. 93–97, 107–9.

55. P. P. Sandford, *Memoirs of Mr. Wesley's Missionaries to America* (New York: G. Lane and P. P. Sandford, 1844), p. 230.

56. "Dummer Academy—Deacon Colman—Master Moody and His 'Manners School,'" *Historical Collections of the Essex Institute* 7 (February 1865), p. 23.

57. Miller, "From the Covenant to the Revival," p. 336.

58. Jacob Green, *A Sermon Delivered at Hanover . . . April 22, 1778* (Chatham, N.J.: Shepard Kollock, 1779), p. 6.

59. Ebenezer Baldwin, *An Appendix . . . ,* in *A Sermon Containing Scriptural Injunctions . . . ,* ed. Samuel Sherwood (New Haven: T. and S. Green, 1774), p. 78.

60. Coffin, *A Sketch,* p. 339.

61. Sandford, *Memoirs,* p. 233. The performance of Rankin, a British Wesleyan, casts doubt on Winthrop D. Jordan's assertion that it was men whose backgrounds were "most explicitly Calvinist" who advanced the equation of slavery and sin. See Winthrop D. Jordan, *White Over Black: American Attitudes Toward the Negro, 1550–1812* (Chapel Hill: University of North Carolina Press, 1968), p. 300.

62. [Benjamin Rush], *An Address to the Inhabitants of the British Settlements in America, Upon Slave-Keeping* (Philadelphia: John Dunlap, 1773), p. 29.

63. [Jacob Green], "On Liberty," *New Jersey Journal,* May 10, 1780 (see Tuttle, "Rev. Jacob Green," pp. 229–30, for Green's authorship); Hopkins, *Works,* vol. II, p. 618; Nathaniel Niles, *Two Discourses on Liberty: Delivered at the North Church, in Newbury-port . . . June 5, 1774* (Newburyport: I. Thomas and H. W. Tinges, 1774), p. 38.

64. For instance, Samuel Cooke, *A Sermon Preached at Cambridge . . . May 30th, 1770* (Boston: Edes and Gill, 1770).

65. A. D. Gillette, ed., *Minutes of the Philadelphia Baptist Association, From A.D. 1707, to A.D. 1807* (Philadelphia: American Baptist Publication Society, 1851), p. 167.

66. Coffin, *A Sketch,* p. 345.

67. Green, *A Sermon,* p. 13.

68. [Rush], *Address,* p. 30.

69. Hopkins, *Works,* vol. II, p. 592.

70. [Rush], *Address,* p. 29.

71. Elhanan Winchester, *The Reigning Abominations, Especially The Slave Trade . . . Delivered in Fairfax County, Virginia, December 30, 1774* (London: H. Trapp, 1788), pp. 17–18. Winchester's writings on universal salvation had an influence on Rush. D'Elia, *Benjamin Rush,* pp. 88–89.

72. Hopkins, *Works,* vol. II, p. 586.

CHAPTER II

1. Peter Kalm, *Travels into North America,* trans. John R. Forster (Barre, Mass.: Imprint Society, 1972), pp. 201–2.

2. Frederick E. Maser and Howard T. Maag, eds., *The Journal of Joseph Pilmore Methodist Itinerant for the Years August 1, 1769 to January 2, 1774* (Philadelphia: Message Publishing Co., 1969), pp. 63–69; hereafter known as Pilmore, *Journal.*

3. H. Richard Niebuhr, *Christ and Culture* (New York: Harper and Row, 1951), pp. 45–82.

4. Pilmore, *Journal,* p. 101.

5. William K. Boyd, ed., "A Journal and Travel of James Meacham," Part I, *Historical Papers,* Trinity College Historical Society, Series IX (1912), p. 67, for example; hereafter known as Meacham, "Journal."

6. Freeborn Garrettson, *The Experience and Travels of Mr. Freeborn Garrettson* (Philadelphia: Parry Hall, 1791), p. 54.

7. Pilmore, *Journal,* p. 31.

8. Nathan Bangs, *A History of the Methodist Episcopal Church* (New York: J. Collard, 1845), vol. I, p. 213.

9. Elmer T. Clark et al., eds., *The Journal and Letters of Francis Asbury* (Nashville: Abingdon Press, 1958), vol. I, p. 115; hereafter known as Asbury, *Journal.*

10. Bangs, *History,* vol. I, p. 215.

11. Ibid., vol. I, pp. 213–14.

12. Asbury, *Journal,* vol. I, p. 252.

13. *Hymns and Spiritual Songs, Collected from the Works of Several Authors* (Newport, R.I.: Samuel Hall, 1766), p. 162.

14. Hunter Dickinson Farish, ed., *Journal and Letters of Philip Vickers Fithian: A Plantation Tutor of the Old Dominion, 1773–1774* (Charlottesville: University Press of Virginia, 1968), p. 72.

15. David Thomas, *The Virginia Baptist* (Baltimore: Enoch Shay, 1774), p. 60.

16. Robert Semple, *A History of the Rise and Progress of the Baptists in Virginia* (Richmond: John Lynch, 1810), p. 26.

17. Ibid., p. 28.

18. Lemuel Burkitt and Jesse Read, *A Concise History of the Kehukee Baptist Association* (Halifax: A. Hodge, 1803), p. 38.

19. Semple, *Baptists in Virginia,* p. 177.

20. Wood Furman, comp., *A History of the Charleston Association of Baptist Churches in the State of South Carolina; with an Appendix Containing*

the Principal Circular Letters to the Churches (Charleston, S.C.: J. Hoff, 1811), p. 71.

21. William Fristoe, *A Concise History of the Ketocton Baptist Association* (Staunton: W. G. Lyford, 1808), p. 149.

22. Dr. William Hill, *Autobiographical Sketches of Dr. William Hill, Together With His Account of the Revival of Religion in Prince Edward County . . .* , Union Theological Seminary Historical Transcripts No. 4 (Richmond: Union Seminary, 1968), p. 10.

23. Jack P. Greene, ed., *The Diary of Colonel Landon Carter of Sabine Hall, 1752–1778* (Charlottesville: University Press of Virginia, 1965), vol. II, pp. 855–56; hereafter known as Carter, *Diary*.

24. L. F. Greene, ed., *The Writings of the Late Elder John Leland* (New York: G. W. Wood, 1845), p. 73; hereafter known as Leland, *Writings*.

25. Asbury, *Journal*, vol. I, p. 335.

26. Thomas, *Virginia Baptist*, p. 55.

27. Fristoe, *History*, p. 153.

28. Burkitt and Read, *History*, pp. 118, 301; Semple, *Baptists in Virginia*, p. 377.

29. Burkitt and Read, *History*, p. 301.

30. Semple, *Baptists in Virginia*, p. 377; Burkitt and Read, *History*, p. 118; Garrettson, *Experience*, pp. 113–14.

31. William T. Youngs, Jr., *God's Messengers: Religious Leadership in Colonial New England, 1700–1750* (Baltimore: Johns Hopkins, 1976), pp. 121–24; Rhys Isaac, "Evangelical Revolt: The Nature of the Baptists' Challenge to the Traditional Order in Virginia, 1765–1775," *William and Mary Quarterly* 3rd series. 31 (July 1974): 345–68. In *Religion in the Old South* (Chicago: University of Chicago Press, 1977), Donald Mathews notes that evangelicalism provided a new form of community with its own standards and social distinctions.

32. Pilmore, *Journal*, p. 109.

33. See Eric McCoy North, *Early Methodist Philanthropy* (New York: Methodist Book Concern, 1914).

34. Pilmore, *Journal*, pp. 63, 100.

35. Ibid., p. 75.

36. Ibid., p. 125.

37. John Wesley, *The Works of the Rev. John Wesley, A.M.* (London: Wesleyan Conference Office, 1872), vol. I, p. 40.

38. Minton Thrift, *Memoir of the Rev. Jesse Lee* (New York: Bangs and Mason, 1823), p. 87.

39. Asbury, *Journal*, vol. II, p. 122. The fast sermons quoted in Chap.

1 show that Presbyterians and Congregationalists also classified blacks with traditional objects of charity.

40. P. P. Sandford, *Memoirs of Mr. Wesley's Missionaries to America* (New York: Lane and Sandford, 1844), p. 228.

41. Pilmore, *Journal*, p. 137.

42. William McKendree, "Diary of Bishop McKendree from 7 May 1790 to 18 February 1791," January 7, 1791 (Vanderbilt Divinity School, Nashville, Tenn.).

43. Ibid., October 5, 1790.

44. Hill, *Autobiographical Sketches*, p. 56; Richard Dozier, "Text Book," April 27, 1789 (Virginia Baptist Historical Society, Richmond, Va.).

45. Garrettson, *Experience*, pp. 76–77.

46. Ibid., p. 76.

47. Meacham, "Journal," part I, p. 75.

48. Asbury, *Journal*, vol. II, p. 77.

49. McKendree, "Diary," August 1, 1790.

50. Thomas, *Virginia Baptist*, p. 59.

51. Ibid.

52. Asbury, *Journal*, vol. I, p. 303.

53. Ibid., vol. I, pp. 310, 189.

54. Ibid., vol. I, p. 184.

55. John Taylor, *A History of Ten Baptist Churches*, in *Religion on the American Frontier*, ed. William W. Sweet, vol. 1, *The Baptists* (New York: Henry Holt, 1931), pp. 136–37.

56. Quoted in Lewis Peyton Little, *Imprisoned Preachers and Religious Liberty in Virginia* (Lynchburg, Va.: Bell, 1938), p. 243.

57. Thrift, *Memoir of Lee*, pp. 86–87.

58. Quoted in Little, *Imprisoned Preachers*, p. 259.

59. Taylor in Sweet, *The Baptists*, p. 134.

60. Quoted in William Lumpkin, *Baptist Foundations in the South: Tracing through the Separates the Influence of the Great Awakening, 1754–1787* (Nashville: Broadman Press, 1961), p. 112.

61. Asbury, *Journal*, vol. I, pp. 9–10.

62. Ibid., vol. I, p. 43.

63. Bangs, *History*, p. 63.

64. Sandford, *Memoirs*, p. 231.

65. See R. S. Crane, "Suggestions Toward a Genealogy of the 'Man of Feeling,'" *ELH: A Journal of English Literary History* 1 (December 1934): 205–30; Walter Jackson Bate, *From Classic to Romantic* (Cambridge: Harvard University Press, 1946), pp. 27–58, 129–59; Hoxie Neale Fair-

child, *Religious Trends in English Poetry* (New York: Columbia University Press, 1939–1949), vol. I, chaps. II, IV, XII; Ernest Bernbaum, *The Drama of Sensibility* (Boston: Ginn and Co., 1915).

66. Quoted in Crane, "'Man of Feeling,'" p. 205.

67. *Pocket Hymnbook Designed as a Constant Companion For the Pious* (New York: William Durell, 1791), p. 121.

68. *Arminian Magazine* 1 (December 1789): 591.

69. Quoted in Wylie Sypher, *Guinea's Captive Kings: British Anti-Slavery Literature of the XVIIIth Century* (Chapel Hill: University of North Carolina Press, 1942), p. 76.

70. Samuel Hopkins, undated ms., Gratz Collection, Case 8, Box 23 (Historical Society of Pennsylvania, Philadelphia).

71. Oliver W. Elsbree, "Samuel Hopkins and His Doctrine of Benevolence," *New England Quarterly* 8 (December 1935): 534–50; David S. Lovejoy, "Samuel Hopkins: Religion, Slavery, and the Revolution," *New England Quarterly* 40 (June 1967): 227–43; Stanley K. Schultz, "The Making of a Reformer: The Reverend Samuel Hopkins as an Eighteenth Century Abolitionist," *Proceedings of the American Philosophical Society* 115 (October 15, 1971): 350–65; and, most importantly, Joseph A. Conforti, "Samuel Hopkins and the New Divinity: Theology, Ethics, and Social Reform in Eighteenth-Century New England," *William and Mary Quarterly* 3rd ser. 34 (October 1977): 572–89.

72. Edwards A. Park, ed., *The Works of Samuel Hopkins, D.D. With a Memoir of His Life and Character* (Boston: Doctrinal Tract and Book Society, 1852), vol. I, p. 398; hereafter cited as Hopkins, *Works.*

73. Ibid., vol. I, p. 399.

74. Ibid., vol. I, p. 397.

75. James O'Kelly, *Essay on Negro Slavery* (Philadelphia: Prichard and Hall, 1789), p. 8.

76. Thomas Haskins, "Journals, 1782 Nov. 7–1785 May 13," Jan. 25, 1785 (Library of Congress, Washington, D.C.).

77. Asbury, *Journal,* vol. I, p. 442.

78. Meacham, "Journal," part I, p. 78.

79. Ibid., part II, *Historical Papers,* Trinity College Historical Society, Series X (1914), p. 94.

80. McKendree, "Diary," February 12, 1791.

81. Hopkins, *Works,* vol. II, pp. 552–53.

82. O'Kelly, *Essay,* p. 21.

83. [David Rice], *Slavery Inconsistent With Justice and Good Policy* (Lexington, Ky.: J. Bradford, 1792), p. 11.

84. Wesley, *Works,* vol. II, p. 76.

85. Levi Hart, *A Christian Minister described, and distinguished from a Pleaser of Men* (New Haven: Meigs and Dana, 1787), p. 28. See also Benjamin Trumbull, *A Sermon Delivered at the Ordination of the Rev. Lemuel Tyler, A.M.* (New Haven: T. and S. Green, 1793).

86. Pilmore, *Journal*, p. 203.

87. Asbury, *Journal*, vol. I, p. 197.

88. Garrettson, *Experience*, p. 102.

89. Ibid., p. 87.

90. Thomas Coke, *Extracts from the Journals of the Rev. Dr. Coke's Five Visits to America* (London: G. Paramore, 1793), p. 15; Garrettson, *Experience*, p. 160.

91. William G. McLoughlin, *Isaac Backus and the American Pietistic Tradition* (Boston: Little, Brown, 1967), p. 46.

92. Fristoe, *History*, p. 57.

93. Garrettson, *Experience*, p. 135.

94. Ibid., p. 166.

95. Elder John Williams, "Journal, 1771," p. 3 (Virginia Baptist Historical Society, Richmond, Va.); David Benedict, *A General History of the Baptist Denomination in America, and Other Parts of the World* (Boston: Lincoln and Edmands, 1813), vol. II, p. 249n.

96. Fristoe, *History*, p. 64.

97. Ibid., p. 90. Rhys Isaac has offered a splendid treatment of the "struggle for allegiance" between the social worlds of the gentry and evangelicals in "Evangelical Revolt" and "Preachers and Patriots: Popular Culture and the Revolution in Virginia," in *The American Revolution: Essays in the History of American Radicalism*, ed. Alfred F. Young (DeKalb: Northern Illinois University Press, 1976), pp. 127–56.

98. Carter, *Diary*, vol. I, p. 378.

99. Ibid., vol. II, pp. 1056–57.

100. Quoted in Little, *Imprisoned Preachers*, p. 259.

101. Meacham, "Journal," part I, p. 94.

102. James Ireland, *The Life of James Ireland* (Winchester, Va.: J. Foster, 1819), p. 135.

103. "Letters of Hon. James Habersham, 1756–1775," *Collections of the Georgia Historical Society*, vol. 6 (Savannah, 1904), pp. 243–44.

104. See Gerald W. Mullin, *Flight and Rebellion: Slave Resistance in Eighteenth-Century Virginia* (New York: Oxford University Press, 1972), for a description of the Tidewater plantation.

105. Allan Kulikoff, "The Origins of Afro–American Society in Tidewater Maryland and Virginia, 1700–1790," *William and Mary Quarterly* 3rd ser. 35 (April 1978): 226–59; Jeffrey J. Crow, *The Black Experience in*

Revolutionary North Carolina (Raleigh, N.C.: North Carolina Department of Cultural Resources, 1977), p. 5.

106. See Peter Wood, *Black Majority: Negroes in Colonial South Carolina From 1670 through the Stono Rebellion* (New York: Alfred A. Knopf, 1974).

107. Charles F. James, *Documentary History of the Struggle for Religious Liberty in Virginia* (New York: Da Capo Press, 1971; originally published 1899), p. 45.

108. Thomas, *Virginia Baptist,* pp. 58–59.

109. Ireland, *Life,* p. 135.

110. Leland, *Writings,* p. 95.

111. Philip Cox to Thomas Coke, July 1787, *Arminian Magazine* 2 (February 1790): 94.

112. Philip Bruce to Thomas Coke, March 25, 1788, *Arminian Magazine* 2 (November 1790): 564.

113. Leland, *Writings,* p. 268.

114. David Barrow, *Involuntary, Unmerited, Perpetual, Absolute, Hereditary Slavery, Examined on the Principles of Nature, Reason, Justice, Policy, and Scripture* (Lexington, Ky., 1808), p. 26n.

115. Meacham, "Journal," part I, p. 94.

116. Rice, *Slavery Inconsistent,* p. 10.

117. O'Kelly, *Essay,* p. 20; Coke, *Journal,* p. 35.

118. Meacham, "Journal," part II, p. 94.

119. Garrettson, *Experience,* pp. 40, 76.

120. Hopkins, *Works,* "Memoir," vol. I, p. 93.

121. Ibid., vol. I, pp. 94, 116, 166.

CHAPTER III

1. William Fristoe, *A Concise History of the Ketocton Baptist Association* (Staunton: W. G. Lyford, 1808), p. 149.

2. Morgan Edwards, "Materials Toward a History of the Baptists in the Provinces of Maryland, Virginia, North Carolina, South Carolina, and Georgia, 1772," vol. 5, p. 3 (copy in the Virginia Baptist Historical Society, Richmond).

3. Ibid., vol. 6, p. 3.

4. James Ireland, *The Life of James Ireland* (Winchester, Va.: J. Foster, 1819), pp. 181–82.

5. Elmer T. Clark et al., eds., *The Journal and Letters of Francis Asbury* (Nashville: Abingdon Press, 1958), vol. I, p. 244; hereafter known as Asbury, *Journal.*

6. Ibid., vol. II, pp. 6, 41. Many southern gentlemen also had

complaints about members of their own class. In the 1760s and 1770s, upper-class radicals urged the gentry to renounce gambling, horse-racing, and ostentatious display in the name of the colonial cause. Thomas Jefferson, Henry Laurens, and Richard Henry Lee recommended the virtues of industry and frugality in such a strenuous manner that one historian has seen them as exemplars of a "Puritan Ethic." Genteel Whigs embraced seemingly Puritan ideals, not out of a devotion to Calvinism or any other religious impulse, but out of a belief that these values were prerequisites of political liberty. In addition, thrift and hard work could also secure a gentleman's place among the elite by helping him to preserve his financial self-sufficiency, or "independence," as he would call it. For a southern gentleman, "independence" from debt or personal obligation was a mark of honor. Thus while evangelicals adopted an austere lifestyle to subdue their pride, a Whig gentleman might advocate austerity as a way to maintain pride. The emphasis on austerity served different needs in each social world, but it formed a basis of understanding that allowed Whig leaders to mobilize evangelicals in support of the patriot movement. See Jack P. Greene, "'*Virtus et Libertas*': Political Culture, Social Change, and the Origins of the American Revolution in Virginia, 1763–1766," pp. 55–108, and Pauline Maier, "Early Revolutionary Leaders in the South and the Problem of Southern Distinctiveness," pp. 3–24, both in *The Southern Experience in the American Revolution*, ed. Jeffrey J. Crow and Larry E. Tise (Chapel Hill: University of North Carolina Press, 1978). See also Edmund S. Morgan, "The Puritan Ethic and the American Revolution," *William and Mary Quarterly* 3rd ser. 24 (January 1967): 3–43.

7. Fristoe, *History*, p. 151.

8. Ibid.

9. David Rice, *Slavery Inconsistent With Justice and Good Policy* (Lexington, Ky.: J. Bradford, 1792), p. 17.

10. William Colbert, "A Journal of the Travels of William Colbert, Methodist Preacher, Through Parts of Maryland, Pennsylvania, New York, Delaware, and Virginia in 1790 to 1838," September 1, 1790 (Library of Congress, Washington, D.C.).

11. Asbury, *Journal*, vol. II, p. 7.

12. Richard Whatcoat, "The Journal of Richard Whatcoat," April 26, 1795 (Garrett-Evangelical Theological Seminary, Evanston, Ill.).

13. Edwards, "Materials," vol. 5, p. 30.

14. Freeborn Garrettson, *The Experience and Travels of Mr. Freeborn Garrettson* (Philadelphia: Parry Hall, 1791), pp. 24–25.

15. Ibid., pp. 28, 34.

16. Ibid., pp. 35–36.

17. Asbury, *Journal*, vol. I, p. 440.

18. Edwards A. Park, ed., *The Works of Samuel Hopkins, D.D. With a Memoir of His Life and Character* (Boston: Doctrinal Tract and Book Society, 1852), "Memoir," vol. I, p. 94.

19. Richard Dozier, "Text Book," September 21, 1783 (Virginia Baptist Historical Society, Richmond).

20. Asbury, *Journal*, vol. I, p. 456.

21. Dozier, "Text Book," September 21, 1783.

22. Lemuel Burkitt and Jesse Read, *A Concise History of the Kehukee Baptist Association* (Halifax: A. Hodge, 1803), pp. 102–3. At this time the Kehukee Association included churches in Virginia and North Carolina.

23. David Rice to unknown correspondent, December 11, 1799 (Shane Collection, Presbyterian Historical Society, Philadelphia).

24. Asbury to Daniel Fidler, June 23, 1793, *Journal*, vol. III, p. 119.

25. Hopkins, *Works*, vol. II, pp. 314–15, 353.

26. Henry Toler, "Diary of Henry Toler, 1782–1784," July 12, 1783 (Virginia Baptist Historical Society).

27. William McKendree, "Diary of Bishop McKendree from 7 May 1790 to 18 February 1791," September 18, 1790 (Vanderbilt Divinity School, Nashville).

28. Asbury to E. Cooper, January 2, 1795, *Journal*, vol. III, p. 133.

29. Elias Smith, *The Life, Conversion, Preaching, Travels, and Sufferings of Elias Smith* (Portsmouth, N.H.: Beck and Foster, 1816), pp. 279–83.

30. Robert Semple, *A History of the Rise and Progress of the Baptists in Virginia* (Richmond: John Lynch, 1810), p. 39.

31. William Hill, *Autobiographical Sketches of Dr. William Hill, Together With His Account of the Revival of Religion in Prince Edward County . . . ,* Union Theological Seminary Historical Transcripts no. 4 (Richmond: Union Seminary, 1968), p. 116.

32. Richard Allen, *The Life Experiences and Gospel Labors of the Rt. Rev. Richard Allen* (New York: Abingdon Press, 1960), p. 22.

33. McKendree, "Diary," September 26, 1790, also September 27, 1790.

34. L. F. Greene, ed., *The Writings of the Late Elder John Leland* (New York: G. W. Wood, 1845), pp. 112–13.

35. Semple, *Baptists in Virginia*, p. 35.

36. Louis Morton, *Robert Carter of Nomini Hall* (Williamsburg, Va.: Colonial Williamsburg, 1941), pp. 234–35.

37. John Rippon, *The Baptist Annual Register for 1790* (n.p., 1793), vol. I, pp. 106–7.

38. Semple, *Baptists in Virginia,* p. 39. Wesley Gewehr pointed to the Baptist successes on Virginia's Northern Neck as one reason for the increased number of gentlefolk in the denomination. See *The Great Awakening in Virginia* (Durham: Duke University Press, 1930), pp. 173, 177.

39. Jesse Lee, *A Short History of the Methodists in the United States of America* (Baltimore: Magill and Clime, 1810), pp. 97, 99.

40. Asbury, *Journal,* vol. II, p. 18.

41. Rice to unknown correspondent, December 11, 1799 (Shane Collection).

42. Quoted in Robert Davidson, *History of the Presbyterian Church in Kentucky* (New York: Robert Carter, 1847), pp. 68–69, 69n.

43. Wood Furman, comp., *A History of the Charleston Association of Baptist Churches in the State of South Carolina* (Charleston: J. Hoff, 1811), p. 26.

44. Semple, *Baptists in Virginia,* p. 196.

45. Strawberry Association Minute Book, 1787–1822, Circular Letter of 1793, p. 63; Circular Letter of 1794, p. 78 (photocopy in Virginia Baptist Historical Society, Richmond). Evangelical alarm about worldliness had parallels in a larger postwar concern about the effects of luxury on the republican character. See Drew R. McCoy, *The Elusive Republic: Political Economy in Jeffersonian America* (Chapel Hill: University of North Carolina Press, 1980), chap. 3.

46. James O'Kelly, *Essay on Negro Slavery* (Philadelphia: Prichard and Hall, 1789), p. 10.

47. Daniel Grant to John Owen, Jr., September 3, 1790, quoted in Duncan J. MacLeod, *Slavery, Race and the American Revolution* (London: Cambridge University Press, 1974), pp. 138–39.

48. Leland, *Writings,* p. 97.

49. Ibid.

50. Asbury, *Journal,* vol. II, p. 280.

51. William K. Boyd, "A Journal and Travel of James Meacham," part II, *Historical Papers,* Trinity College Historical Society, Series X (1914), pp. 92–93; hereafter known as Meacham, "Journal."

52. O'Kelly, *Essay,* p. 14.

53. Ibid., p. 18.

54. Meacham, "Journal," part I, *Historical Papers,* Trinity College Historical Society, Series IX (1912), pp. 82, 67.

55. McKendree, "Diary," February 9, 1791.

56. John Asplund, *The Annual Register of the Baptist Denomination, In North America; To the First of November, 1790* (Philadelphia: Dobson,

1792), pp. 56–57. The other four items requiring attention were contributions to the ministers and the poor, attendance at worship, the encouragement of ministers, and the constitution of churches.

57. *Minutes of the Portsmouth Association . . . 1796* (n.p., n.d.), p. 5 (copy in the Virginia Baptist Historical Society).

58. David Rice to unknown correspondent, December 11, 1799 (Shane Collection).

59. See, for instance, McKendree, "Diary," October 9, 1790; Colbert, "Journal," August 6, 1791; Thomas Coke, *Extracts from the Journals of the Rev. Dr. Coke's Five Visits to America* (London: G. Paramore, 1793), April 1, 1785, p. 33. See also Kenneth L. Carroll, "Religious Influences on the Manumission of Slaves in Caroline, Dorchester, and Talbot Counties," *Maryland Historical Magazine* 56 (June 1961): 176–97.

60. Carlos R. Allen, Jr., ed., "David Barrow's Circular Letter of 1798," *William and Mary Quarterly* 3rd ser. 20 (July 1963): 445n.

61. Quoted in Joseph F. Tuttle, "Rev. Jacob Green, of Hanover, N.J., As an Author, Statesman, and Patriot," *Proceedings of the New Jersey Historical Society* 2nd ser. 12 (1893): p. 225.

62. Joshua Coffin, *A Sketch of the History of Newbury, Newburyport, and West Newbury* (Boston: S. G. Drake, 1845), p. 350.

63. Hopkins, *Works*, "Memoir," vol. I, p. 157, vol. II, p. 604.

64. *Records of the Presbyterian Church in the United States of America, Embracing the Minutes of the General Assembly and General Synod, 1706–1788* (New York: Presbyterian Board of Publication, 1904), p. 540.

65. *Minutes of the General Assembly of the Presbyterian Church in the United States of America From Its Organization A.D. 1789 to A.D. 1820 Inclusive* (Philadelphia: Presbyterian Board of Publications, 1847), pp. 103–4, 104n.

66. Lee, *History*, pp. 101–2; Donald G. Mathews, *Slavery and Methodism* (Princeton: Princeton University Press, 1965), pp. 10–12; N. C. Hughes, "The Methodist Christmas Conference: Baltimore, Dec. 24, 1784–Jan. 2, 1785," *Maryland Historical Magazine* 54 (September 1959): 272–92.

67. *Minutes of the Baptist General Committee . . . May, 1791* (Richmond: John Dixon, 1791), p. 5. The records of this session contain the only reference to the resolution of 1785.

68. Quoted in W. Harrison Daniel, "Virginia Baptists and the Negro in the Early Republic," *Virginia Magazine of History and Biography* 80 (January 1972): 66.

69. Semple, *Baptists in Virginia*, pp. 303–4.

70. *Minutes of the Baptist General Committee . . . 1790* (Richmond: John Dixon, 1790), p. 5.

71. Ibid., p. 7.

72. Roanoke Association Minute Book 1789–1831, Minutes for June 1790, pp. 39–40 (Virginia Baptist Historical Society).

73. Strawberry Association Minute Book, Minutes for May 1792, p. 45 (Virginia Baptist Historical Society).

74. *Minutes of the Baptist General Committee . . . 1793* (Richmond: T. Nicolson, 1793), p. 4.

75. Freeborn Garrettson, *A Dialogue Between Do-Justice and Professing Christian* (Wilmington: Peter Brynberg, n.d.), p. 8.

76. Ibid., pp. 47, 34.

77. Ibid., p. 44.

CHAPTER IV

1. See Gordon S. Wood, *The Creation of the American Republic, 1776–1787* (Chapel Hill: University of North Carolina Press, 1969), pp. 114–24; Bernard Bailyn, *The Ideological Origins of the American Revolution* (Cambridge: Harvard University Press, 1967).

2. Wood, *Creation*, pp. 10–22; Bailyn, *Ideological Origins*, pp. 33–44; J. G. A. Pocock, "Virtue and Commerce in the Eighteenth Century," *Journal of Interdisciplinary History* 3 (Summer 1972): 119–22. For an analysis of the literature on republicanism, see Robert E. Shalhope, "Toward a Republican Synthesis: The Emergence of an Understanding of Republicanism in American Historiography," *William and Mary Quarterly* 3rd ser. 29 (January 1972): 49–80.

3. Robert Semple, *A History of the Rise and Progress of the Baptists in Virginia* (Richmond: John Lynch, 1810), pp. 359–60; James B. Taylor, *Lives of Virginia Baptist Ministers* (New York: Sheldon and Co., 1860), pp. 161–63.

4. Carlos R. Allen, Jr., ed., "David Barrow's Circular Letter of 1798," *William and Mary Quarterly* 3rd ser. 20 (July 1963): 445n.

5. David Barrow, *Involuntary, Unmerited, Perpetual, Absolute, Hereditary Slavery, Examined on the Principles of Nature, Reason, Justice, Policy, and Scripture* (Lexington, Ky., 1808), p. 9.

6. Ibid., pp. 10–11.

7. Ibid., p. 11; "Diary of David Barrow of his Travels through Kentucky in 1795," June 24, 1795, p. 11 (Filson Club, Louisville, Ky.).

8. Barrow, "Diary," June 24, 1795, p. 10.

9. Barrow, *Slavery Examined,* pp. 38–39. The insertions, of course, are Barrow's. Cf. Luke 4:18, 19 and Isaiah 61:1–2.

10. Barrow, *Slavery Examined,* p. 49.

11. Ibid., pp. 18–19.

12. Ibid., p. 22n.

13. Semple, *Baptists in Virginia,* p. 360; Barrow, "Circular Letter," p. 445.

14. Barrow, "Diary," May 18, 1795, p. 2; June 25, 1795, p. 12.

15. Ibid., May 17, 1795, p. 2.

16. Ibid., May 22, 1795, p. 3; June 15, 1795, p. 7.

17. Ibid., July 10, 1795, p. 18.

18. Ibid., July 30, 1795, p. 26.

19. Charles Franklin Kilgore, *The James O'Kelly Schism in the Methodist Episcopal Church* (Mexico City: Casa Unida de Publicaciones, 1963), p. 5. In his *Essay on Negro Slavery* (Philadelphia: Prichard and Hall, 1789), p. 19, O'Kelly refers to Virginia as "my native country." See also Frederick Abbot Norwood, "James O'Kelly—Methodist Maverick," *Methodist History* 4 (April 1966): 14–28.

20. Kilgore, *O'Kelly Schism,* pp. 5–6; [James O'Kelly], *The Author's Apology for Protesting Against the Methodist Episcopal Government* (Richmond: John Dixon, 1798), p. 4.

21. Kilgore, *O'Kelly Schism,* pp. 6–7; Frank Baker, *From Wesley to Asbury: Studies in Early American Methodism* (Durham: Duke University Press, 1976), pp. 102–3.

22. Elmer T. Clark et al., eds., *The Journal and Letters of Francis Asbury* (Nashville: Abingdon Press, 1958), vol. I, pp. 364–65; hereafter known as Asbury, *Journals.*

23. Kilgore, *O'Kelly Schism,* p. 5. Asbury, *Journals,* vol. I, p. 488. See also Richard K. MacMaster, "Liberty or Property? The Methodist Petition for Emancipation in Virginia, 1785," *Methodist History* 10 (October 1971): 44–55.

24. O'Kelly, *Apology,* p. 11.

25. Fredrika Teute Schmidt and Barbara Ripel Wilhelm, eds., "Early Proslavery Petitions in Virginia," *William and Marry Quarterly* 3rd ser. 30 (January 1973): 145, 142.

26. O'Kelly to unknown correspondent, April 1787, in Asbury, *Journals,* vol. III, p. 52.

27. Kilgore, *O'Kelly Schism,* pp. 12–15; O'Kelly, *A Vindication of the Author's Apology* (Raleigh: Joseph Gates, 1801), p. 60.

28. O'Kelly, *Essay,* "To the Reader."

29. Ibid., p. 22.

30. Ibid., p. 18.

31. Ibid., p. 10.

32. Ibid., p. 21.

33. Ibid., p. 24.

34. Ibid., pp. 26–27. Cf. Isaiah 2:4, 60:1.

35. Ibid., pp. 31, 32.

36. O'Kelly, *Apology*, p. 78.

37. O'Kelly, *Vindication*, p. 54.

38. O'Kelly, *Apology*, pp. 2, 38.

39. O'Kelly, *Vindication*, p. 60.

40. O'Kelly, *Apology*, p. 47.

41. Quoted in Robert Paine, *Life and Times of William McKendree* (Nashville: Publishing House, Methodist Episcopal Church, South, 1922), p. 87. See Kilgore, *O'Kelly Schism*, pp. 28–31.

42. Kilgore, *O'Kelly Schism*, pp. 34, 37.

43. O'Kelly, *Apology*, p. 119.

44. Robert H. Bishop, *An Outline of the History of the Church in the State of Kentucky . . . Containing the Memoirs of Rev. David Rice* (Lexington, Ky.: T. T. Skillman, 1824), p. 14.

45. William Henry Foote, *Sketches of Virginia, Historical and Biographical* 2nd ser. (Philadelphia: J. B. Lippincott, 1856), p. 78.

46. Samuel Davies, *Religion and Public Spirit* (New York, 1761), p. 5.

47. Ibid., p. 4.

48. David Rice, Sermon ms., undated (Shane Collection, Presbyterian Historical Society, Philadelphia).

49. Rice, *Slavery Inconsistent With Justice and Good Policy* (Lexington, Ky.: J. Bradford, 1792), p. 35.

50. Ibid., pp. 35–36.

51. Foote, *Sketches*, p. 79.

52. Bishop, *Memoirs of Rice*, pp. 57, 63, 92–93; Foote, *Sketches*, p. 327.

53. Bishop, *Memoirs of Rice*, pp. 68–70.

54. Rice, *Slavery Inconsistent*, pp. 23, 37.

55. Ibid., p. 5.

56. Ibid., p. 40.

57. Quoted in David Brion Davis, *The Problem of Slavery in Western Culture* (Ithaca: Cornell University Press, 1966), p. 120.

58. Rice, *Slavery Inconsistent*, p. 11.

59. Ibid., p. 14.

60. See Winthrop D. Jordan, *White Over Black: American Attitudes Toward the Negro, 1550–1812* (Chapel Hill: University of North Carolina Press, 1968), pp. 377–80, for responses to the St. Domingo uprising.

61. Rice, *Slavery Inconsistent,* p. 17.

62. Ibid., p. 26.

63. Ibid., pp. 41, 43.

64. John Mason Brown, *The Political Beginnings of Kentucky* (Louisville: John P. Morton, 1889), pp. 229–30, 230n.

65. Rice to William Rogers, November 4, 1794, Pennsylvania Abolition Society Committee of Correspondence, Letterbook, Vol. 2, 1794–1809, pp. 19–20 (Historical Society of Pennsylvania, Philadelphia).

66. Rice to unknown correspondent, December 11, 1799 (Shane Collection, Presbyterian Historical Society, Philadelphia).

67. Edwards A. Park, ed., *The Works of Samuel Hopkins, D.D. With a Memoir of His Life and Character* (Boston: Doctrinal Tract and Book Society, 1852), "Memoir," vol. I, pp. 33–35; hereafter known as Hopkins, *Works.* Perhaps the most telling assessment of Hopkins' pastoral abilities came from a layman who said that the minister "told people to come to Christ, but never told them how to come" (p. 35). See also the journal entry for December 28, 1754 ("Memoir," vol. I, p. 36). Hopkins thought of his preaching as "poor, low and miserable." See Stephen West, ed., *Sketches of the Life of the Late Rev. Samuel Hopkins, D.D.* (Hartford: Hudson and Goodwin, 1805), p. 88.

68. Hopkins, *Works,* "Memoir," vol. I, pp. 52, 66.

69. Edmund S. Morgan, *The Gentle Puritan: A Life of Ezra Stiles, 1727–1795* (New Haven: Yale University Press, 1962), pp. 118–20.

70. Wood, *Creation,* pp. 59–60, 113–14; Kenneth A. Lockridge, "Social Change and the Meaning of the American Revolution," *Journal of Social History* 6 (Summer 1973): 424, 434. Joseph A. Conforti advances a similar interpretation of Hopkins in "Samuel Hopkins and the New Divinity: Theology, Ethics, and Social Reform in Eighteenth-Century New England," *William and Mary Quarterly* 3rd ser. 34 (October 1977): 572–89.

71. Hopkins, *Works,* "Memoir," vol. I, pp. 116, 119.

72. Virginia Bever Platt, "'And Don't Forget the Guinea Voyage': The Slave Trade of Aaron Lopez of Newport," *William and Mary Quarterly* 3rd ser. 32 (October 1975): 601–18; Stanley F. Chyet, *Lopez of Newport: Colonial American Merchant Prince* (Detroit: Wayne State University Press, 1970), pp. 66ff; James B. Hedges, *The Browns of Providence Plantations: The Colonial Years* (Providence: Brown University Press, 1968), pp. 70–81; and Gilman Ostrander, "The Making of the Triangular Trade Myth," *William and Mary Quarterly* 3rd ser. 30 (October 1973): 635–44.

73. Hopkins, *Works,* vol. II, p. 559n.

74. Ibid.

75. Ibid., vol. II, p. 619.

76. Ibid., vol. II, p. 615.

77. Ibid., vol. II, p. 624.

78. Ibid., "Memoir," vol. I, pp. 122–23; Arthur Zilversmit, *The First Emancipation: The Abolition of Slavery in the North* (Chicago: University of Chicago Press, 1967), pp. 156–57.

79. Hopkins, *Works,* "Memoir," vol. I, p. 158.

80. Ibid., vol. I, pp. 158–59.

81. Quoted in ibid., vol. I, p. 208.

82. Ibid., vol. II, p. 275.

83. Ibid., vol. II, p. 285.

84. Ibid.

85. Ibid., vol. II, pp. 322–23, 325.

86. Ibid., vol. II, p. 312.

87. Ibid., vol. II, p. 359.

88. Ibid., vol. II, pp. 604, 609. For background on the Providence Society, see Mack Thompson, *Moses Brown: Reluctant Reformer* (Chapel Hill: University of North Carolina Press, 1962), pp. 195–202.

89. Hopkins, *Works,* vol. II, pp. 600–601.

90. Quoted in ibid., "Memoir," vol. I, p. 208.

91. Gustav A. Koch, *Republican Religion: The American Revolution and the Cult of Reason* (New York: Henry Holt and Co., 1933).

CHAPTER V

1. See Thomas R. Moseley, "A History of the New York Manumission Society, 1785–1849" (Ph.D. diss., New York University, 1963), and Arthur Zilversmit, *The First Emancipation: The Abolition of Slavery in the North* (Chicago: University of Chicago Press, 1967), pp. 162–65.

2. Morse was born in Connecticut, and Dwight in Massachusetts; Morse later moved to Massachusetts, while Dwight eventually took up residence in Connecticut. See James King Morse, *Jedidiah Morse: A Champion of New England Orthodoxy* (New York: Columbia University Press, 1939), and Charles E. Cuningham, *Timothy Dwight, 1752–1817* (New York: Macmillan, 1942).

3. Morse, *Morse,* pp. 26–28.

4. Compare his remarks on slavery in *Geography Made Easy* (New Haven: Meigs, Bowen, and Dana, 1784) with those in *The American Universal Geography* (Elizabethtown: Shepard Kollock, 1789).

5. Morse, *Universal Geography,* pp. 144–48.

6. Ibid., pp. 251, 292, 313, 347.

7. Ibid., p. 352.

8. Ibid., pp. 387, 390.

9. Ibid., pp. 390–91.

10. Ibid., p. 417.

11. Ibid., pp. 432–33.

12. For related themes, see Linda Kerber, *Federalists in Dissent: Imagery and Ideology in Jeffersonian America* (Ithaca: Cornell University Press, 1970), chap. 2; Eric Foner, *Free Soil, Free Labor, Free Men: The Ideology of the Republican Party before the Civil War* (New York: Oxford University Press, 1970), pp. 47–49.

13. Zilversmit, *First Emancipation*, pp. 113–15, 123.

14. Timothy Dwight, *Greenfield Hill* (New York: Childs and Swaine, 1794), part I, line 158, page 15. Hereafter, all quotations from the poem will be referred to by part, line, and page number, respectively.

15. Ibid., I, 243–46, 18; I, 154–57, 15.

16. Ibid., "Notes to Part I," p. 170.

17. Ibid., II, 193–94, 36–37.

18. Ibid., II, 205–6, 37.

19. Ibid., II, 209–12, 37.

20. Ibid., II, 204, 37.

21. Ibid., II, 247–48, 38.

22. Ibid., II, 253–60, 38.

23. Ibid., II, 279–83, 39.

24. Ibid., II, 319–27, 40.

25. Ibid., II, 347, 41.

26. Kenneth Silverman, *Timothy Dwight* (New York: Twayne Publishers, 1969), p. 71.

27. Dwight, *Greenfield Hill*, "Notes to Part II," p. 172.

28. Ibid., "Notes to Part II," p. 173.

29. In "The Dove and the Serpent: The Clergy in the American Revolution," *American Quarterly* 31 (Summer 1979), Emory Elliot argues that after the Revolution, Congregational and Presbyterian clergymen used benevolent associations as vehicles to disseminate clerical wisdom, court the favor of the influential, and "reassert their importance for the general progress of the society" (p. 200).

30. *Records of the General Association of the Colony of Connecticut* (Hartford, Ct.: Case, Lockwood, and Brainard, 1888), pp. 68–104, especially p. 91.

31. Quoted in Edmund S. Morgan, *The Gentle Puritan: A Life of Ezra Stiles, 1727–1795* (New Haven: Yale University Press, 1962), p. 315. In an attempt to refurbish the image of the New Divinity men, Richard D. Birdsall inadvertently pointed up their failure to attract a popular

following. In "Ezra Stiles versus the New Divinity Men," *American Quarterly* 17 (Summer 1965), Birdsall compared the New Divinity men to "the Neo-Orthodox young clergymen who flock from our divinity schools preaching the astringent doctrines of Kierkegaard, Barth, and Reinhold Niebuhr" (p. 253).

32. General Association, *Records*, p. 114.

33. Ibid., p. 116.

34. Ibid., p. 127.

35. *New Haven Gazette and the Connecticut Magazine*, October 9, 1788.

36. *American Mercury*, September 1, 1788.

37. Henry F. May, *The Enlightenment in America* (New York: Oxford University Press, 1976), p. 122; Morgan, *Gentle Puritan*, p. 415.

38. General Association, *Records*, p. 121.

39. Richard J. Purcell, *Connecticut in Transition, 1775–1818* (Washington, D.C.: American Historical Association, 1918), p. 69.

40. James Mudge, *History of the New England Conference* (Boston: The Conference, 1910), pp. 30, 452.

41. Morgan, *Gentle Puritan*, pp. 412–19.

42. Richard D. Birdsall, "The Second Great Awakening and the New England Social Order," *Church History* 39 (September 1970): 345.

43. General Association, *Records*, p. 138. It should be noted that the clergy's major offensive against infidelity was yet to come. See Gary B. Nash, "The American Clergy and the French Revolution," *William and Mary Quarterly* 3rd ser. 22 (July 1965): 392–412.

44. Tryon Edwards, ed., *The Works of Jonathan Edwards, D.D., Late President of Union College* (Andover: Allen, Morrill, and Wardwell, 1842), vol. II, pp. 161–62, 170.

45. Benjamin Trumbull, *A Sermon Delivered at the Ordination of the Rev. Thomas Holt, A.M., . . . June 25, 1789* (Worcester, Mass.: I. Thomas, 1790), p. 31. Cf. Trumbull's *Sermon Delivered at the Ordination of the Rev. Lemuel Tyler, A.M. . . . May 7, 1789* (New Haven: T. and S. Green, 1793), p. 18, where Trumbull declares: "Make connections with ingenious and good men."

46. Ms. copy of constitution [ca. August 6, 1790], Box 6, Baldwin Family Papers (Yale University Manuscripts and Archives Room).

47. The membership has been reconstructed from lists in the following collections: October 20, 1790, Box 6, Baldwin Family Papers; September 13, 1792, Box 7, Baldwin Family Papers; September 12, 1793, Box 4, Benjamin Trumbull Papers (Beinecke Library, Yale University); May 11, 1791, in Emily E. F. Ford and Emily E. F. Skeel, eds., *Notes on the Life of Noah Webster* (New York: Kathleen Turle et al., 1912), vol. II, p. 480.

48. See scattered minutes for the Connecticut Society in Box 6 of the Baldwin Family Papers.

49. Purcell, *Connecticut in Transition,* pp. 325–26.

50. Theodore Dwight, Chauncey Goodrich, and Zephaniah Swift would all one day attend the Hartford Convention. Purcell, *Connecticut in Transition,* p. 292.

51. Minutes of October 31, 1791, Box 6, Baldwin Family Papers; H. Channing to Simeon Baldwin, November 22, 1790, Box 6, Baldwin Family Papers.

52. Elnathan Beech to Jonathan Edwards, Jr., December 7, 1791, Box 6, Baldwin Family Papers; William Law and Elnathan Beech to Simeon Baldwin, April 26, 1792, Box 7, Baldwin Family Papers; Benjamin Trumbull to John Lewis, March 19, 1792, Box 7, Baldwin Family Papers.

53. Minutes of January 10, 1791, Box 6, Baldwin Family Papers.

54. Jonathan Edwards, Jr., *The Injustice and Impolicy of the Slave Trade, and of the Slavery of the Africans* (New Haven, T. and S. Green, 1791), p. 28; H. Channing to Simeon Baldwin, November 22, 1790, Box 6, Baldwin Family Papers.

55. Zephaniah Swift, *An Oration on Domestic Slavery* (Hartford: Hudson and Goodwin, 1791), pp. 18, 19.

56. Ibid., p. 17.

57. Theodore Dwight, *An Oration, Spoken Before the Connecticut Society for the Promotion of Freedom and the Relief of Persons Unlawfully Holden in Bondage* (Hartford: Hudson and Goodwin, 1794), pp. 20, 22.

58. Edwards, *Injustice and Impolicy,* pp. 36–37.

59. Dwight, *Oration,* pp. 15–16, 19–20.

60. This antislavery society served purposes remarkably similar to the New England moral societies that were being formed at this time. According to Donald M. Scott, *From Office to Profession: The New England Ministry, 1750–1850* (Philadelphia: University of Pennsylvania Press, 1978), the moral societies were nonpartisan organizations which enabled ministers to carry on their role as public guardians. At the same time, these moral societies promoted "moral solidarity" among members of the elite (pp. 31–35).

61. *The Public Records of Connecticut* (Hartford: Case, Lockwood, and Brainard, 1894–1967), vol. VIII, pp. xviii, xix–xx.

62. *Minutes of the Proceedings of the Second Convention of Delegates From the Abolition Societies* (Philadelphia: Zechariah Poulson, 1795), pp. 18–19, and minutes for the next several years.

63. Winthrop D. Jordan, *White Over Black: American Attitudes Toward the*

Negro, 1550–1812 (Chapel Hill: University of North Carolina Press, 1968), pp. 344, 373.

64. Duncan J. MacLeod, *Slavery, Race and the American Revolution* (London: Cambridge University Press, 1974), pp. 36–37; Jordan, *White Over Black*, p. 373.

CHAPTER VI

1. William Fristoe, *A Concise History of the Ketocton Baptist Association* (Staunton: W. G. Lyford, 1808), p. 59; Robert B. Semple, *A History of the Rise and Progress of the Baptists in Virginia* (Richmond: John Lynch, 1810), p. 39, for example.

2. John Rippon, *Annual Register for 1790* (n.p., 1793), vol. I, p. 105.

3. Synod of the Carolinas, Minutes, vol. I, p. 168 (Union Theological Seminary of Richmond, Richmond, Va.).

4. Winthrop D. Jordan, *White Over Black: American Attitudes Toward the Negro, 1550–1812* (Chapel Hill: University of North Carolina Press, 1968), pp. 380–82.

5. *Minutes of the General Baptist Committee . . . 1793* (Richmond: T. Nicolson, 1793), p. 4.

6. L. F. Greene, ed., *The Writings of the Late Elder John Leland* (New York: G. W. Wood, 1845), p. 174.

7. Quoted in Garnett Ryland, *The Baptists of Virginia, 1699–1926* (Richmond: Virginia Baptist Board of Missions and Education, 1955), p. 154.

8. Robert Davidson, *History of the Presbyterian Church in Kentucky* (New York: Robert Carter, 1847), p. 336.

9. Synod of the Carolinas, Minutes, vol. II, pp. 22–23.

10. William Warren Sweet, ed., *Religion on the American Frontier*, vol. II, *The Presbyterians, 1783–1840: A Collection of Their Source Materials* (New York: Harper and Brothers, 1936), pp. 163, 169–70.

11. Synod of Virginia, Minutes, September 27, 1800 (Union Theological Seminary of Richmond, Richmond, Va.).

12. Ibid.

13. Presbytery of South Carolina, Minutes, July 20, 1796 (Microfilm at Union Theological Seminary of Richmond, Richmond, Va.).

14. Synod of the Carolinas, Minutes, vol. I, pp. 268–69.

15. Jonathan Edwards, Jr., to Reverend Robert Wilson, November 7, 1798 (Shane Collection, Presbyterian Historical Society, Philadelphia).

16. William Birney, *James G. Birney and His Times* (New York: Negro University Press, 1969; orig. pub. 1890), p. 433; George Howe, *History*

of the Presbyterian Church in South Carolina (Columbia, S.C.: George Duffie and Company, 1870), pp. 627–28.

17. *Journals of the General Conference of the Methodist Episcopal Church* (New York: Carlton and Phillips, 1855), vol. I, p. 22; Donald G. Mathews, *Slavery and Methodism: A Chapter in American Morality, 1780–1845* (Princeton: Princeton University Press, 1965), pp. 20–21.

18. Wood Furman, comp., *A History of the Charleston Association of Baptist Churches in the State of South Carolina* (Charleston: J. Hoff, 1811), p. 149.

19. Gerald W. Mullin, *Flight and Rebellion: Slave Resistance in Eighteenth-Century Virginia* (New York: Oxford University Press, 1972), pp. 143–49, quotation on p. 149. Mullin points out that Gabriel himself remained aloof from evangelical religion (pp. 156–61).

20. Henry W. Flournoy, *Calendar of Virginia State Papers and Manuscripts* (Richmond: James E. Goode, 1875–1893), vol. IX, p. 152.

21. Mullin, *Flight and Rebellion*, pp. 153–54, 201–2.

22. *Letter to a Member of the General Assembly of Virginia on the Subject of the Late Conspiracy of the Slaves, with a Proposal for their Colonization* (1801), quoted in Mullin, *Flight and Rebellion*, p. 203. Mullin attributes the *Letter* to St. George Tucker, but Jordan asserts that it was the work of George Tucker (*White Over Black*, p. 562n).

23. George A. Phoebus, comp., *Beams of Light on Early Methodism, Chiefly Drawn from the Diary, Letters, Manuscripts, Documents, and Original Tracts of the Rev. Ezekiel Cooper* (New York: Phillips and Hunt, 1887), p. 334; David J. McCord and Thomas Cooper, eds., *The Statutes at Large of South Carolina* (Columbia, S.C.: A. S. Johnston, 1836–1841), vol. VII, p. 441; Jeffrey J. Crow, "Slave Rebelliousness and Social Conflict in North Carolina, 1775–1802," *William and Mary Quarterly* 3rd ser. 37 (January 1980): 79–102.

24. *An Address of the General Conference . . . Baltimore, May 20, 1800* (Broadside).

25. Phoebus, *Beams*, pp. 330, 332–33.

26. Henry Pattillo, *The Plain Planter's Family Assistant* (Wilmington: James Adams, 1787), p. 23.

27. Ibid., p. 26.

28. Ibid., p. 22; Mullin, *Flight and Rebellion*, p. 19.

29. Pattillo, *Family Assistant*, pp. 46–52.

30. Pattillo to William Williamson, December 4, 1799 (Shane Collection).

31. Pattillo, *Family Assistant*, p. 22.

32. Synod of the Carolinas, Minutes, vol. I, pp. 267–68.

33. Dover Association, Minutes, 1796, 1797 (Virginia Baptist Historical Society).

34. *Minutes of the Bethel Association . . . August 1794* ([Charleston]: n.p., 1794).

35. Quoted in Anne C. Loveland, "Richard Furman's 'Questions on Slavery,'" *Baptist History and Heritage* 10 (July 1975): 180.

36. David Benedict, *A General History of the Baptist Denomination in America, and Other Parts of the World* (Boston: Lincoln and Edmands, 1813), vol. II, pp. 210, 211–13.

37. Phoebus, *Beams,* p. 205.

38. Elmer T. Clark et al., eds., *The Journal and Letters of Francis Asbury* (Nashville: Abingdon Press, 1958); Asbury to George Roberts, February 11, 1797, vol. III, p. 160.

39. Ibid., vol. II, p. 591.

40. Jedidiah Morse, *A Sermon Delivered at the North Church in Boston, in the Morning, and in the Afternoon at Charlestown, May 9, 1798 . . .* (Boston: Samuel Hall, 1798).

41. See Vernon Stauffer's still useful *New England and the Bavarian Illuminati* (New York: Columbia University Press, 1918), and Gary B. Nash, "The American Clergy and the French Revolution," *William and Mary Quarterly* 3rd ser. 22 (July 1965): 392–412.

42. Theodore Dwight, *An Oration Spoken at Hartford . . . July 4, 1798* (Hartford: Hudson and Goodwin, 1798), p. 16.

43. Timothy Dwight, *The Duty of Americans, at the Present Crisis . . .* (New Haven: T. and S. Green, 1798), p. 21.

44. Ibid., p. 30.

45. Samuel Hopkins to Levi Hart, September 12, 1798, Case 8, Box 23 (Gratz Collection, Historical Society of Pennsylvania, Philadelphia).

46. Jedidiah Morse, *A Sermon, Exhibiting the Present Dangers and Consequent Duties of the Citizens of the United States of America* (Boston: Samuel Etheridge, 1799), pp. 19, 14.

47. For a perceptive treatment of countersubversive movements, see David Brion Davis' introduction to *The Fear of Conspiracy: Images of Un-American Subversion from the Revolution to the Present* (Ithaca: Cornell University Press, 1971).

48. John B. Boles, *The Great Revival, 1787–1805: The Origins of the Southern Evangelical Mind* (Lexington: University Press of Kentucky, 1972), pp. 12–24; Charles Roy Keller, *The Second Great Awakening in Connecticut* (New Haven: Yale University Press, 1942), pp. 49–50.

49. Bennett Tyler, *New England Revivals, As They Existed at the Close of*

the Eighteenth, and the Beginning of the Nineteenth Centuries (Boston: Massachusetts Sabbath School Society, 1846), p. 158.

50. Ibid.

51. *Acts and Proceedings of the General Association of Connecticut* (Hartford: Hudson and Goodwin, 1801–1807), p. 10.

52. P. P. Sandford, *Memoirs of Mr. Wesley's Missionaries to America* (New York: G. Lane and P. P. Sandford, 1844), p. 373.

53. Boles, *Great Revival,* pp. 53–57. John McGee, a Methodist preacher, also participated in the Gasper River meetings.

54. Ibid., pp. 63–69.

55. Davidson, *Presbyterian Church in Kentucky,* p. 161.

56. James Hall, *A Narrative of a Most Extraordinary Work of Religion in North Carolina . . .* (Philadelphia: William W. Woodward, 1802), p. 21.

57. Ibid., p. 20.

58. *Virginia Religious Magazine* 1 (March 1806): 126.

59. *Massachusetts Missionary Magazine* 1 (December 1803): 317–18; see Julia Post Mitchell, *St. Jean de Crèvecoeur* (New York: Columbia University Press, 1916), pp. 346–49, for a list of publications which reprinted this account.

60. *Massachusetts Missionary Magazine* 1 (August 1803): 160.

61. *General Assembly Missionary Magazine* n.s. 1 (July 1807): 47–48.

62. Ibid., p. 48.

63. Ibid. n.s. 1 (December 1807): 257.

64. Ibid., p. 258. See also "The Pious Negro," *Massachusetts Missionary Magazine* 5 (June 1807): 29–31.

65. Charles D. Mallary, *Memoirs of Elder Edmund Botsford* (Charleston: W. Riley, 1832), pp. 45, 107.

66. Mallary, *Botsford,* p. 225; *Sambo and Toney* (New York: American Tract Society, n.d.; orig. pub. 1808), p. 2.

67. *Sambo and Toney,* p. 12.

68. Ibid., p. 19.

69. *Virginia Religious Magazine* 3 (May and June 1807): 161–70.

70. Ibid. 2 (September 1806): 293.

71. Ibid., pp. 293, 295.

72. Quoted in Loveland, "Richard Furman," p. 178.

73. Edwards A. Park, ed., *The Works of Samuel Hopkins, D.D. With a Memoir of His Life and Character* (Boston: Doctrinal Tract and Book Society, 1852), "Memoir," vol. I, p. 22; hereafter known as Hopkins, *Works;* "A Narrative of the rise & progress of a proposal and attempt to send the gospel to Guinea," Case 8, Box 23 (Gratz Collection).

74. William Patten, *On the Inhumanity of the Slave Trade* (Providence, R.I.: Carter, 1793), p. 11.

75. Hopkins, *Works*, vol. II, pp. 603–7; "Memoir," vol. I, p. 144.

76. Hopkins, *Works*, vol. II, p. 607.

77. *New York Missionary Magazine* 2 (1801): 28.

78. *Massachusetts Missionary Magazine* 2 (July 1804): 66.

79. Ibid., pp. 67–68.

80. Ibid., p. 69.

81. *Connecticut Evangelical Magazine* 5 (April 1805): 394–95.

82. Ibid., pp. 396–97. The minutes of the proceedings for 1805 also reveal no efforts on behalf of Africans. See ibid. 6 (June 1806): 476–77.

83. Timothy Dwight, James Dana, and Benjamin Trumbull to Granville Sharp, December 14, 1797, Box 4, Benjamin Trumbull Papers (Beinecke Library, Yale University, New Haven, Ct.).

CHAPTER VII

1. *Extracts of Letters Containing Some Account of the Work of God Since the Year 1800* (New York: J. C. Totten, 1805), p. 43; William Warren Sweet, ed., *The Rise of Methodism in the West, Being the Journal of the Western Conference, 1800–1811* (New York: Methodist Book Concern, 1920), p. 23.

2. Lorenzo Dow, ed., *Extracts From Original Letters to the Methodist Bishops . . . Giving An Account of the Work of God, Since the Year 1800* (Liverpool: H. Forshaw, 1806), p. 15.

3. *Western Missionary Magazine* 1 (January 1804): 436.

4. William Colbert, "A Journal of the Travels of William Colbert, Methodist Preacher, Through Parts of Maryland, Pennsylvania, New York, Delaware, and Virginia in 1790 to 1838," November 8, 1800 (Library of Congress, Washington, D.C.).

5. Ibid., December 6, 1801.

6. William Warren Sweet, ed., *Religion on the American Frontier*, vol. 1, *The Baptists, 1783–1830* (New York: Henry Holt, 1931), pp. 328–29, 330. Five years later, Winney was restored to fellowship (p. 372).

7. By now the literature on slave resistance is quite substantial, but for suggestive treatments of the way Christianity enabled blacks to endure the brutalities of the system, see Eugene Genovese, *Roll, Jordan, Roll: The World the Slaves Made* (New York: Pantheon Books, 1974), pp. 161–284; and Donald G. Mathews, *Religion in the Old South* (Chicago: University of Chicago Press, 1977), pp. 185–236.

8. In 1800, Kentucky had 40,343 slaves in a total population of

220,959, or about 18 percent slaves, while Virginia had 322,199 slaves out of a total population of 676,682, or about 47 percent slaves, and South Carolina had 146,151 slaves out of a total population of 345,591, or about 42 percent slaves. See *Return of the Whole Number of Persons of the Several Districts of the United States* (Washington, D.C.: William Duane, 1802), p. 89, "Enumeration of Persons." There is a very slight discrepancy between the figures for Kentucky on p. 89 and on p. 84.

9. Robert B. Semple, *A History of the Rise and Progress of the Baptists in Virginia* (Richmond: John Lynch, 1810), p. 354. In *A General History of the Baptist Denomination in America, And Other Parts of the World* (Boston: Lincoln and Edmands, 1813), David Benedict stated that a "flood of Baptist emigrants" poured into Kentucky after the war, "mostly from Virginia" (vol. II, p. 228).

10. Asa Earl Martin, *The Anti-Slavery Movement in Kentucky Prior to 1850* ([Louisville, Ky.], 1918), p. 31.

11. Robert Davidson, *History of the Presbyterian Church in Kentucky* (New York: Robert Carter, 1847), p. 336; Synod of Virginia, Minutes, September 27, 1800 (Union Theological Seminary of Richmond, Richmond, Va.).

12. David Rice to unknown correspondent, December 11, 1799 (Shane Collection, Presbyterian Historical Society, Philadelphia).

13. Donald G. Mathews, *Slavery and Methodism: A Chapter in American Morality, 1780–1845* (Princeton: Princeton University Press, 1965), pp. 20, 298.

14. Quoted in Hiram Mattison, *The Impending Crisis of 1860* (Freeport, N.Y.: Library Press, 1971; orig. pub. 1853), pp. 16–17; A. H. Redford, *History of Methodism in Kentucky* (Nashville: Southern Methodist Publishing House, 1870), vol. I, p. 456.

15. Mattison, *Impending Crisis*, p. 17; Mathews, *Slavery and Methodism*, pp. 20, 298–99.

16. Peter Cartwright, *Fifty Years a Presiding Elder* (Cincinnati: Hitchcock and Walden, 1871), p. 53; Sweet, ed., *Rise of Methodism in the West*, p. 147.

17. Robert Paine, *Life and Times of William McKendree, Bishop of the Methodist Episcopal Church* (Nashville: Publishing House, Methodist Episcopal Church, South, 1922), p. 131.

18. Sweet, ed., *Rise of Methodism in the West*, p. 148. On background of committee members John Sale, Benjamin Lakin, and William Burke, see Redford, *Methodism in Kentucky*, vol. I, pp. 156, 206, 295.

19. Cartwright, *Fifty Years*, p. 54; Mathews, *Slavery and Methodism*, p. 32.

20. Elmer T. Clark et al., eds., *The Journal and Letters of Francis Asbury* (Nashville: Abingdon Press, 1958), vol. II, p. 580.

21. J. H. Spencer, *A History of Kentucky Baptists* (Cincinnati: n.p., 1885), vol. I, p. 184; Martin, *Anti-Slavery Movement in Kentucky*, p. 19.

22. Spencer, *Kentucky Baptists*, vol. I, p. 184.

23. Sweet, ed., *The Baptists*, p. 508.

24. Ibid., p. 338; Spencer, *Kentucky Baptists*, vol. I, p. 185.

25. Benedict, *General History*, vol. II, pp. 232, 235–36; Spencer, *Kentucky Baptists*, vol. I, p. 189. Sweet, however, gives 1791 as the date for the Tarrant schism (*Baptists*, p. 81).

26. Quoted in David Barrow, *Involuntary, Unmerited, Perpetual, Absolute, Hereditary Slavery, Examined on the Principles of Nature, Reason, Justice, Policy, and Scripture* (Lexington, Ky., 1808), p. 22.

27. Barrow, *Slavery Examined*, p. 30n. Spencer described the North District's expulsion of Barrow as an act of "papal arrogance" (*Kentucky Baptists*, vol. I, p. 196).

28. Benedict, *General History*, vol. II, p. 247; Sweet, ed., *The Baptists*, pp. 83–84.

29. Benedict, *General History*, vol. II, p. 248; Sweet, ed., *The Baptists*, p. 84.

30. Spencer, *Kentucky Baptists*, vol. I, pp. 188–97.

31. Ibid., vol. I, p. 190.

32. Semple, *History*, p. 357; Spencer, *Kentucky Baptists*, vol. I, pp. 190–91; A. H. Dunlevy, *A History of the Miami Baptist Association* (Cincinnati: George S. Blanchard, 1869), p. 138.

33. Barrow, *Slavery Examined*, pp. 23, 45.

34. Sweet, ed., *The Baptists*, p. 569.

35. Barrow, *Slavery Examined*, p. 47n.

36. Sweet, ed., *The Baptists*, p. 568.

37. Ibid., p. 569.

38. Benedict, *General Hisotry*, vol. II, p. 248; Spencer, *Kentucky Baptists*, vol. I, pp. 163, 186; Sweet, ed., *The Baptists*, p. 354.

39. Benedict, *General History*, vol. II, p. 248; Spencer, *Kentucky Baptists*, vol. I, pp. 186.

40. Kentucky Abolition Society, Circular Letter of 1810, in *Abolition Intelligencer and Missionary Magazine* 1 (October 1822): p. 84.

41. Ibid.; Benedict, *General History*, vol. II, p. 246.

42. In the late 1790s and early 1800s, however, inhabitants of the Indiana Territory petitioned Congress for a suspension of the article prohibiting slavery. See Duncan J. MacLeod, *Slavery, Race and the American Revolution* (London: Cambridge University Press, 1974), pp. 50–53.

43. John M'Lean, *Sketch of Rev. Philip Gatch* (Cincinnati: Swormstedt and Poe, 1856), p. 95; Josiah Morrow, ed., "Tours into Kentucky and the Northwest Territory: Three Journals by the Rev. James Smith of Powhatan County, Va., 1783—1795—1797," *Ohio Archaeological and Historical Society Publications* 16 (1907): 364, hereafter known as Smith, "Tours." Smith actually combined the sentiments of two prophets in this quotation. Cf. Jeremiah 9:2 and Habakkuk 3:16.

44. Smith, "Tours," p. 377.

45. Ibid., p. 396.

46. Ibid., p. 382.

47. M'Lean, *Gatch*, p. 96; Smith, "Tours," p. 351.

48. Smith, "Tours," pp. 378, 390–91.

49. William Birney, *James G. Birney and His Times* (New York: Negro University Press, 1969; orig. pub. 1890), pp. 432–34.

50. William Williamson to Warren Beuford [Benford?], June 24, 1805 (Shane Collection, Presbyterian Historical Society). William Birney's date for Williamson's removal is evidently in error (Birney, *James G. Birney*, p. 434).

51. Benedict, *General History*, vol. II, p. 258n; Dunlevy, *Miami Baptist Association*, pp. 132–33.

52. Quoted in Dunlevy, *Miami Baptist Association*, p. 48.

53. Benedict, *General History*, vol. II, p. 258n.

54. William Birney, *James G. Birney*, pp. 432–34.

55. For a literary analysis of Branagan, see Lewis Leary, "Thomas Branagan: Republican Rhetoric and Romanticism in America," *Pennsylvania Magazine of History and Biography* 77 (July 1953): 332–52.

56. For biographical details on Branagan, see his own *The Penitential Tyrant*, 2nd ed. (New York: Samuel Wood, 1807), pp. 1–38, or Leary, "Branagan," pp. 332–35.

57. Branagan, *A Beam of Celestial Light* (Philadelphia: n.p., 1814), p. 295.

58. Branagan, *Penitential Tyrant*, p. 27.

59. Branagan, *Celestial Light*, pp. 294–95.

60. Ibid., p. 296. From his *A Concise View of the Principle Religious Denominations in the United States of America* (Philadelphia: John Cline, 1811), it appears that Branagan was originally a Methodist. He devoted more space to a discussion of Methodism than any other denomination, and he displayed an insider's familiarity with their practices. Although he did not agree with the Methodists ("at least in some things"), he believed that "no society in the same number of years, ever done [sic] so

much good as they unquestionably have done in Europe and America"
(p. 57).

61. Branagan, *Penitential Tyrant*, pp. 72–74.

62. Ibid., pp. 141–42; Branagan, *Avenia: or, A Tragical Poem, on the Oppression of the Human Species, and Infringement on the Rights of Man* (Philadelphia: Engles and Wood, 1805), p. 308.

63. Branagan, *A Preliminary Essay on the Oppression of the Exiled Sons of Africa* (Philadelphia: John W. Scott, 1804), pp. 31–32; David Brion Davis, *The Problem of Slavery in Western Culture* (Ithaca: Cornell University Press, 1966), p. 357.

64. Branagan, *Avenia*, p. 22.

65. Branagan, *Preliminary Essay*, p. 23.

66. Branagan, *Avenia*, pp. 16–21.

67. Ibid., p. 172.

68. Branagan, *Penitential Tyrant*, p. 80.

69. Ibid., p. 77.

70. Branagan, *Serious Remonstrances* (Philadelphia: Thomas Stiles, 1805), p. 68.

71. Ibid., p. 92.

72. Ibid., p. 79. Branagan certainly benefited from his own contact with blacks: Richard Allen, a black Methodist minister, paid the printer's bill for *A Preliminary Essay*, and he, another black minister named Absalom Jones, and a wealthy black sails-maker named James Forten helped to raise money for the publication of *Avenia*. See *Avenia*, p. 310n, and *Preliminary Essay*, "Proposals."

73. Branagan, *Serious Remonstrances*, p. 24.

74. Branagan, *Celestial Light*, pp. 298–99.

75. Leary, "Branagan," p. 350.

EPILOGUE

1. Winthrop D. Jordan, *White Over Black: American Attitudes Toward the Negro, 1550–1812* (Chapel Hill: University of North Carolina Press, 1968), p. 373. In *Slavery, Race and the American Revolution* (London: Cambridge University Press, 1974), Duncan J. MacLeod observes that many Americans regarded slavery and the slave trade as an organic whole, and they believed that slavery could not survive if the slave trade were abolished (pp. 36–37).

2. Jedidiah Morse, *A Discourse Delivered at the African Meeting House . . . in Grateful Celebration of the Abolition of the African Slave Trade* (Boston: Lincoln and Edmands, 1808), pp. 17–18.

3. Ibid., pp. 24–25.

4. Quoted in Anne C. Loveland, "Richard Furman's 'Questions on Slavery,'" *Baptist History and Heritage* 10 (July 1975): 180–81. In the letter, Furman alluded to the fact that the slave trade would end "with the present year" (p. 179).

5. Donald G. Mathews, *Slavery and Methodism: A Chapter in American Morality, 1780–1845* (Princeton: Princeton University Press, 1965), p. 33; Willard C. MacNaul, *The Jefferson-Lemen Compact* (Chicago: University of Chicago Press, 1915).

6. The phrase is taken from the title of Alice Dana Adams' book, *The Neglected Period of Anti-Slavery in America (1808–1831)* (Gloucester, Mass.: Peter Smith, 1964; orig. pub. 1908).

7. See David Brion Davis, "The Emergence of Immediatism in British and American Antislavery Thought," *Mississippi Valley Historical Review* 49 (September 1962): 209–30.

8. Ronald G. Walters, *The Antislavery Appeal: American Abolitionism After 1830* (Baltimore: Johns Hopkins University Press, 1976), pp. 37–53; Donald G. Mathews, *Religion in the Old South* (Chicago: University of Chicago Press, 1977), chap. 4; Donald M. Scott, *From Office to Profession: The New England Ministry, 1750–1850* (Philadelphia: University of Pennsylvania Press, 1978), chap. 6.

9. Mathews, *Religion in the Old South*, pp. 136–64; Scott, *Office to Profession*, pp. 104–6.

10. James H. Moorhead, *American Apocalypse: Yankee Protestants and the Civil War* (New Haven: Yale University Press, 1978), pp. 92–96.

11. James B. Stewart, *Holy Warriors: The Abolitionists and American Slavery* (New York: Hill and Wang, 1976), pp. 33–43; Walters, *Antislavery Appeal*, pp. 80–81.

12. Walters, *Antislavery Appeal*, pp. 80–84, 112–13; James D. Essig, "The Lord's Free Man: Charles G. Finney and His Abolitionism," *Civil War History* 24 (March 1978): 25–45.

13. Essig, "Lord's Free Man"; William G. McLoughlin, Jr., *Modern Revivalism: Charles Grandison Finney to Billy Graham* (New York: Ronald Press, 1959), pp. 113–19. In no way did these revivals work to undermine the emerging industrial order. As Paul Johnson has shown, the revivals in Rochester granted it legitimacy by relieving the anxiety of middle-class entrepreneurs, encouraging work habits essential to the success of the new order, and providing a vision of society based on voluntary self-restraint. See *A Shopkeeper's Millennium: Society and Revivals in Rochester, New York, 1815–1837* (New York: Hill and Wang, 1978).

14. The phrase is borrowed from Ian C. Bradley, *The Call to Serious-*

ness: The Evangelical Impact on the Victorians (New York: MacMillan, 1976).

15. Walters, *Antislavery Appeal,* chap. 5; Scott, *Office to Profession,* pp. 89–91; Essig, "Lord's Free Man."

16. Leonard L. Richards, *"Gentlemen of Property and Standing": Anti-Abolition Mobs in Jacksonian America* (New York: Oxford University Press, 1970); Walters, *Antislavery Appeal,* p. 113; Silvan S. Tomkins, "The Psychology of Commitment: The Constructive Role of Violence and Suffering for the Individual and His Society," in Martin Duberman, ed., *The Antislavery Vanguard* (Princeton: Princeton University Press, 1965), pp. 270–98.

17. James B. Taylor, *Lives of Virginia Baptist Ministers* (New York: Sheldon and Co., 1860), pp. 165–77; Frank E. Maser, ed., "Discovery," *Methodist History* 9 (January 1971): 35.

18. Robert Paine, *Life and Times of William McKendree* (Nashville: Publishing House, Methodist Episcopal Church, South, 1922), pp. 131–32.

19. Edwards A. Park, ed., *The Works of Samuel Hopkins, D.D., with a Memoir of His Life and Character* (Boston: Doctrinal Tract and Book Society, 1852), "Memoir," vol. I, pp. 162–64; Hiram Mattison, *The Impending Crisis of 1860* (Freeport, N.Y.: Library Press, 1971; orig. pub. 1853), p. 22.

20. John Robinson, *The Testimony and Practice of the Presbyterian Church in Reference to American Slavery* (Cincinnati: Thorpe, 1852), pp. 123–24; David Rice, *A Kentucky Protest Against Slavery* (New York [1864]); William Birney, *James G. Birney and His Times* (New York: Negro University Press, 1969; orig. pub. 1890), pp. 432–34.

21. See, for example, Dwight Lowell Dumond, *Antislavery: The Crusade for Freedom in America* (Ann Arbor: University of Michigan, 1961).

INDEX